My Mini Cooper it's

My Mini Cooper

it's part in my breakdown

Copyright © 2013 & 2022 James Ruppert
www.foresightpublications.com
www.bangernomics.com
All rights reserved.
ISBN 978-0-9559529-5-1

James Ruppert

How not to buy, run or restore a classic car, and why owning one might be some form of unwellness, a short history of the small car from 1885 to 2000 plus an examination of what came before, during, but not after the Mini including the fairly complete story of the Mini and Mini Cooper from 1959 to 2000 and just how a small car managed to conquer some of the world...

Contents

My Mini Cooper it's part in my Breakdown

An apologetic introduction...I've got a terrible confession to make...

My name is James and I shouldn't be trusted with an old car. I may have owned a Mini Cooper for over 30 years, but for most of that time it has been off the road gathering dust, invoices and rust bubbles.

Sometimes it was under repair, occasionally being bodged by me, mostly though the Mini wasn't going anywhere at all. I did though make sure that it was always comfortable and dry. The very least I could do was put a blanket over the Cooper whilst it waited for the MOT to expire, the test to be booked or some spare part to arrive through the post.

Consequently miles wasn't something that my Mini actually accrued over the years. I'm not quite sure how few miles it has done, but by the end of the book I should have worked it out along with just how much it cost to mostly stand still. The resulting calculation won't be very pretty especially when it comes to the miles/money equation. At least spreading it all over thirty odd years should help me feel a bit better. It won't though make me look very normal because running a classic car isn't a very sensible thing to do.

For every classic car owner who takes their Ford Anglia on an epic road trip, win dice with other period racers in competition or compete in a concours (beauty) competition with their Aston Martin, there are thousands like me who just muck about pointlessly with theirs for years on end. That's until it rusts to bits, becomes the subject of divorce proceedings, or takes root in the garden. That's right we achieve nothing, enjoy very little and drive no more than a few yards, if we are lucky. A classic car is something to waste money on and generally fret about which means that for some the act of owning a classic triggers what could be regarded as a mental unwellness.

Now I would not want to trivialise mental illness, which is a very debilitating problem for many people, but some of the very odd things I have done and then justified on the grounds that it will help the restoration of my car defy belief. For instance I've bought other Minis I didn't need, sometimes selling and giving away large chunks of

3

them. I've reduced Minis to their constituent parts and then lost some of the most important bits. Indeed, a Mini may appear to be a rather miniscule vehicle, but once dismantled the resulting pile of bits fill an awful lot of cardboard boxes. These boxes are easy to mislay.

So whilst some people have the inclination and the ability to collate, record and refurbish those parts they never lost in the first place, before planning a detailed rebuild over a strict twenty-four month period. Others just get a little bit depressed and overwhelmed by it all. They might have been keen and indeed capable of making it all good once upon a time, but age and real life has overtaken them. Maintaining a roof over your head and more importantly steering a meaningful relationship between obstacles that are shaped like Mini body shells, is rather more important.

Owning a classic car certainly isn't a logical thing to do. It's a vehicle you don't actually need, designed for an era and motoring conditions that no longer exist. Most of these classics also have all the durability you would expect from something hammered together in the Midlands fifty years ago. If it hasn't been rebuilt twice already, the old banger is certainly going to need plenty of TLC if it is intended to be a going concern, rather than being mostly stationary and a large drain on resources.

Yes classic cars have a habit of hanging around. That's partly because they can't be moved as a fuse has blown or the tyres are flat. Often it isn't that simple. Sometimes a car won't work because the engine is at the opposite end of the garage sitting in its own pool of oil. The car's owner, does not see a problem, only a future where it really will work. They can polish it for that concours (beauty) contest. That engine they rebuild is likely to be better than new and perfect for taking to Goodwood and entering races. To top it all off and to make up for all those years when their classic did not go anywhere, they are planning to go on some epic road trip.

Obviously none of this deluded dreaming is ever likely to become reality. The sufferer is quite likely to keep the classic and even add to the collection with more hulks and more dreams. Trouble is even if the owner wants to kick the habit a half-bodged classic car can be difficult to get rid of. No one else would be stupid enough to take it on. That's why a certain type of classic car owner will continue to stockpile parts, useful magazines and books. Slowly it dawns on him, and I guarantee that it will be a him, (as women are far too sensible to waste their lives and money on something like this) that perhaps buying a finished classic, like those pretty ones in the colourful classic car adverts would be a good idea.

However, buying a fully restored classic car may seem like a solution to one sufferer it is perversely the bitter end for another. Mostly they will be selling under some sort of duress. If the rebuild has been properly done it is unlikely that the amount it sells for would even begin to cover the restoration costs. That's the reality, because only in exceptional circumstances, if say the vehicle is a Bugatti Royale, rather than a Vauxhall Royale, is there any potential to make a profit. Financially there is little justification for this hobby, but is it actually a hobby?

No, it's an obsession and often a slightly unhealthy one at that. The hours spent in unheated garages, or open driveways must increase the likelihood of arthritis. Hands submerged in used engine oil are more likely to cause cancer than exfoliate clogged pores. Then they're the other health and safety issues involving axle stands, hydraulic jacks and over eager pets that could result in a Hillman Minx being parked on your head. Yes classic cars can be very bad for your physical as well as mental health.

I believe that I am more than qualified to tell you how not to restore and care for a classic car, even though I am not the biggest offender in that respect. In fact, I've never paid storage fees, neither have I lost a finger, got divorced or been declared bankrupt as a result of owning my Mini or any other old car. But then I did think it just might be possible to tell the great little car's story whilst detailing my own mistakes and misadventures. Especially as the Mini is celebrating fifty glorious years....hold on that was 2009. Oh dear. It's a good job I've got a Cooper then. That model came out in 1961....oh so I've missed that anniversary too. Well actually January 1962 is when the Austin Se7en Cooper was renamed the Austin Mini-Cooper, but then you'd have to be reading this in 2012 and

My Mini Cooper it's part in my Breakdown

I'm still writing it. All right then 1963 is when aluminium suspension trumpets replaced the steel ones. So it's the 50th anniversary of that. Except that in November 1963 the first 998cc Cooper engine was built which would ultimately replace the 997cc version. As this book progresses the relevance of that rather dreary fact will become apparent. So here it is then, a book to celebrate the 50th anniversary of the 998cc Cooper engine, but it is about a lot of other things besides.

So I stand corrected and really don't want to retread too many of the old stories. Indeed, as well as following the lack of progress on restoring my Mini Cooper we will be putting the Mini in context. Just what it was up against at the various stages of its 40-year career, which doesn't happen often.

Right now the original Mini and Mini Cooper have never been more relevant or in demand. In 2012 as I write some idiot, sorry investor, has just paid £40,250 for a rusty old Mini. On that reasoning someone will surely pay £12.99 for a spanking new book about Minis, with no signs of corrosion at all. To be fair the old Mini in question was a piece of history. A 1959 Austin Mini Seven De Luxe it is believed to have been the eighth off the production line, which was three months before the model was officially launched. It also hadn't done much in the way of mileage clocking up just 30,041. Finished in Farina grey paint and it has to be said, rust, the driver's door had been replaced, but otherwise it was original. One old lady owner Gladys Hobro and then inevitably a bloke, called David Gallimore wisely parked in his garage and left it there untouched. I wish I had done the same with mine.

Let's move onto more cheerful things, the foreword by the late great comedian Les Dawson. He should really have been Sir Les. He loved cars and Jaguars in particular. Indeed, when I was asked to write a series of silly books back in the '80s for Haynes Publishing he kindly wrote a foreword for the Jaguar one. He must have liked the book because I saw it on his desk many years later after his death when a TV documentary showed it taking pride of place on his desk. Here you can read how he was just as consumed by the need to bring yet another big cat back to life. In his case it was a V12 E-Type

6

but it could have been any old car at all. Like all of Sir Les's scripts, books and performances it is very funny and you can hear his distinctive voice as you read it.

So far I may have given the impression that old cars were rubbish. Well, many are, but the Mini and Mini Cooper in particular are different. Reinvented by BMW who not only massively increased the size of their version of the Mini, they also made it all upper case. The MINI is not a Mini it's a smallish BMW. A sort of 0.75 Series. However the residual goodwill that the original Mini had carried over to the brand new car. MINI may be good to drive, but the similarities with the lowercase Mini ends there. Ultimately the three door MINI is a 2.25 seat hatchback with a wafer thin boot. It really isn't that useful, or that Mini. The original was a smidgen over 10 foot and just 4 feet 7 inches wide, whereas the MINI, is an inch shy of 12 foot in length and an unforgivably porky 6 foot 4 wide. Yes the MINI has the wrong badge, but one badge, which helped the image no end.

BMW may have bought the rights to all the BMC names including Lord of the Rings like Elf, Moke and Hornet but chose to use the most valuable of all, Cooper. Cooper meant a Mini that was fast. Cooper meant a Mini that looked cool. Everyone wanted a Cooper, or to make their Mini look like a Cooper. That name meant world champion Formula One cars, rally and race track wins against seemingly impossible odds and of course Michael Caine blowing those bloody doors off. Whilst an original Mini is classless, practical, economical and surprisingly spacious, the Cooper was just a bit more special. Indeed, the Mini Cooper S was even more special, and that S could have stood for special but is quite likely that it is actually Sport, though no one seems to know. Just as no one seems to know, least of all me, why my Mini has taken so long to restore.

So because there are long periods of complete inactivity, whilst my Cooper festers in various garages it seemed to like a splendid opportunity to tell the whole Mini story. After all, without the Mini, you can't have the Cooper and by the end of the Mini's life, it was pretty much all about the Cooper. The Mini and Mini Cooper offers a fascinating tale of how one man's vision was turned into a perfectly formed car.

The Mini story, which really should be part of the school curriculum. It's inspirational proving that one obstinate genius (Alec Issigonis) can get his own way and change the way that small cars are made forever. Then along comes another maverick (John Cooper) who has already rewritten the formula one blueprint switching the engine from front to rear, sprinkles his own go faster fairy dust over the Mini to make the Cooper.

I think can tell the story partly because Minis have been an integral part of my life. From the time in 1962 when I first rode in my Uncle Charles's brand new Austin Mini Seven, to buying my sister's very used Austin Mini Super De Luxe to driving my mum's automatic Mini Clubman, then buying a few more and creating an utterly spurious tuning company called **Rüpp**_Speed_®. There has not been time when a Mini wasn't somewhere or other in my life, even if it was in bits, rusting, or just unwell.

I think I should have done better when it comes to finishing my Cooper off, because over the years I have interviewed some classic car owners who have been heroically dedicated to their cars. Some have completed restorations in lock ups with no electrical power. Others to the joy of their neighbours have rebuilt a car in the street. Many have burnt out several drills grinding away the rust. The hardcore would take a week off work to prepare their car for competitions. Others excavated their garage so that they had an inspection pit, all better to buff the track rod ends to a brilliant sheen that few could have appreciate, unless they had an angled mirror on the end of a stick, like the bomb squad. Indeed, some garages were fantastic shrines to their classics with posters, pictures, models in glass cases and in one case a Union flag painted onto the pack of their garage door. Mine is just grey primer with a garnish of cobweb and ingrained dirt.

Hopefully there will be a happy ending to all this. Not just a Mini Cooper I can drive, but a Mini Cooper that I really want to drive. When I first started this book years and years ago the Mini didn't look good. It had no MOT, a recently seized rear brake, and a Mini Metro engine where the real, even more leaky one should have been. Fast-forward to right now and the body has been rebuilt and painted. I know because I've seen it. The original engine is complete too, but as yet, not actually bolted inside the body. I've asked for all the bits to be scooped up and put into boxes so I will try and finish it myself like a great big Airfix kit. But I don't fancy my chances. Every time I've tried to do anything constructive with my Mini it's all ended in tears, burglary and financial irresponsibility. But you can read about all that later.

In the meantime my name is still James and whatever happens by the end of this book, I really shouldn't be trusted with an old car.

The Mini Books I've Read

I've bought and read them all. The first one I got was Mini by Rob Golding which is excellent, I loved Amazing Mini by Peter Filby and I've got cuttings and road tests from dozens of car magazines including Autocar and Car Magazine, Autosport and What Car?

Probably one of the best books I've read, which wasn't just about the Mini was written by Gillian Bardsley and called 'Issigonis The Official Biography' published in 2005. She is now a senior archivist at the British Motor Industry Heritage Trust. Gillian was instrumental in letting me rummage around the files. She made far better use of them and quite rightly emphasised the point that every chronicler of the Mini story has missed, which is that it's been made up. Many of the quotes and stories over the years have been designed to tell a tale. So all of those "We must drive these bloody awful bubble cars," quotes need to be taken with a huge pinch of new specification MINI Salt. Which means that The Mini Story by Laurence Pomeroy, which I thought was all-true, probably isn't. That's journalists for you.

Mini Thanks

Brian Luff, an ex Lotus engineer who gave me many Mini pictures and explained Issigonis from the engineer's perspective. The late Alan Bridle for working on my Mini in the 1980s. Mark Nolan at Bank Garage for looking after my Mini in the '90s. Ted Sparrow at the East Anglian Mini Centre for actually finishing my Mini, I hope.

My Mini Cooper it's part in my Breakdown

Car Magazine for allowing me to dip into their archive many years ago, in particular Nick Elsden and Richard Bremner. Kevin Jones and Dennis Chick at Rover when it existed, for their help and the Rover group copyright photographs. Also at Rover in the old days it was Pam Wearing who very kindly took me around Longbridge and introduced me to everyone on the production line, including the remarkable Geoff Powell and Brian Dipple. Gillian Bardsley, Karim Ram and Phillip Zanella at the British Motor Industry Heritage Trust who couldn't have been more helpful. All the people who have let me photograph their Minis over the years especially Lynn Thompson, Kate Perrins, Malcolm Harbour and Clive Powell.

Thanks to my Mum and Dad for putting up with lots of Mini bits around their house over the years. Finally my wife Dee who also tolerates a lot of Mini related nonsense and copes with my fragile mental state and when it all got too depressing said, 'just get the damned thing finished'. Which I may have done. Oh and before I forget, Olivia who will inherit the Cooper whether she wants to or not.

Dedication
To Marion. For selling me her old Surf Blue 850cc Mini in 1977 for fifty quid and starting all this nonsense.

Foreword by the late, great comedian and classic car enthusiast Les Dawson which doesn't actually mention Minis, but that's not the point.

My Mini Cooper it's part in my Breakdown

To freely confess to once having had a passionate love affair
with a motor car, could I suppose invite an investigation into
one's moral and physical condition by worried relatives. But
I did have such an encounter and it was to say the least: a
smouldering relationship.

It happened quite a few years ago when financial ruin often
stared me bleakly in the face. At the time, I tottered about
in a venerable Morris saloon that was so old, it had a secret
passage in the boot, and it did'nt have a hand brake...it was
a pike staff.

When that noble metal patriarch finally wheezed into a death-like
state in Urmskirk, I cursed life roundly and vowed never to give my
heart to another saloon car, especially ones that required a major
service at Lourdes. But of course fickle fate or whatever, saw
things in a very different light, and one morning as a watery sun
bled it's feeble rays over a Manchester abbatoir complex, in a
car showroom...I fell hopelessly, head over heels in love with a
second hand Jaguar X J Six. It lay in wait; throbbing like Blake's
tiger"Burning Bright".

                    .

Her paintwork shone and glittered....the loveliest blue I had ever
seen; the bumpers sparked off fragments of shimmering atoms...
To hell with ruin...I had to possess that Jaguar.
There is no point in going on about how I got my hands on the car,
suffice to say that I did without actually creating a crime wave to
raise the cash.(Although frankly, at one stage I thought seriously of
selling two of my kids for the deposit) That Jag and I were lovers;
we purred the lanes together, we roamed the hills together and we
darted through traffic like minnows together. That first Jaguar of mine
gave me four years of unbridled bliss before juddering to a halt one
night in Bayswater, never to move a sprocket again. I've ran Jags
for years, I love 'em but I swore I'd never show my emotions so
openly, and I meant it....But now in my garage there is a 1973
12 cylinder fixed head "E" Type...Here I go again.

Date: Mileage: 0 Amount spent: £0 Minis in my Life: None MOT: n/a

Here is the Mini Cooper instrument binnacle that will appear when I start spending money on the Mini Cooper. As you can see the engine hasn't been started, warmed up or even ticking over. In fact my Mini, or indeed any of my Minis have yet to be built.

By way of explanation the oil pressure gauge shows how well the Mini is actually running, if at all. The water pressure flickers with my interest level ranging from hot to stone cold. The fuel gauge indicates roughly how much money I'm pumping into the thing, E symbolises an empty wallet and F must stand for fortune. Finally the speedometer is the best guide as to just how finished the Mini Cooper is. I think 30mph at least means it is one piece. I'll add another 30mph for a current MOT (roadworthiness certificate), a further 20mph if it especially tidy and only when it hits full speed, 100mph, will it be officially finished. You'll have to wait until the end of the book to see if we reach the magic ton.

My Mini Cooper it's part in my Breakdown

And there will be more silly drawings, because at the end of the chapters there will be Minis. Here in chronological order will be the Minis in my life. They will change, sometimes be subtlety updated and may even be rebuilt to reappear later. The featured Mini or Minis will be larger than the others and the story will revolve around them.

1. **A History of the World in Small Cars – here's the proof that cars started small but then got much bigger, more exclusive and unobtainable. It's a good job then that the whole complicated world of cycle cars, light cars and three wheelers arrived to fill that gap. Here are just some of the odd modes of transport from way before the Mini ever existed...**

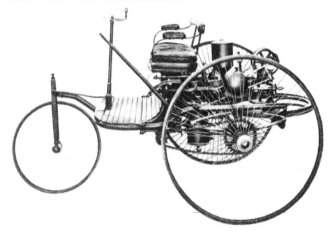

The first Benz, much smaller than a Mini and arguably just as pure, but makes do with just the three wheels.

Imagine for a moment the world without the Mini? Course you can't, but once upon a time there weren't any Minis or indeed any cars. Except that the very first car, was in its own way, also the first Mini.

In 1885 Karl Benz put together the elements that made up the first car, which was minimal in every sense of the word. It was just 93.5 inches long (2378mm) and weighed in at 584lbs (265kg). To make it really manoeuvrable Benz made do with just the one wheel up front. Pushing it all along was a tiny three quarter horsepower engine. It certainly wasn't quick (12mph tops), but when it is so small and light you really don't need a big power plant. Yes the Benz was the blueprint for

15

the Mini except that it had one less wheel and only seated two.

The world though was not exactly ready for this brilliant new invention. The Mannheimer Zeitung newspaper described it as "useless, ridiculous and indecent". They also went further and asked this important question, "Who is interested in such a contrivance as a horseless carriage so long as there are horses for sale?"

Well, actually just about everyone would want to get on board their very own personal transportation device, but it hadn't exactly been proven yet, which is where Mrs Benz came in. Motoring needs more heroines and Frau Benz fits the bill. Her role in the birth of the motor car has been largely overlooked. Yet Berta was with her husband all the way, whether it was postponing financial disaster by using her families money, or just being there to support, encourage and be involved in the first ever car crash (the out of control Benz hit a wall). She would spend evenings on her sewing machine treadle, not repairing Karl's work shirts, but driving a generator, which was charging up batteries. And most significantly of all, Frau Benz was instrumental in proving that cars would be our future, as the world's first test driver.

In summer 1888 Berta along with their two sons, Eugen (15) and Richard (13) didn't just undertake an epic journey from Manheim to Pforzheim, this was also the earliest incidence of taking and driving away. Husband Karl was tucked up in bed when the rest of the Benzes made a break for it in order to visit relatives.

This journey was not just significant, but truly epic and who knows, it may well have been embellished or largely made up, but I doubt it. There were no roads, just cart tracks. Hills were a problem as there were no gears on the early Benz, so Frau Benz and her larger son would have to get out and push. No petrol stations, just the odd chemist that would sell them fuel by the tin. No garages, so a cobbler added leather to the face of the wooden brake block. Indeed, the Benz's were very resourceful. A hatpin cleared a blocked fuel jet and a garter was used to hold together a faulty electrical circuit. So this very first 'Mini' tricycle car completed a major day long journey with plenty of incident. Clearly there was no going back to the horse and cart.

Companies that had previously built bicycles and carriages saw an opportunity by simply adding an engine and in some cases extra wheels to what they already made. So the history of the early small car becomes complicated as hundreds of models were designed and built.

Benz added a fourth wheel in 1893, Gottlieb Daimler built a quadracycle (effectively a four wheeled cycle) in 1889. Edward Butler patented the first British vehicle in 1887 a motor tricycle that he called the 'petrol' cycle, the first recorded use of that word. Frederick Lanchester was keen to distance this new invention from the horseless carriage and in 1896 designed a unique frame and the four wheel car, which significantly had the first steering wheel. In the same year across the Atlantic Henry Ford built his first car, which was a quadricycle. These early models were all small, light and innovative just like the Mini from 1959. Then suddenly they put on weight.

Motoring never had been for working people and as engine technology improved and could shift bigger bulks around, cars got suitably massive. Made of steel with huge engines, only the landed gentry, industrialists and idle rich could afford them. They were also reluctant to do anything as grubby as actually drive them. This meant a whole new breed of automotive servants, or chauffeurs engaged to steer these huge land yachts around. Then came a worldwide economic depression in 1907, just the sort of crises that led to the creation of the Mini in the 1950s. Then came Henry.

The Ford Model T was at the 1908 Olympia Motor Show, which went on sale for £225. It was relatively light, tough and easy to drive and everyone loved it. Here was the world's first people's car, a title that only the Volkswagen Beetle and later the Mini, truly deserved. The T was the first car designed to reap the benefits of mass production and it was certainly built down to its own low price. In the first year four hundred Model Ts were sold and it encouraged Ford to establish a production plant in Trafford Park Manchester. For European manufacturers

this new car was so cheap they could not possibly compete. There was though a new type of vehicle, which did allow them to fight back, cycle cars. Part cycle, part car, part motorcycle, but mostly a cheap, draughty and uncomfortable way to get around.

A year after the T made its debut the Bedelia, surfaced in Paris as one of the cheapest, crudest, most difficult to drive and ridiculous little cars ever built. It had tandem seating, one behind the other, a narrow wooden chassis and a belt drive from the single cylinder air-cooled engine drove the rear wheel. It was though very cheap, selling for 56 guineas in Britain. And the British were quick to cash in on the craze for these so-called cyclecars. Ron Godfrey and Archie Frazer Nash produced the G.N. cycle car and production began in 1911 and they were quickly joined by H. F. S. Morgan designed a distinctive motorcycle based car. The former company's three wheelers would eventually prove to be more durable and popular than the fad for cycle cars.

However, Europe needed a more grown up rival to the Model T and what became known as the 'Light Car' emerged yet again in France. A motoring magazine L'Auto encouraged smaller racing cars to compete for a trophy which led to smaller four cylinder engines being developed for the road. Most famously Ettore Bugatti designed a car that he sold to Peugeot and called the Bébé when it was

18

launched in 1912. In Germany there was Wanderer who came up with the Puppchen that translated means Doll.

A cyclecar. Not all of them were as elegant as this one, which DKW used to test out their motorcycle engines in a four wheel application.

In Britain Singer had moved in from bicycles to cyclecars and then light cars. William Morris who had simply been retailers of cars and builder of his own bicycles produced his own model, the Oxford, in 1913, which proved popular, not least because it only cost £175. Cleverly Morris used the techniques he had learnt building bikes and applied them to cars. So he simply acquired parts from specialists and assembled them. However, it was still £25 more than the Model T, which had been steadily dropping in price. Then the Great War got in the way.

Germany may have lost the war, but they were enthusiastic pioneers and consumers of the kleinwagen, or small car. That's because there was a shortage of materials and a surplus of designers forbidden by the Treaty of Versailles to build aircraft or weapons. Although there were aircraft designers like Hans Grade who built three wheelers, the established industrial manufacturers all downsized in order to survive.

Adam Opel was the founder of the family business. A mechanic, he first built sewing machines, but it was his five sons passion for cycling, which led him to manufacture bicycles in 1886. He died in 1895 and left a company big in bikes and sewing machines and looking for a new product. After several false starts an agreement to build French Darracqs in 1900 proved successful. A fire wiped out the factory and it was decided to concentrate solely on cars.

After the First World War a decision to build another French car kick started their recovery. It was called the Laubfrosch, which is German for tree frog on account of the fact that it was painted bright green and moved a bit jerkily. However, that didn't stop it selling in decent numbers of around 120,000 during its seven-year production run. Weighing in at just 600 kilograms in Germany and 1,322 pounds in the UK, it was introduced in 1924 and looked not unlike the Austin Seven, which had arrived two years earlier.

1931 Austin Seven and remarkably this is the long wheelbase version.

Herbert Austin realised that there was a gap in the market for a small affordable family friendly car that wasn't a Model T, in fact it would be even cheaper. However, his own car company didn't think much of the idea, so he went to his country pile with a draughtsman, Stanley Edge and set about designing the simplest car possible. It comprised of a chassis, basic suspension, a tiny four-cylinder engine, whilst the bodywork was made up of steel panels and some aluminium over an ash frame. That made it light and very simple and most of all it really was cheap. The starting price was just £225 making it the 'motor for the millions' according to the advertising blurb.

My Mini Cooper it's part in my Breakdown

So for the price of a motorcycle and sidecar combination buyers could get a proper four seat open top car that had no discernable trace of cycle in it.

By 1926 the price had dropped to just £145 and by 1929 it had sold a staggering 100,000. With over a third of the UK car market the Seven had blossomed into a complete range models including saloons, sports cars, and delivery vans. The Austin Seven became the nations' favourite car because it was so adaptable and just so damned cute and useful. Suddenly more people could enjoy the delights of motoring with their family in a car that was easy to own and cheap to run. Not only that, here was a sports car that in competition humbled much larger and more expensive machinery. It was the perfect car to brighten up the otherwise depressing 'Depression'. Wonder if that would ever happen again?

Not everyone thought the Seven was so brilliant. Motorcycle manufacturer BMW were growing steadily, successful in competition and looking for acquisitions. So when they took over the Dixi Automobil Werke in 1928 they also picked up the licence to build the Austin Seven and with it a large slice of German small car market.

BMW were not impressed by the level of engineering in the Austin Seven, redesigning significant parts before pulling out of the agreement to build the car. Sixty years later BMW were just as non-plussed when they took over Rover (which included the Austin marque), being very embarrassed by the dated Austin Metro. They were compelled to cancel what was effectively a coffin on wheels according to crash test results.

That's fast forwarding a bit too much, but future BMW rivals Audi, back in 1928 known as AUDI Werke AG was acquired by JS Rasmussen, the head of the DKW Empire famous for its motorcycles. Essentially Audi was dumbed down to develop simpler and cheaper cars. Indeed, Rasmussen gave a brief to designers to build a small car powered by a DKW motorcycle engine, front wheel drive and a wooden body - to be developed in just six weeks. Amazingly the brief was completed and the car, the P 15 went on to sell over 250,000, making it Germany's most popular car at the time.

My Mini Cooper it's part in my Breakdown

Back in Blighty, there was always much love for the Seven, which technically became the very first Jaguar, well sort of. Company founder William Lyons and his neighbour in Blackpool, Thomas Walmsley built a motorcycle sidecar. They went into partnership to form the Swallow Sidecar Company in 1922. In 1927 they went on to fit new bodies to Austin Sevens which they then called Austin Swallows, all for just £175.

The finish was superb. On a saloon you would find cloth covered trim, distinctive fresh air trumpets behind the bonnet and two-tone paintwork, usually the preserve of luxury cars. Remarkable as it may seem now, buyers were also treated to a full set of instruments. Usually on basic Sevens owners would have to make do with simple warning lights. William Lyons soon learnt that keen pricing and great styling was a recipe for success. So tarting up a Seven was a money-spinner, a trick that of course would work a treat with Minis.

Yet again we are jumping ahead when again we should be looking at the other countries in Europe that appreciated, celebrated and produced, brilliant small cars. France was there right at the beginning and it is worth taking the time out to consider one designer in particular.

Gabriel Voison is an often overlooked engineer of quite staggering genius, producing a range of planes, cars and even prefabricated houses that were at times brilliant, and at others just very weird indeed. In engineering terms he not only predicted the layout of future cars he built them too. Obsessed by saving weight and aerodynamics he nonetheless designed huge cars with large V8 and V12 engines that the rich and famous loved. Dedicated to reducing weight reduction he used timber and aluminium with mixed results in the styling department. Due to poor sales his company lurched from one financial crisis to another and this meant he wasn't always in full control. Despising American styling and chrome he built eccentric prototypes including a front wheel drive V8 car in 1930. Built in collaboration with André Lefévre, the rights to the car were later sold on. Lefévre later joined Citroen and soon after the groundbreaking Traction Avant was born, a highly advanced front wheel drive saloon. We will leave Voison there for a moment, along with the Citroen 2CV, which may have been designed in '30s, but didn't actually break cover until the next decade.

A Fiat Topolino. Italy's own Austin Seven and just as lovable.

However, what did appear in the 1930s (1936) was a lovely little Italian and arguably the closest in spirit to the Mini. This 'baby' Fiat, the 500, best known as the 'Topolino' (little mouse, apparently a reference to Mickey Mouse) was easily the smallest mass-produced car of its time. With just two seats, a 13bhp 569cc engine and a 2000mm wheelbase, it was conceived to bring motoring to the Italian masses. Not surprisingly it proved to be an incredible success. In its original form the car stayed in production until 1948, when more than 110,000 had been sold. During that long run relatively few changes were made and the only notable modification for those who care about such things was the change from transverse-leaf independent suspension to a quarter elliptic set-up from the middle of 1938.

Another place where small cars were popular is Japan. Although the emphasis was on military vehicles which the government subsidised. The small cars though mainly looked like copies of Austin Sevens. The First Datson, (Datsun) in 1931 was almost identical whilst later versions looked like the Topolino. Imitation was the sincerest form of flattery, but at the time few cared about an insular nation knocking off Europe's greatest hits.

Except that Austin bought one to see if they had grounds to sue. We will return to the Far East later.

A continent not usually associated with tiny cars is America. There is a clue in the firm's name, because Bantam was officially known as the American Austin Car Company, which sprang to life in 1929 and built modified Austin Sevens under licence. Essentially these were blinged Sevens. America didn't understand the Seven and the firm, which had already been bought out, went bankrupt in 1934. It became American Bantam in 1936 and the cars sold through to 1940, but they never made a profit.

Incredibly, America did have their own homegrown Mini in the oddly styled Crosely. Powel Crosley Junior who was better know for building refrigerators and radios, built not just America's smallest, but also cheapest and most frugal (50mpg) cars from 1939. With an unreliable air-cooled engine it would briefly make sense for anyone who was affected by wartime 'gas' rationing.

America may never have understood the small car, but then they never needed too. It would not however stop designers, manufacturers and importers telling the public what they should be buying. The story of the small car isn't over just yet.

First Mini Memory? Well that would be the back of Uncle Charlie's Mini. It was an Almond Green Austin that he bought brand new in 1962. The first thing he did was take all of the hubcaps off and put them in a clear plastic bag, on the grounds that they would easily get lost or damaged. As a result the Austin Se7en looked rather hard. A bit like the owner. Docker and amateur boxing referee Uncle Charlie fitted Issigonis's Mini buyer profile perfectly, with the little car parked outside the working man's cottage, except in this case it was outside our house. Uncle Charlie and Auntie Flo loved upstairs in our house, which was brilliant. That meant I could go out on jobs with Uncle Charlie. He was a proper bloke and I remember him getting into a fight in a car park and what upset him the most was someone shouting, 'leave the old fella alone' when he was prone on the bonnet. I think it spurred him on to a knockout victory.

As his passion was boxing he would regularly put up fight posters around the east end of London and sometimes I would be in the back. I am not quite sure whether it was all strictly legal in a Bill Posters will be prosecuted terms, but there was paste, rolls of posters and brick walls. The little A Series engine ticking over in between pastings as I handed out another poster. This is one of my earliest and freshest memories that I have and the point when I thought that owning a Mini would be huge fun. After that all I ever wanted was Mini.

Aunt Flo climbs aboard the trusty Austin Mini.

My Mini Cooper it's part in my Breakdown

**Uncle Charlie in full flight and obviously playing to the
camera because in the next frame he tuck and rolls,
then jumps back on board without breaking sweat.**

2. **Bubbles, Three Wheelers and Rubber Bands...more cars that weren't actually called Mini, apart from the Bond Minicar and just why there were so many transportational tiny tots between 1945 and 1959.**

The conditions that created the small car in the past, namely economic depression and a scarcity of materials would once again spawn a brand new generation of ever smaller cars which all predated the Mini by several significant years.

In many ways the spiritual home of the small car was Italy. Fiat Topolino production restarted after the war and the 500B looked identical to the old model, but the changes were all under the skin. The engine got an extra 3.5bhp and the brakes, suspension and electrical equipment were all improved. Also in 1948 an estate version, the 500 Giardiniera-Belvedere made the small car more practical because it was finally able to carry four people in its longer body made from steel, wood and plastic.

In 1949 there were more changes as the 500C model arrived with a new front end and engines with aluminium cylinder heads. These models were also the first Fiats to have interior heating systems, proving that the basic Topolino had come a long way after some 131,000 had been built. What came next though was truly innovative, stylish and with the Multipla a real lesson in small car packaging.

Fiat 600, a lot more 500.

Introduced in 1955 the 600 had a monocoque body with two B pillar hinged 'suicide' doors (the doors opened backwards) and seated four. Powered by a 633cc (21.5bhp) water-cooled four-cylinder engine located behind the rear seats, driving the rear wheels and running on independent suspension.

Multipla. Perfect for family picnics, the world's smallest, and only, people carrier.

A year after the saloon, a full-length canvas sunroof became an option, but more significantly a new type of vehicle was also launched. The Multipla is arguably the first people carrier, albeit a very small one. This had three rows of seats and could accommodate a total of six people. In addition the two rear pairs of seats could be folded into the floor, leaving a large flat loading area. To cope with the expected extra weight the brakes, suspension and steering were all uprated.

What the whole of Italy had been waiting for though was a successor to the legendary 'Topolino', here was the vehicle that really mobilised the masses over three decades. Probably the biggest part of the model's appeal was its ability to cruise easily at 55mph yet deliver an astounding 53mpg. The handling was good too with wonderfully direct steering and a very chuckable nature.

Just in case you wondered, it's a Fiat 500. This is a later one with proper doors.

The 'Nuova 500' adopted a similar layout to the 600, so there was a rear mounted engine driving the rear wheels with independent suspension on all four wheels and those rear hinged 'suicide' doors. A first for Fiat was the air-cooling of the engine, which was a two cylinder 479cc unit producing 13bhp. This was attached to a four speed manual gearbox with a floor-mounted gear lever. Initially it was not the great success that Fiat had been expecting. This prompted them to launch two distinctive versions, the 15bhp 'Economica' and 'Normale'. Essentially the 'Economica' was as the original 'Nuova 500', but with a more powerful engine but at a lower price. As for the 'Normale' this also had the revised engine plus various other upgrades that made the small car easier to live with including opening door windows and a more usable rear seat.

Italy wasn't just Fiat. In 1957 Vespa made a passable small car that looked not unlike the 500, and also had a similar name, the 400. Also in the same year the Bianchina was equally 500 inspired and spawned a range of coupe, convertible, saloon and estate variants.

Then there was the Autobianchi and here is an interesting story. Like many car companies it is possible to trace their roots back to bicycle manufacturing. Bianchi was established in 1885, and they progressed graduated to proper cars from 1905 to 1939. After the war it was challenge to get back into the motor business but engineer Ferrucio Quintavelle managed to drum up interest from Fiat and tyre manufacturer Pirelli to form a new company in 1955. The motives behind this alliance seemed to be guaranteed tyre sales and for Fiat a free hand to design more upmarket and experimental vehicles. That last point is important and we will come back to that later. For the moment though the Bianchina models were extremely popular, effectively Fiat 500s with subtle flecks of chrome trim, fashionable wings and two-tone paintwork. The Bianchina meant very little in the UK, but Alec Issigonis was a fan.

A DAF, not at all daft and propelled by rubber bands.

Even the Dutch had their own little people's car in the shape of the DAF. Indeed, the DAF range of small cars, culminating in the 33 was every bit as innovative and well loved as all those other European icons like the Beetle, 500 and 2CV. In 1959, seven years after the start of the

DAF Truck production line, they started the production of passenger cars with the DAF 600, which was fitted with an air-cooled 2 cylinder 4-stroke engine. The unique selling point was its so-called "Variomatic" transmission, which used huge rubber bands. For the more technically minded it was essentially an automatic transmission that didn't have any actual gears. It was constructed out of a centrifugal clutch attached to a system of two belt driven sets of conical metal wheels that were separately adjustable at the engine and at the rear wheel.

Japan was bringing out some intriguing small cars that pre-date the Mini and its love affair with the Brit built baby. The 1955 Suzuki Suzulight was a step up from the motorcycles that the company was famous for with its 360cc two stroke, twin cylinder engine. Only 43 were made but it was a promising start.

Subaru's first car the 360 was an amazing rear engined creation from 1958, which resembled a micro Beetle. Part of the midget car movement that meant with a 360cc engine it was possible to park kerbside whilst bigger cars were banished to the garage. In fact the teeny 360 was just 9.8ft (2.99m) long.

The miniscule Austin A35.

America still had Croseys, which actually grew two feet (60cm) longer, but was still resolutely subcompact by their standards. 1948 was a great year for sales and there were sporty convertibles that must have made some sort of sense. The joke though started to wear thin and Crosley Junior went back to doing what he did best in 1952, making fridges and radios.

In Britain the spirit of the Austin Seven lived on in the Austin A30, and the A35. We will look at those in more detail later so instead let's spend some time with the hatch backed Austin A40 which had arrived in 1958. Yes you read correctly, a hatchback, well two-box shape anyway, because the true hatchback would not arrive for another year. BMC had realised that in order to break away from the dull models they had been serving up in the '50s they needed some Italian flair.

Now the A40 Farina may have looked simple, uncluttered and smart on the outside, but otherwise it was BMC business as usual with an engine from an A35 and also instrumentation on the inside from that model too. The outside was pure Italian and the design house involved with Pinin Farina, hence the model's name. It pioneered the two-box shape, with a small one at the front for the engine and a big one for both the people and their luggage and no boxy boot tacked on the back. Large doors meant that it was easy to get in and out of. The original saloon had a tailgate that opened downwards from waist height whilst the rear seats could be folded back to give almost estate car load capacity. In 1959 the Countryman model was a true estate car as the lower tailgate not only dropped down, but the upper one that incorporated the rear window could be lifted up. The A40 Farina symbolised a new era for BMC and it meant that Pinin Farina would get a decades worth of work from them.

**Austin A40. In Countryman format
pretty much a hatchback.**

Here was a truly groundbreaking car and
obviously twenty years ahead of it's time. The Farina sold
in decent numbers, some 340,000 over the next nine
years, but it was never seen as a particularly important
car at the time.

Otherwise the small car market that existed in
the UK of the '50s was a very strange one. Lots of British
companies in the 'never had it so good' era seemed to
fancy having a crack at building small cars. What many of
them had in common were sundry motorcycle
components, a plastic body, a complete absence of style,
oh yes and a very silly name. Most of these were not so
much Mini as micro cars and it was like the cyclecar craze
had come back again, but with added hallucinogenic
drugs.

Take the Astra Utility (1956-60), originally
badged as a Jarc it looked like a little van and was
powered by an Anzani engine mounted underneath the
floor and a three-speed gearbox. More successful was the
Bond Minicar (1948-65), with a very prescient name, a
three-wheeler which originally had a front mounted
Villiers two-stroke motorcycle engine driving the single
front wheel by a chain. Then there was the Fairthorpe
Atom (1954-57) a four-wheeled Brit bubble and BSA twin
powered Atomota (1958-60). How about the Frisky
Sport? Built from 1958-59. Yes it lasted that long and

33

came with (front hinged) suicide doors and a small Villiers engine.

Opperman (1956-59) sounded a bit German, but only had a low fuel consumption going for it, otherwise the Opperman was just a dull plastic body and a buzzy engine. The Powerdrive (1956-58) was a three-wheeler with two wheels at the front. As opposed to the Austin Seven powered Reliant Regal (1951-62), which had just the one at the front. The Scootacar (1957-65) was an upright egg of a tri-scooter at just 81" (205cm) long. More madness with the non-sweary Tourette (1956-57) which was another eggy design inspired by the German Mopetta, with a single chain driven rear wheel.

The Germans had the upper hand when it came to building what became widely known as Bubble Cars.

Uphill struggle for the Bubble car (this is a BMW Isetta) but only after the Mini arrived.

Indeed, the illustrious name of BMW was attached to the Isetta (1955-65) the quintessential bubble. When the war ended all of BMW's manufacturing plants were either dismantled, confiscated, or on the other side of the iron curtain. So they made anything from kitchen pots to coal scuttles and did not produce a car, the 501 which was not remotely Mini, until 1951. However, BMW got the rights to build the Italian Isetta Bubble car which proved to be a money-spinner for them, it was even built under licence in Brighton. However, this was not enough to save the company from going bankrupt in 1960.

As for the Germans that were not BMW. Glas (a company that BMW would eventually buy in the middle '60s) Goggomobils (1955-67), were almost roomy, but had mini-sized wheels. After the Isetta the best-known three-wheel bubble car was the Heinkel (1956-65), eventually built in Britain by Trojan. Messerschmitt (1953-64) was a tandem seat scooter, although the later Tiger had an extra wheel and a frightening amount of power. Nobel Fuldamobil (1959-61) a classic egg shape three wheeler that was also built by Lea Francis in Britain.

NSU-Fiats existed in the 1930s building Fiat Topolinos under licence and also Ferdinand Porsche and English designer Walter Moore produced some rear engined prototype cars that were recognisably the forerunners of the Volkswagen Beetle. NSU started building cars again in 1958 with the nicely proportioned rear engined Prinz range.

Behind the iron curtain a nationalised consortium called IFA brought together all the car plants in the East and went on to build rehashed versions of the pre-war DKW Meisterklasse. An all-new car though arrived in 1957 and was called Trabant, which meant satellite. That's because the Soviets had just launched the first satellite in the shape of Sputnik, a name that on reflection might have been name for the car.

The Trabant had a steel chassis and frame that was made on huge presses which stamped out the basic shapes in a dangerously poisoness and deafening atmosphere. The bodywork was thought to be fibreglass, but it was hardly as sophisticated as that. Duroplast sounded good but the ingredients were actually shredded plastic, brown paper and cotton waste, all soaked in resin. Overall these was not ideal working conditions and if the workers themselves survived all that and some didn't, they would then have to wait up 14 years to get to the front of queue to buy one. So was the Trabant worth waiting for? Three million were made so they must have been good.

My Mini Cooper it's part in my Breakdown

Powered by a small 499cc, which grew five years later to a massive 594cc, it could not operate as a four-cycle engine thanks to Soviet restrictions. So just like a noisy, smelly, old two stroke motorbike it ran on a combination of petrol and lubricating oil. Despite that the Trabant could hit a top speed of 62 mph, but take all day to get there. Hardly stylish to me it resembles a late model Morris Oxford, with just two doors that had been shrunk in the wash and given a lawnmower engine transplant. Its specification was equally bad for all citizens. No one got a fuel gauge or an interior light because they were never an option. For most of its existence the Trabant made do with motorcycle type 6-volt electrics, although a decadent, capitalist automatic gearbox was eventually offered.

It is probably worth mentioning the Beetle at this point which is not at all Mini as far as Europe is concerned, but certainly counts as sub compact for the American market, where it spend the next 20 years as their favourite import.

Meanwhile the French were offering us the Vespa (1958-61), which was an Italian design, from Piaggio but well built in France and a big hit in the Channel Isles apparently.

Remember Voison? Well he never let his concept of a front wheel drive, transverse engined car die. Instead he continued with the concept and the so-called Biscooter, or even Biscuter was made under licence in Spain. Built from 1951 to 1958 it used a 197cc Hispano-Villers 2-stroke engine and around 5,000 were sold before the Spanish population could afford something much better. At one point a sexy fibreglass body on a sporting model was introduced but no one fell for that. Here though is the clearest indication that before the Mini arrived a transverse front wheel drive layout would work, even with a big V8 engine. Whilst the Biscooter suggested that a lightweight small size would make it practical, cheap and manoeuvrable. Voison who lived to the great age of 93 (he died in 1973) was certainly around to witness the success of the Mini. Like Issigonis he kept on developing his small car and even designed a bigger 1300cc prototype car with four wheel steering. It would certainly have been interesting to see how the French Mini would have fared.

36

Instead the Brit Mini went on to colonise Paris in the '60s and '70s.

Actually what did colonise Paris and was even built there is the Citroen 2CV. Some might argue that it is not a particularly small car and it has four doors, but it is significant because of its simplicity, lightness, practicality and personality. Also the first official name it had was Toute Petite Voiture or Very Small Car. Oh and the fact that a decade ahead of the Mini, it was the front wheels which did all the driving.

The 2CV story is a suitably long and illustrious one, with all sorts of thrillerish twists and turns. The original proposal by managing director Pierre Boulanger in 1936 specified that Citroen would make a car which could carry two French farmers in clogs and 50Kg (110lbs) of potatoes at 30mph and 90mpg. "If a box of eggs were placed in the car and it was driven over a ploughed field, not a single egg would be broken." It should be "four wheels and an umbrella". However, the war got in the way and the prototype 2CVs were hidden away in case the Germans wanted to add the vehicle to their line up of people's cars.

Just as the Volkswagen had an affectionate nick name (Beetle) that stuck, the 2CV got a more sarcastic one, that didn't. So the Tin Snail was finally launched in 1949 and only available in grey until colour paint arrived in 1959. The French press called it Citroen's biggest mistake, yet almost four million were been built around the world, including unfashionable Slough in the '50s. It didn't catch on though. The 2CV only became a hit when re-imported in the '70s and the sandal wearing, Chardonnay sipping intellectuals adopted it as their own and started referring to it as the Deux Chevaux.

Here was the most unpretentious and classless car ever built, which like the Mini was embraced by those higher up the social order. What was so attractive was its simplicity, an air cooled, flat twin engine didn't provide much in the way of performance but that wasn't the point. The suspension was equally uncomplicated, a single shock absorber for each, which were interconnected, meant a sublime ride and the ability to delicately off road with ease. A roll back roof didn't just let the weather in, it meant that odd shaped loads could easily be accommodated. Actually not only could it take planks of wood, the simple hammock seats could be taken out to give a large van like load space. In production for 42 years until 1990, like the Mini it proved that the simplest of concepts have plenty of life in them. Not a small car by Mini standards, but an innovative, lovable and lightweight one. It left the UK market for the first time just as the Mini made its debut.

Mini Toys. My First Mini was a Corgi. The reference number that was printed on the box and on the bottom of the model was 226. I also remember a Matchbox gold Mark 2 model with Superfast wheels that I remember more clearly. It had a large 29 decal on the doors. Obviously these were used and abused to destruction. Mum would indulge me by letting donating some flour so I could play mini Monte Carlo Rally.

I used to enjoy modifying the models and as all the best go faster companies had Speed in their name, Broad(Speed)Well, so I thought that **Rüpp***Speed*® might work. Only later did I add the umlaut in tribute to the European origins of my name. Also my customers may think I had a Teutonic approach to the way I re-engineered the little models.

I then left small Minis behind until my sister made me a clay model of my first Mini for my 20th Birthday. Sadly as it was drying the Mini Model sunk on it's artificial rubber, so it has four flat tyres.

My Mini Cooper it's part in my Breakdown

3. **Issigonis the difficult genius and just how he came up with such a big idea for a small car. Also a guest appearance by Lenny Lord the great dictator, plus a Mosquito and a Dragonfly...**

Alec Issigonis. Mini. Inseparable and synonymous. You can't have one without the other. The genius and his Mini masterpiece.

One man with one automotive vision is a rare thing these days. Unfortunately there are plenty of other bodies waiting to get in the way of an innovative car. Opinionated stylists. Mad marketing gurus. Cautious corporate bean counters. Confused customer clinics. If it is impossible today to find a single person guiding the development of a new car, back in the '50s it was equally rare to find a mass market player like the British Motor Corporation (BMC) entrusting a design brief to just one man. But that is exactly what happened. Alexander Arnold Constantine Issigonis did not know it in 1956, but he was about to make history and invent the modern motor car.

My Mini Cooper it's part in my Breakdown

Born in the Greek City of Smyrna in 1906, Issigonis had a cosmopolitan background, his father being a naturalised Briton of Greek descent whilst his mother was German. Incredibly this family maintained a close connection with the motor industry through former BMW Chairman and Volkswagen director Bernd Pichetsreider, ultimately controller of Rover's destiny in the 1990s and his first cousin once removed.

In 1922 Issigonis came to England with his widowed mother having lost their home as a result of war between Turkey and Greece. Smyrna is now part of Turkey. Setting up home in London Issigonis enrolled at Battersea Polytechnic to study automotive engineering. After graduating in 1928 he joined a London design office and worked as both draughtsman and salesman on a project to incorporate an automatic clutch release on the gear stick. Later the Rootes Group proved to be more interested in Issigonis and in 1933 he went to Coventry to work for them, concentrating on independent suspension systems for Humber and Hillman. Issigonis furthered his suspension credentials at Morris Motors in Cowley from 1936. He was responsible for an independent front suspension system, which was tested on a Morris Ten in 1939, but because of the outbreak of war was not seen in production until 1947 on the MG Y-Type.

During hostilities he worked on a number of projects for the war department. A priority though was a new small Morris car. Work began in 1942 on what was initially known as the 6hp and soon after code named 'Mosquito'. A radical design it incorporated a large number of important innovations. The body construction was unitary rather than the conventional separate chassis. At the front was independent suspension with torsion bars, plus responsive rack and pinion steering. Its engine was placed ahead of the front axle and the car ran on smaller than normal 14" wheels. The styling was heavily influenced by the 1941 Packard Clipper, the most up to date motor car of the period. Although the power plant was scheduled to be a flat four engine, the existing Morris 8 unit was installed as a cost consideration. For aesthetic and practical reasons Issigonis, carved up the prototype and inserted an extra four inches width into the

41

prototype. This last minute action dramatically improved the interior accommodation and exterior proportions. The first Issigonis masterpiece had been born.

The Morris Minor was one of the stars of the 1948 London motor Show and went on to become Britain's most popular car. During it's long life, 23 years, the basic car changed very little. Power plants were updated a couple of times, but essentially Issigonis had the concept right first time, a trick he was to repeat with the Mini. With the Morris Minor he touched an important nerve with buyers who wanted simple transportation, but also appreciated the lively handling, reliability and durability. Despite this success Issigonis left Morris in 1952 for Alvis in Coventry. There he worked on a large saloon, which was the antithesis of the Minor. This V8 engined car had many innovative features including hydraulic interconnected rubber suspension units, which were developed by Alex Moulton, a long time friend of Issigonis. However, Alvis shelved this saloon to concentrate on the more profitable production of army vehicles. Consequently Issigonis decided to leave in 1955 and took up an offer from Leonard Lord, the boss of BMC.

When Issigonis started to sketch the Mini he was following in the great British tradition of building small cars. Obviously narrow roads, short journeys and a motoring public keen on economy are all conducive to small car culture, but the vehicle has to be a good one before it is accepted. Britain's own Model T which revolutionised the previously expensive pastime of car ownership was as we have already seen, the Austin Seven. This is what Sir Herbert Austin had to say in 1929: "I look back on the year 1922 as one that marks an important milestone in my life, for it was then that I introduced the now famous Seven which has made motoring possible for thousands who could not otherwise have enjoyed its advantages. The Seven has done more than anything previously accomplished to bring about the realisation of my ambition to motorise the masses. Of course, my little car was treated with a good deal of ridicule at first, but it cheers me up to notice that the appreciation which the Baby meets today is just as hearty as the erstwhile smiles were broad."

My Mini Cooper it's part in my Breakdown

Austin could have been talking about the Mini. In fact there are a remarkable number of parallels between the development and success of the Seven and Mini. Firstly the two men were both practical engineers. Like Issigonis, Austin was responsible for much of the car's design and both produced detailed sketches to express their ideas. Not only that, the prevailing economic circumstances in the post war 1920s and 1950s had similarities. Denied new cars, the public were eager to buy almost any form of transport. In the '20s that meant a strange and unsatisfactory cycle cars. In the '50s the emphasis was on economy after the Suez crisis and the country was flooded by mainly German two stroke, three wheelers, generically referred to as 'bubble cars'. What the Seven and Mini did was wipe out these small car pretenders at a stroke and motorise a group of the population who could not otherwise afford four wheeled, four seat transportation. In the words of Sir Herbert, "A decent car for the man who, at present, can only afford a motor cycle and sidecar, and yet has the ambition to become a motorist. It is also for the vast hordes of motorists who realise that, owing to taxation and the high cost of living, they are paying ridiculously for the privilege of using their car."

Like the Mini, the Seven became a British institution and went on to enjoy a glorious competition career. In fact, Issigonis built his Lightweight Special based on parts from an Austin Seven Ulster, which had independent suspension and rubber springing. This brilliant little car was discontinued in 1939. Then the war got in the way of any model development, but there was an interesting interlude in the late '40s when Austin bought a prototype car called the Duncan Dragonfly. This was a technically interesting two seater, which was powered by a transversely mounted two-cylinder engine, which drove the front wheels. Suspension was rubber. Does that sound a little familiar?

Well instead of pursuing this groundbreaking concept Austin came up with the A30. However, as this Dragonfly prototype existed at Longbridge at the time of the Austin Morris merger there is a strong suggestion that this vehicle could have influenced Issigonis thoughts when it came to devising a brand new small car. Surviving records curiously make no mention of the Dragonfly and the part it played, if any in the development of the Mini. Surely though it is too much of a coincidence for an existing transversely mounted two cylinder engined, front wheel drive car not to have had a bearing on a transversely mounted two cylinder engined, front wheel drive Mini prototype which first emerged in 1957?

The Duncan Dragonfly - The Mini's grandad? Quite possibly. Transverse engine, front wheel drive and rubber suspension.

Remarkably Austin entered the post-war car market without a small car, which was almost unthinkable at the time. Their big rival Morris had already scored a huge success with the Issigonis designed Minor. Then in the same year as the two companies merged, the A30 was unveiled at the 1951 Earls Court Motor Show. Like the Minor it was virtually an all-new car and the body was the first unitary construction body built by Austin. Under the bonnet was a new overhead valve four cylinder engine which became known as the A series which went to power every small car from BMC to

Leyland. Sadly it was in a pathetic state of tune, as the 803cc unit developed just 28bhp. Ultimately the A30 was less sophisticated than the Minor although the independent coil spring and wishbone front suspension was a nice touch and much better than the Minor's complicated torsion bars and threaded trunnions. What let the A30 down though was the indirect worm and peg steering, which was less than a match for the Minor's rack and pinion. Interior space was at a premium with just 48 inches of shoulder room across the front seats.

A range of A30 models soon emerged in 1952 with a four-door saloon followed by a two door a year later and in 1954 a van and Countryman estate. Specifications were basic to say the least on early models. Just the one windscreen wiper and sun visor, on the driver's side naturally, whilst the front windows were counterbalanced rather than having some complex winding mechanism and claustrophobically the rear windows were fixed. Not ones to miss a marketing trick Austin called the A30 the new Seven. Obviously it wasn't. Neither was its successor, the revamped A35.

Austin at least dropped the pretence of calling the A35, a Seven. It addressed many of the original car's shortfalls, especially in the power department, when they increased the capacity of the engine by a massive 18% to 948cc. Gearbox ratios were also revised and it became a much torquier and faster car. Whereas the A30 struggled to 60mph, the A35 romped up to 72mph. There were proper indicators rather than trafficators, the rear window was enlarged for improved rearward vision and all round it was a much better car. In all 546,672 were built, it proved to be a sturdily built and reliable little car. The A35 was surprisingly successful in competition too. However, with the introduction of the Pininfarina styled A40, with its revolutionary two-box shape the A35 looked a little frumpy and twee. Not surprisingly it was discontinued in 1959 and replaced by you know what.

XC 9001, Issigonis pre-Mini pet project that spawned the 1800. Note the Mini resemblance embodied in the roof panel, windscreen surround, rounded rear end and rather longer front end incorporating a very familiar grille shape and arrangement of lights.

Issigonis joined what was now BMC in 1955 and Chairman of the Corporation, Leonard Lord envisaged Issigonis devoting himself primarily to advanced product design. With this in mind a small team was assembled, including Chris Kingham and John Shepherd who had also been at Alvis. Jack Daniels, a brilliant draughtsman who had worked with Issigonis at Morris pre-war and had done the detail work on the Minor. The first project was a rear wheel drive family saloon, which was to feature Moulton's Hydrolastic independent suspension with a two box body. Code-named XC 9001 it was destined to be the 1800 model. A downsized version XC 9002 would eventually become the 1100. However, these projects were promptly dropped in March 1957 when a more important brief cropped up.

My Mini Cooper it's part in my Breakdown

Gotten Himmel! As they used to say in those War! Magazines. It's a Heinkel at 2 o'clock, which seems to have swallowed up a large British family. That's why Leonard Lord hated them then...

According to legend Sir Leonard Lord was offended by the sight of the mostly German produced bubble cars. The Suez crisis in September 1956 was the result of Egypt's dictator Nasser, closing the Canal and Syria cutting the main oil pipeline that crossed their country. This crisis had ushered in petrol rationing and it looked like this dire situation would continue indefinitely. Not surprisingly the British public put their faith in multiple mpg, motorcycle engined, three and four wheeled, plastic bodied, so called bubble cars. However, Lord reckoned that a small economical car did not have to be cramped and crude and told Issigonis so with the words "God damn these bloody awful bubble cars. We must drive them out of the streets by designing a proper Miniature car". No one is certain he actually said that, but it sounds good.

His requirements were simple: BMC's small car had to be a full four seater, use an existing engine, be smaller than any other car they made and be introduced at the earliest possible opportunity. Issigonis constrained himself even further by mentally drawing a rectangular box measuring ten feet (3.04m) in length by four foot (1.21m) wide and high. He decided that 80% of this available space should be dedicated to the four occupants and their luggage, resulting in a passenger compartment of just 8ft 6in (2.59m). Out of that tight brief which could have caused problems came several brilliant solutions, which made the Mini unique. The most obvious were the wheels, shrunk to an unusually small 10" (25.4cm) so that they did not intrude into the cabin. The suspension was also rethought as an independent system was always going to be a more compact package. According to Issigonis's calculations it left just 18in (45.7cm) to accommodate the power train. So a little lateral thinking led to the engine being mounted transversely, driving the front wheels via a gearbox and final drive built into the sump of the engine. Brilliant. All he had to do was make it work, in just two years.

Leonard Lord was effectively the Mini's Godfather. Born in Coventry in 1896, the home of the British Motor Industry, Lord went on to become arguably the most outstanding and successful car company bosses. His origins were humble, but he obtained a scholarship which got him to Bablake, Coventry's old established public school. The ambitious Lord worked initially as a draughtsman for Courtaulds and then went on to Daimler and Hotchkiss. When William Morris bought the latter company the exceptional Lord was difficult to miss and he was soon transferred from the drawing office to help reorganise Wolseley and from there he went to Morris.

Although Lord looked unassuming with spectacles, bald head and a cigarette permanently positioned in the corner of his mouth, he was a real corporate bruiser, "If the door isn't open, then you kick it open." He fell out with Morris and switched allegiance to Austin. He transformed Austin's production methods and introduced important new models like the Big Eight and Ten. By 1950 he was in a position to propose a merger with his old firm. This eventually happened in 1952 with the creation of the British Motor Corporation.

According to Mini legend without Lord there would certainly have been no Mini. He was the catalyst for the whole concept, he asked Issigonis to come up with a solution, which was exactly what Issigonis wanted: the smallest car with the largest payload space. Issigonis only had to produce some of his famously detailed sketches to get the go ahead. Lord set an incredibly tight deadline, just two years. In the end it took 25 months. This was partly due to the brilliance of Issigonis and his team, but the other crucial element was Lord's complete commitment to the project. Anything that the team needed he provided paper authority for it to be done, which amounted to immediate attention from any part of the BMC organisation. As he said to Issigonis after their decisive ride around the factory in the first prototype and is reported to have said, "I shall sign the cheques, you get on with getting the thing to work."

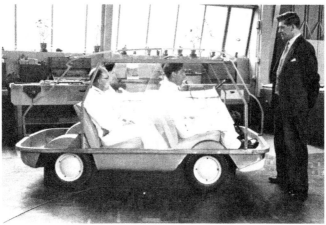

DO19 a radical small car proposal from within BMC trying to second-guess what the competition could come up with once the Mini was launched. Although rejected it is certainly a glimpse into the far future full of people carriers. Or it's a Multipla with less bodywork.

Lord retired in 1961 to become vice president and a year later was elevated to the House of Lords. "Lord Lord would sound bloody stupid" was his typically blunt comment at the time, so he became Lord Lambury. His successor George Harriman respected his old boss so much that he left Lord's office untouched and unoccupied until his death in 1967.

Issigonis was not the only designer given a clean sheet to come up with a brand new small car. Leonard Lord did not get where he was without being very shrewd. Consequently he invited ERA, the famous racing car company that also did contract work for the industry, to work to a similar brief. They were assisted by Laurence Pomeroy, technical editor of Motor and constant agitator for engineering change. With Pomeroy acting as the ideas man, they came up with the Maximin. This was a rear engined, air cooled proposal with the engine cast in aluminium and mounted transversely. Interestingly NSU arrived at the same conclusion with the 1000 just a few years later. For BMC though, the concoction would have been too costly and complex to build. The suspension was based on Firestone air bags with a constant height regulator whilst an otherwise conventional gearbox was shifted into gear automatically at set speeds. At least BMC must have thought that the name 'Maximin' had some potential.

Over at Cowley there was yet another project. BMC technical director Sidney Smith wanted to build a car for under £300. Charles Griffin responded with a rear-engined car powered by a two cylinder A series unit. With high silled bodywork and a sliding canopy in place of doors, they came in under budget whereas Issigonis missed by about £20. Griffin was also in charge of yet another alternative Mini project a few years later, before the new car entered production. It was decided to think like the enemy and come up with a rival small car, which would hit back at the Mini by being just as revolutionary and even better space utilisation. He came up with the fascinating DO19, a one-box design that may have resembled contemporary Fiat Multiplas, but actually predicted the people carrier. The engine was rear mounted and the sliding doors were made of Perspex. It actually was roomier than a Mini, but considered dangerous in an accident with the front occupants seated far too close to any impact.

Faced with all these alternatives, Lord it seems, picked the right one.

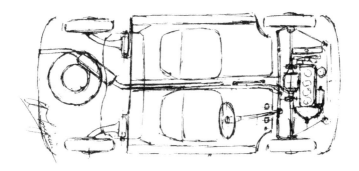

An early Issigonis sketch which shows the familiar layout with a transverse engine, trailing rear suspension, radiator on the nearside, but no subframes.

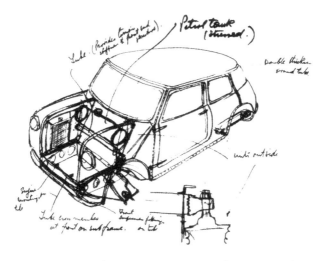

Bodywork style is now clearly emerging along with the front subframe, but the petrol tank would eventually relocate to the boot.

**XC9003 effectively a very scaled down XC9001, but
distinctively Mini and remarkably close
to the finished article.**

Initially the code name for the Mini was XC9003, but this was eventually changed to ADO (Austin Drawing Office) 15. This small car project was not the first time that Issigonis had experimented with front wheel drive, having studied both contemporary Citroen and pre-war DKW systems whilst at Morris. For him, stability especially with a small car meant placing the maximum amount of weight over the driven wheels.

Issigonis even went so far as to build a front wheel drive Minor by turning the engine and gearbox through 90 degrees. The car was completed just before Issigonis left for Alvis in 1952 so there was not much opportunity to see how it performed. In his absence Jack Daniels had driven the car in ice and snow and found the handling remarkable. It worked because the driveshafts to the front wheels incorporated constant velocity joints. This design feature had initially proved to be a big problem as their original proposal had resulted in a hub bearing that was as big as a brake drum and consequently very heavy. However, MG designer Syd Enever sent Issigonis a drawing of a Hardy-Spicer Birfield joint. This turned out to be a part for submarine control gear that also proved to be perfect for adaptation into a vehicle driveshaft. In fact, its origins could be traced back to 1926 and Czech, Hans

Rozeppa. Front wheel drive not only made sense as a concept, it was also a practical proposition for this new small car, but there was still a major problem to overcome.

Although there was enough room for an end-on gearbox in the Minor's big engine bay, the diminutive ADO15 presented a big accommodation problem. The stroke of genius was to site the gearbox beneath the engine. A specially designed clutch went outboard on one side of the engine so at least it was still reasonably accessible. The differential gear for the final drive was built into the sump at the rear of the power unit. Equal length drive shafts incorporated inner universal joints and Rozeppa constant velocity joints at their outer ends.

ADO 15, or more affectionately know to the testers as an 'Orange Box' one of the development hacks with an A35 'disguise' grille which actually worked and also provided excellent access to an engine which at this point is the 'wrong' way round.

There was not time to develop a brand new engine, so the power unit chosen was the well established A series, first seen in the Austin A30 in 1951. However the team did experiment with a two cylinder version simply by cutting the existing unit in half. In theory a smaller one would save space and money, but in practice

My Mini Cooper it's part in my Breakdown

it proved that a two cylinder A series could perform very inefficiently, noisily and roughly. Back with four cylinders, the engine 948cc engine proved to be dangerously quick for the time and long before the Cooper had even be considered, was topping 90mph. As a result the decision was made to cut the engine's output by 100cc. Initially the carburettor and manifolding faced the front whilst the ignition and electrical equipment was positioned at the back. This layout was subsequently reversed for the production car, the official reason given, was that this was warmer and stopped the engine icing up, even though later tests revealed that there was only about 1 degree in temperature difference. However, the engineers discovered that the large primary gears between the clutch output and gear train actually caused too much inertia for the synchromesh to cope with.

With the engine turned around an idler gear effectively reduced the size of the gearwheels. Routine servicing could be tortuous enough in that tight bay on the production model, but hiding the electrics away would at least have stopped the little car drowning itself when negotiating puddles. Experiments with the gear lever placement included a dashboard mounting which looked too quirky for British tastes, despite the 2CV precedent and was also thought to be less than direct. However once the engine was turned around and the lever located in its 'magic wand' position the change actually became even more vague. Only the later remote system restored the 'feel'.

An often overlooked yet crucial element in the overall success of the Mini were the tiny wheels and tyres. They helped keep the wheel arches down to Minimum dimensions so increasing interior space. Small tyres reduced the car's unsprung weight and also helped the car to look aesthetically correct. Issigonis could never understand why wheels needed to be so large and during a meeting with Dunlop indicated with his hands just how small they should be. That gap was measured as eight inches (20.3cm), but realistically the company settled on making tyres for a ten inch (25.cm) wheel. That was the easy part. However, making a small tyre, which could cope with high rotational speeds, not disintegrate, provide reasonable tyre life, great grip and stay on the rim was going to be a challenge.

Dunlop proved to be up to the task. Revised compounds made the tyres durable. A tubeless design with a wide ledge meant better security and a safety shoulder dampened down the liveliness of the steering. Development mileage was racked up using a German Glas Goggomobil, because prototype Minis were unavailable at the time whilst the Glas had equally tiny wheels.

In fact, tyre development went hand in hand with the car's future success, from radial ply to rally winning Coopers. Just as Dunlop had come up with well engineered and innovative solutions Lockheed had to solve the problem of making the smallest hydraulic brake system to date. For the standards of the time, the performance was remarkable.

Independent suspension came late to the shores of Britain. Although popular on the continent in pre-war years incredibly the first British mass produced car to have this feature was the Triumph Herald. Launched in 1959 it was quite primitive relying on transverse leaf springs and swing axles at the rear. By contrast the ADO15 had rubber cones with fully trailing arms at the back. This was a joint project also involving Alex Moulton, the Issigonis team at Longbridge and Dunlop who made the moulded rubber elements. Moulton's rubber cone system had been developed at Alvis and effectively provided a clever solution to the problem of independent suspension, which could have intruded into the passenger department. The principle at work here was that the doughnut like circular rubber diaphragms were effectively reduced to minimal thickness in the centre as they were compressed between two cones. One of them was attached to the subframe whilst the other was linked to a suspension arm. As a result this set up produced a steeply progressive rate according to the number of passengers and weight of the luggage. In addition, rubber has excellent self-damping qualities, which decreased reliance on the dampers, making the whole system both light and compact. Issigonis had long been convinced of the inherent properties of rubber as a suspension medium. His independently sprung and rubber suspended

Lightweight Special, which he built and used in competition was proof of that. He realised that for its weight the energy content of rubber was excellent, compact and cost effective. Even so, the proposed Issigonis-Moulton system for the Mini was to have been based on interconnected reservoirs, but there was no time to develop them. Eventually the Hydrolastic system would be launched on the 1100 in 1962 and the Mini in 1964.

There was even some experimentation with a rear beam axle, although it proved too intrusive, as it would have reduced that 80% of interior room fairly significantly. Even so, the Mini's amazing handling capabilities were no happy accident, Charles Griffin the chief development engineer can be roundly credited with creating the overall set up. He experimented for a long time with the relative geometrics at the front and rear of the car. As a result the rear wheels had a marked toe in, which reduced understeer. Added to this was the highly responsive rack and pinion steering which had done so much to make the Minor handle with such aplomb, though it was still considered unusual at the time.

Late ADO15 prototype with fixed van style grille as originally envisaged by Issogonis, a big fan of austerity.

My Mini Cooper it's part in my Breakdown

With all the mechanical problems addressed, Issigonis could get on with planning the bodywork which from bumper to bumper was to be a mere 10ft (3.04m). Of course, the Mini was not so much styled as evolved around the mechanical components. Form truly followed function. This really was Minimalism, an intended but accurate pun. As Issigonis once said, "Styling is designing for obsolescence." He was proved right by the Clubman, a late '60s update which added length and a square front end for marketing rather than mechanical reasons. It was no surprise that the Clubman dated rapidly and the original '59 design soldiered on undiluted.

As Issigonis commented years later, "The Mini was never meant to be styled. It is a functional thing....A car should take its shape entirely from the engineering that goes into it...The thing that satisfied me most was that it looked like no other car." So this shape was the smallest, simplest and most practical way of accommodating four people. The rounded panels looked natural whilst the external welding seams were incorporated for ease of manufacturing. Although it is true that Lord bankrolled the project, there were still strict budgets. Issigonis did not have enough money for jigs, so had to make his own, hence the seams around the roof and down the pillars. These are jigging ribs, which allowed the car to be spot welded together cost effectively. No wonder the ADO15 only cost £100,000 to develop.

Indeed, two-box styling was becoming a BMC trademark and was first pioneered by Austin with the A40 Farina model in 1958. Above all the Mini looked right with its tiny wheels at each corner and not an ounce of wasted weight, or metalwork. In fact, it was decided to increase the width of the body almost at the last minute by a further two inches to boost interior room and because it looked right. Interestingly Issigonis had made a similar late decision with the Minor although those four extra inches were much more obvious because of a crude plate spacing the front bumper! Any lingering doubts that Leonard Lord might have had about the shape were dispelled by celebrated stylist Pininfarina who uttered an immortal phrase, "Don't change it." They never did.

My Mini Cooper it's part in my Breakdown

As we have already seen, the Mini took shape in a remarkably short time. Just four months from Lord's orders a wooden mock-up of the body and major mechanical parts were ready. By October of 1957 two prototypes were already on the road. In July of 1958 Lord took a test drive in the car and then told Issigonis to get it into production within 12 months. Which of course was achieved. The first two prototypes were nicknamed orange boxes because of their bright colour scheme and were sent to work at Chalgrove aerodrome. Negotiating the poor perimeter road during a 30,000 mile, 500 hour test led to a major revision of the design. Although the bodywork was going to be unitary, it was decided to fit subframes front and rear to accommodate the power unit and suspension. The original arrangement involved bolting and welding these parts directly to the bodywork, but dangerous metal fatigue set in. The subframe solution however, also helped to isolate the passenger compartment from the worst of the vibration and noise caused by the engine and road conditions. Also it was found that whilst braking on an incline the rear wheels were unweighted and locked up. So not only was a brake limiter introduced, as only 40psi pedal pressure was needed to stop the car within 75ft (22.8m) at 30 mph, to improve weight distribution and balance, the battery which had been located under the bonnet was moved to the boot. Yet another reason for the Mini's excellent handling.

Pre production testing despite the tight timescale was very thorough. Some problems did emerge though. Firstly there was a slipping clutch caused by oil from the sump getting onto the plates. Noise was still getting into the passenger department via the gear lever this time. Torque steer made the steering somewhat lively under acceleration. And then there was that unusually hot and dry summer of 1959...

58

My Mini Cooper it's part in my Breakdown

You don't have to read any further if you don't want to, because this section of the Mini proves what the whole point of the car was, packaging. Not an inch of space was wasted, it was all about the passengers and their luggage.

That Mini Film. Now I love films. Films with cars in them though can be a bit hit and miss. Best if the car provides the supporting roles. Me and my mate Keith were the only two paying customers in the Rialto Leytonstone to watch Le Mans. We sat right down the front and felt a bit ill after and had to sit further back to avoid feeling racing car sick. And then there was The Italian Job.

Keith and me were there, but quite a few friends from school made it along too. Then I had to go and see it again and the only way I could do that was convince my parents to take me. Well, I convinced them that we should all go. It was in a brilliant double bill with the brilliant

My Mini Cooper it's part in my Breakdown

Monte Carlo or Bust which like The Italian Job came out in 1969. The venue was the Odeon in South Woodford. Unfortunately one row in front of us was a young couple that were not watching the film full time. Dad wasn't happy and he referred to their 'wrestling match' in the loudest possible voice more than once but I didn't care, because I got to see the Italian Job again.

Any film that can bring together the talents of Hollywood star Michael Caine, music hall stalwart Fred Emney, the bawdy humour of Benny Hill and the stiff upper lip of Renaissance man Sir Noel Coward, had to be brilliant. On one level the film itself was an amusing insight into the Brits abroad. Union Jacks, beer, football and the Mafia portrayed as uppity waiters. Of course, the Minis were the perfect cars for the bullion job. No other UK car would fit the bill, a limp Imp? Nope. A brutish Escort, don't think so. It had to be a Mini, for a start they were ripping off Fiat and there was no better way to show up those Polizi Alfas (Giulia Super 116bhp) than with a pack of screaming Cooper Ss (76bhp). Which er, would have been much quicker even with all that bullion in the back surely?

The swinging '60s bit you can ignore. The Noel Coward's home from home prison is preposterous. Irene Handel is briefly brilliant. Benny Hill is Benny Hill. It even has a cliffhanger ending. I'm not spoiling it for you because you've already seen it. At least seventy-three times.

4. **It's 1959 when the Austin Se7en and Morris Mini Minor were born and very soon after they sprang leaks, rattled a bit and then came over all Super De Luxe and Hydrolastic. Here's everything that happened up to 1967.**

Longbridge in 1959, sharing the line with the Austin A40 as production of the Austin Se7en begins.

According to Mini legend the first example was hand built by production foreman Albert Green. The order had come through from George Harriman to build three prototype cars. A new assembly line at Longbridge was earmarked for production, but no workers had been allocated to it. There was no alternative, Green, along with his chief inspector, Freddie Finch, set about their task. Green laid out all the components adjacent to 220 yards (201m) of assembly line and worked his way along it, with Finch inspecting every stage of production. Seven hours later, the car was driven off the line by Green, chassis number 101, engine number 101, painted white and destined to be registered 621 AOK and become the most famous Mini of them all. But in the week ending April 4th it was one of just two pre-production prototypes to emerge and it still had an awful lot to prove. Nothing happened at the Cowley Plant in Oxford until ten Minis were built during the week ending May 9th. Now that production had started preparations could now be made for the launch of this remarkable little car.

Managing Director George Harriman had first teased the press at a 1957 Motor Show luncheon in London by stating that the Corporation's statisticians and market researchers had discovered that the public did not want bubble cars, but a low priced, fully engineered car. "Obviously if the Corporation can produce such a car which will sell more cheaply, they will do so."

The launch venue was the Fighting Vehicle Research and Development Establishment at Chobham, Surrey and the date was August 18th 1959. The British Motor Corporation had invited the world's press to drive their new small car. After the old fashioned A35, journalists were asked to marvel at the brave new world of the Morris Mini-Minor and Austin Se7en. This secret army testing ground was a secluded location, which would not pre-empt the public launch and there were winding tracks, all the better to demonstrate the Mini's superb agility. There was the chance to thrash around the track at speed where Grand Prix winning journalist Paul Frere set an impressive 2 min 2 sec lap time on the foreign press launch two days later. Not only that there was the chance to tackle a one in four gradient from a rolling start no less. Then it was on to the dry skidpan and the revelation of vice free oversteer.

As far as the public was concerned the Mini hit the headlines on the 26th August. In keeping with the badge engineering principles of the time there were two distinct advertising campaigns for the brands. Either the names used on these all new cars referred back to a previous, or current greatest hit, hence Austin Se7en intended to conjure up an image of Austin's pre-war bouncing baby car. The Morris Mini Minor of course was alluding to the post war success of the rather larger Issigonis designed Minor. In fact, the new car was to have been christened the Austin Newmarket in keeping with the county theme adopted by BMC at the time.

Back in the glamorous world of advertising the Morris Minor was promoted as 'Wizardry on wheels! Far more room in far less space.' Alternatively, 'From Austin - a new breed of small car!' For once all the advertising puffery was actually backed up by hard facts that emphasised all the Mini virtues that the buying public would eventually come to appreciate: 40mpg, 70mph+, front wheel drive, independent suspension and a seriously space efficient interior. There was even a neat little plan view of the car to explain the east-west layout of the engine. O.K. so Morris lied about the 'big holiday size boot!', but otherwise the Mini delivered what it promised.

The Austin Se7en and Morris Mini-Minor were available in two levels of trim, Basic and De Luxe. There were also just three colours per model for the first three years: Speedwell Blue, Tartan Red and Farina Grey for the Austin and Clipper Blue, Cherry Red and Old English White for the Morris. Another distinction between the two marques were the grilles: Austin versions had eight horizontal wavy bars which were chromed and Morris models had 7 vertical and 11 horizontal barred item painted white. The basic car had fixed rear quarter windows, fixed passenger seat, rubber floor mats, one sun visor, cloth upholstery, no screen washers and not much else. Well, what could you expect for just £497?

All the launch press photos seem to feature Austins, so here's another suggesting that you could squeeze plenty inside, but surely not seven bodies from the publicity department?

An extra £40 bought you the De Luxe version and not surprisingly the vast majority of Mini buyers opted for the luxury trim and equipment. Compared to the basic Mini, the interior of the De Luxe was almost sumptuous. It comprised two tone vinyl upholstery, foam seat cushions, vinyl covered dashboard, a chrome surround on the switch panel, fleck design trim, chrome kick plates on the doors, pile carpets, a rubber mat in the boot and head lining which extended to the C pillars. The equipment level was just as dizzying as the front seat passenger benefited from an adjustable seat and sun visor. Fresh air was easier thanks to opening rear quarter lights, but there was less danger of freezing as a result of a heater and demister. On the outside, the De Luxe was just as distinctive. Chrome was lavished on the fuel filler cap, rear number plate surround and on the Morris version, the grille. There were also bright plastic inserts in the windscreen rubbers and rear windows. The bumpers had overriders, the wheel trims were full width and bright trim, which ran over both wheel arches, was joined together at the sill.

Another Austin in Basic trim, it gets admiring glances, but will it ever make a profit?

At just £496 19s 2d the Mini was a cheap car, possibly too cheap. At the time the cheapest mass-produced car was the Ford Popular at £419 on the road. The Pop was a dull, utterly conventional domestic appliance, with cart springs, side valve engine and three-speed gearbox. Yet the Mini was clearly being priced down to compete directly with it. The Mini also undercut its stablemates in the shape of the A35 by £41 and the Morris Minor by £93. More dramatically it knocked the exotic competition into touch by being £116 cheaper than the Fiat 600, also undercutting the Renault Dauphine and VW Beetle by a whopping £219. So the emphasis was on shifting units which began leaving Longbridge at some 3000 a week in an attempt to claw back some of the £10m invested.

John Barber who went on to become managing director of British Leyland was working as a senior accountant at Ford in 1959 and claimed that the American company was so astounded by the low price they bought a Mini and took it to pieces. According to their costings it was impossible for BMC to make a profit, estimating a £30 loss on every one. By contrast, Ford launched their completely conventional Anglia a year later, safe in the knowledge that at £93 more it would make money and appeal to a loyal core of committed buyers.

At the heart of the problem for the Mini was the fact the BMC still had not quite worked out exactly who was going to buy it. Issigonis had envisaged, quite wrongly, that this was a car for the workers. Those who needed basic, no-nonsense transportation. It wasn't. The complex mechanicals frightened them off. Potential buyers were scared of the technical advances and would

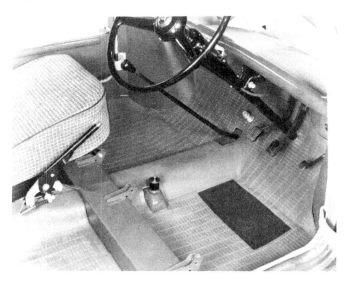

Spartan interior, rubber mats, no heater and a push button start. No passenger seat either, which was an option on the van.

rather stick with what they knew. Even a little further up the social ladder the aspirant lower middle classes were put off by the sight of an offensively small car. Small meant cheap, which it was. Not only that there were plenty of well publicised teething troubles and for a while there the Mini teetered on the edge of a very public and expensive failure. The Mini just did not add up.

Strangely it was saved by the press, high society and a bunch of racing drivers.

The reception given to the new small car was very enthusiastic. BMCs achievement in putting together such a revolutionary model at such an absurdly low price sent the press into raptures. This was not just a bunch of old motoring hacks towing the patriotic Brit cars are best line, they really meant it.

Motor Sport picked up on the new concept straight away identifying that they "Seem to belong to a new class of family vehicle - dimensionally they are very small - in fact Mini-cars." The magazine went on to applaud the innovation of the design and the bravery of BMC in allowing a proper 'clean sheet' approach. After years of banging on about not being left behind by the continental competition, with some fresh thinking, the magazine felt vindicated after being accused of having shares in VW's Wolfsburg factory. They were flabbergasted by the sensationally low price and summed up by conceding that BMC "appear to lead the world in small car design."

No shortage of storage space inside a Mini. These are Johnny Walker Red Label bottles, these days it would be milk cartons.

Sporting Motorist joined the Mini fan club. They appreciated the fact that Issigonis was not about to sacrifice ride at the expense of road holding. The magazine thought that the "Accurred benefit from the rubber suspension and independent rear springing gives rear seat passengers the most comfortable ride we have yet experienced in a very small car." Even in the wet they could corner the car on the limit with little roll and no hint that the car would break away. They found it quick too, "With only one up the little car accelerates away in the most sparkling fashion." They achieved better performance figures than BMC but admitted they probably had 'two up' at the time. Weirdly enough they were under the impression that the Mini had had an eight-year development period. Obviously a BMC PR officer reckoned that no one would swallow the two year and one month truth! The magazine went so far as to inform its readers that they were planning to buy a Mini-Minor so that they could report back on the day-to-day pleasures to their readers.

Over at Autosport John Bolster "Knew at once that this would be by far the best machine that the Corporation has ever produced." He liked all those features that for so long had been regarded as continental, which meant independent suspension and front wheel drive. Not convinced by the styling, he believed that, "One soon grows used to it, and the sheer good sense of its design appeals enormously." The outstanding feature turned out to be the suspension that despite the small wheels and poor road surfaces was "superb". The ability to corner at speed impressed, as did the quick, yet light steering. Overall he found the car well finished and despite the price, the build quality was not cheap. He concluded "I am so happy that at last patriotism may be combined with enjoyable motoring, and I have expressed my appreciation by signing an order form."

Autocar gave the car a dry write up, but still considered it to be outstanding which "Set new standards of comfort and road worthiness in the very small family car class." They saw most of its potential as a town car excelling in heavy traffic and proving to be a doddle to park. The magazine's editorial leader however, was an enthusiastic endorsement of the new model in particular and front wheel drive in general. "The road test report will gladden many hearts, for it offers great economy, lively performance, comfort for four grown ups and exceptional safety of handling, in a car costing home buyers around £500 total."

Motor had an Austin Seven De Luxe on test for 1,900 miles and reckoned that all the unconventional features: 10in wheels, rubber springs, transverse engine and front wheel drive "have justified themselves by results." The biggest miracle however was the packaging in a car that could be so roomy.

In fact, a lot of hacks were interested enough to enquire what the delivery situation was like on this radical new car. Engineer, motor journalist, builder of a rival Mini prototype and author of the first Mini book, 'The Mini Story', Laurence Pomeroy went a stage further and wrote to George Harriman suggesting that brother journalists should be given priority if they ordered a Mini. Harriman seized the opportunity and offered Minis on a twelve-month loan with an option to purchase at a fair price once the period was up. The long-term test car had been born.

BMC certainly needed all the good press they could get. In all 80 Minis were loaned out and they certainly got used. According to John Bolster of Autosport who reported back after six months of Mini-Minor motoring, although offered this extended loan, Bolster persuaded BMC to part with the blue car registered 981 GFC for cash. At the time of his report, Bolster had racked up a huge 10,000 mileage covered in the UK and France. He suffered from damp carpet syndrome of course, but the service department apparently put that right. Otherwise it proved to be mechanically reliable, never missing a beat. "Only an idiot or maniac could possibly have an accident." In short, the Mini-Minor proved to be nimble and practical. An interesting postscript to this piece was provided by Gregor Grant who reassured readers that a Mini could cope with long distances. He took his wife and three children, aged 16 (6ft tall!), 14 and 9 to Scotland complete with luggage, much of it packed onto a Portarack roof rack. He clocked up 1000 miles, averaged 44 mpg and the Mini used no oil, or water. He calculated that second class rail fares would have cost more than £22, whereas the cost of petrol for the 810 miles romp from London to Glasgow and back was a paltry £3 7s 6d. Now if that did not convince readers of the benefits of Mini motoring, what on earth would?

"It was a bit like having a damp Labrador in the back" commented an early Mini owner. The combination of water and carpets mixed to produce a soggy, musty and distinctly uncomfortable environment for anyone with their new Se7en, or Minor. Longbridge could hardly believe the reports when they came through as they had been very diligent in subjecting prototypes to water splash testing. In fact a brand new water splash was built outside the production plant to help solve the problem. Several theories surfaced as the production process was scrutinised. There was the 'differential pressure theory' where it was suggested that a combination of an open window, the road and the interior created conditions conducive to the build up of moisture. Then it was pointed out that the prototypes had been hand sprayed whilst the production Minis were baked suggesting that the sealing material between the floor joints must have disintegrated.

Minis having a splashing time. The water test became an unwelcome ritual as engineers struggled to discover why the cars filled up every time it rained.

Finally the tendency of the Mini to provide its occupants with unwelcome foot baths was traced to a late revision in the design. Originally when the power plant was going to be smaller, two cylinders in fact, a simple floor pressing with outward facing flanges was proposed. However, as the larger and more powerful four-cylinder engine was employed it was decided to strengthen the overall structure by effectively boxing the outer edges. Unfortunately the floor pressing lapped the wrong way. The first quick fix involved taking a newly built Mini to an area of the assembly hall where the sills were drilled and then injected with expanding foam (3Ms heat gelling sealer, type UK 3455 to be precise). It cost ten shillings and not only stopped water going in, it also added a useful amount of torsional stiffness to the whole structure. The ultimate cure was a revised pressing so that the water entered the enclosed space and could then drain out again.

Yes there was a whole bunch of what can only be described as Mini niggles. So never mind about periodic and unwelcome soggy sock syndrome, the original Mini owners also had a lot of other development work to do for BMC.

Firstly there were ventilation issues. The idea had been for air to flow through the sliding windows from a high-pressure area around the windscreen pillar, and then depart through low-pressure quarter lights. In fact the location was a high pressure one so they slammed shut. A locking window button soon stopped this. However condensation was a worry until a fresh air heater in 1961 was added to the options list.

Chattering from the window channels was caused by ill-fitting catches, which could even come adrift. They were redesigned.

The exhaust downpipe fractured because it was used as a locating member for the engine on its mountings. The torque of the engine meant that it jumped about. So to stop the bottom bracket breaking, it was changed and the gauge of the down pipe increased whilst the rubber joints in the horizontal stabilising bar were made stiffer.

And finally the brakes. The rear shoes in particular were prone to sticking in position and this was finally cured when Issigonis insisted on a heavy-duty pull off spring.

A very special Austin Se7en and Mini-Minor was launched in September 1961 and was clearly based on the contemporary Mini-Cooper, a sort of sheep in wolfish clothing. The Super Se7en and Super Mini-Minor had a duo-tone colour scheme, with the roof painted a contrasting white, or black. The Austin grille was a unique slatted version with 12 straight vertical bars and 9 wavy horizontal ones and the Morris version had 10 horizontal bars. However, the rest was pure Cooper: stainless steel window surrounds, sill finishers and bumpers complete with overriders and 'tubular extensions', the corner piece sections. Inside, the trim was all two tone, carpets, boot board, extra soundproofing, courtesy light and oval instrument binnacle. The Cooper touches extended to black faced instruments, chrome door levers instead of the string pulls and black vinyl on the dashboard. Mechanically the modifications were minor, the anachronistic separate floor starter was replaced by a combined ignition/starter key. The engine may have been standard Mini 848cc, but a Cooper 16-blade fan replaced the inadequate four blade item and was so successful in improving cooling and reducing engine noise it was extended to the rest of the range within a few months.

**The very rare Super had Cooper trimmings. This is a
Morris version for a change.**

This is one of the rarest models that remained in production for just over a year to be replaced by the less Cooperish Super De Luxe.

In 1962 the Se7en name was dropped for the Austin model. Hardly surprising as the name conjured up a tiny, pre war, vintage car, rather than a iconoclastic, swinging '60s, at the cutting edge of automotive technology type urban transportation. So it was dramatically rebadged Austin Mini. By contrast, the Morris Mini-Minor stayed the same. Significantly the Mini part of its moniker had been plucked out as the defining name and would survive the already nebulous marque identities.

The Super De Luxe arrived in October 1962 and in spite of retaining overiders and tubular extensions on the bumpers it largely reverted to standard Mini specification with some chrome knobs on, to set it apart from the Cooper. Inside there was the luxury of Vynide upholstery, chrome hinged sun visors and lidded ashtrays.

The most significant change to the Mark 1 Mini occurred in September 1964 with the introduction of Hydrolastic suspension. First used on the 1100 range it was the logical development of the original suspension. Rubber was still used as the springing medium which linked the two ends of the car by transmitting the deflecting forces through fluid in a pipe. At the front transverse links carried the front wheels acting on Hydrolastic units housed in the sub frame. When a road wheel struck a bump the tapered piston was forced into the cylinder and because fluid cannot be compressed, pressure was passed on to the conical rubber spring. The piston became larger as the diaphragm rolled off the walls of the cylinder on to its tapered crown making the spring progressive so that it stiffened up at an increasing rate. Damping was actually built in by forcing the fluid through a separating member between the upper and lower parts of the cylinder. The fluid could go through a bleed hole that copes with small deflections, or through the two rubber flap valves which operate as dampers for bump and rebound. The fluid used was 50/50 water and alcohol anti-freeze with some rust inhibitor and even a Customs and Excise additive to make it undrinkable! Not only that, it would also not be affected by any changes in temperature. The same Hydrolastic units were at the back, but they are laid horizontally within the sub frame and worked by bell cranks from the trailing arms. Pipes connecting the units run on each side of the car, rather than side to side which meant there was a degree of resistance to roll. There was a host of minor improvements too.

1964 models received a number of other modifications. Inside, the interior light switched on automatically once the door was opened. There was an oil warning light and for safety reasons crushable sun visors and plastic rimmed rear view mirror. Mechanically the gearbox was strengthened to Cooper specification. The mainshaft had needle roller bearings instead of plain bronze bushes and wider teeth in the gears, whilst a diaphragm spring clutch and new speed change forks completed the transmission revisions. In addition there were twin leading shoe front brakes and less importantly the Super De Luxe was shortened to De Luxe.

It must always be remembered that the Mini was a team effort and a crucial member of that team was the now late Doctor Alex Moulton who died at the end of 2012 when I was still writing this book. He met Issigonis for the first time in 1948 when they talked about Moulton's proposal to develop a rubber suspension system.

When Issigonis left Morris to join Alvis, the big car he designed for them called the Diablo, featured Moulton's rubber suspension. At the same time Moulton was also doing work for Morris and with Jack Daniels, a prominent member of the original Mini team, was converting a Morris Minor to use a new Flexitor rubber front suspension system. Meanwhile the Alvis was developed further when Moulton filled the hollow cones used in the suspension system and then linked the front and rear ones together so that the fluid could be displaced hydraulically. This was the beginning of the Hydrolastic and much later Hydragas suspension.

However, when it came to developing the Mini, there was not time to miniaturise those cones. The stopgap measure was to cut them in half to use them as a sort of buffer. Moulton and Issigonis though, still dreamt of using a much more sophisticated interconnected system. Hydrolastic suspension was introduced in 1964. Unfortunately the system was expensive to produce and on mainstream Minis was used until 1969, although it was fitted to the Cooper to use up existing units until 1971.

Moulton though continued to come up with revolutionary suspension solutions which were sadly compromised by production, or budgetary constraints. In 1973 the Hydragas system was fitted to the Allegro that lacked sub frames and so prevented the inclusion of anti-dive and anti squat geometry. The system as fitted to the Metro from 1990 regained the system's credibility. Moulton though went as far as equipping his own 1966 Cooper S with Hydragas (spheres filled with nitrogen and connected front to rear) and A shaped tubular lower suspension arms, rubber bushed and inclined to provide a degree of anti dive. Rubber bushes on the upper transverse arm reduced road roar and also friction to the axially mounted bushes cutting down road noise. At the back the rear suspension has a pair of slim helper springs just like Hydrolastic cars to prevent the rear end sagging under heavy loads. The result is a smooth and quiet ride.

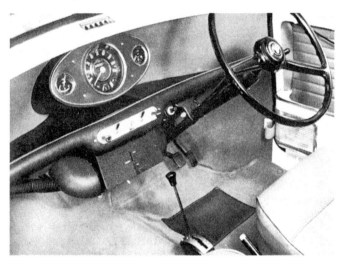

Inside a Mini automatic. A massive statement of the obvious.

An interesting new option from 1965 was four-speed automatic transmission, even though production did not start for some time it proved to be very popular. Autocar tested one in October when they noted the fuel consumption penalty of around 10 per cent and did not like the high price. Performance matched the manual car to as just a 2 mph sacrifice in top speed with just climbed by 0.5 a mph over 70mph. There was nothing to compare it with except the unique and slightly bizarre DAF from Holland. By contrast with the Minis 4-speed torque converter based system, the DAF had driving belts on expanding and contracting pulleys with an infinite variation of ratios. That made the DAF system smoother, but hardly as versatile as the Mini. "BMC's baby has developed into a much more civilised product than the original" they concluded.

At the heart of Issigonis quest for a simple, usable small car, was an automatic gearbox. Having begun his career as the one and only draughtsman in a London based engineering consultancy trying to market a semi automatic gearbox obviously left an impression. The technology never existed at the Minis launch although Automotive Products were tackling the problem. A bevel gear device designed by Hugh Reid was the breakthrough as it acted like a torque converter to link both the engine and gearbox.

A two speed version, with no reverse worked well in a Humber Hawk. Then Austin A50 Cambridge were fitted with a three-speed system and like the Mini, lubrication was shared by both engine and gearbox. Just as the Mini was launched, AP saw the potential and created a three-speed gearbox only slightly larger than the manual version that fitted in the same location. Issigonis was delighted, especially when an extra gear could be added at Minimal cost. For the technically minded the clutch was replaced by a torque converter attached to the crankshaft. The drive was then transmitted by primary gears to the bevel gear within the transmission. Two clutches are then employed, one for the forward gear, the second coming in when top is engaged which also transmits reverse. From the clutch, the power goes to the differential, driveshafts and then to the road wheels.

The disadvantages were Minimal, obviously it cost more, at £90 12s 6d. There was also a slight performance penalty despite a larger carburettor, caused by the power consumed by the torque converter that depressed top speed and fuel consumption by around 10 per cent. However, this unit remained as the only gearbox in the world suitable for cars under 1.3 litres. Yet another Mini first.

Four door Mini from the early '60s. It would have harmed 1100 sales, but never got beyond the prototype stage. Interesting though.

So what else happened to the Mark 1 Mini over the years? Well in 1965 the external door handles now had small protective safety bosses to prevent pedestrians from being injured were first seen on Morris versions in 1965 and Austins in '66. A new clutch meant a smoother operation whilst sealed beam headlamps were standardised.

By 1967 when the last few Mark 1s were leaving the production lines the Mini had clearly come a very long way. It had started life as a technically interesting oddball. Sales were slow and the problems were plentiful, although a necessary evil of a short development run was a few post production problems. However, BMC were quick to respond, fix the glitches and watch production climb rapidly from 19,749 in 1959 to 237,227 in 1967. On the showroom floor it was a big hit right from the start. As Bill Preston who later became sales director at one of Rover's longest serving dealers, G.Kingsbury remembers: "So many people said to me, 'you'll never sell that.' They laughed out loud. Not for long though, we could not get

78

enough of them, some people almost came to blows in the showroom when it came to allocating the first Minis."

Other manufacturers were surprisingly slow to follow suit with their own 'Mini' cars. Maybe they had good reason to be cautious, had done their sums and were biding their time mindful of the aphorism, 'Mini cars make Mini profits'. After all, Ford did not dip their toes in the small car waters for another seventeen years.

Mini Sister. The next real Mini in my life was my sister's Surf Blue 1963 Austin Super De Luxe. It had started life as a Birthday present. The lucky recipient was the wife of an accountant and it was all tied up in red ribbon outside their house in Loughton. It then passed on to one of his clients, Mr Hoffman who bought it for his daughter Ursula who later sold it to my sister. Being a Mini it was of course already getting rusty and I remember we unbolted the original bumpers that were crumblier than a crusty baguette. I never thought of it as very fast having just an 848cc engine, but it was nippy enough to earn my sister a speeding ticket. 34mph in a 30mph zone.

My Mini Cooper it's part in my Breakdown

**My sister behind the wheel of her Austin Mini. And
definitely not speeding.**

5. **Imps, Prinz, Zaporozhets, and Bijous - what the rest of the World came up with between 1959 – 1967 to take on the Mini...**
Minis Made in 1959 19,749 • 1960 116,677 • 1961 157,059 • 1962 216,087 • 1963 236,713 • 1964 244,359 • 1965 221,974 • 1966 213,694 • 1967 237,227

Car manufacturers now knew what they had to beat. However, in the early days the Mini didn't look like it was going to be much of a threat. Because it wasn't an instant hit, the oddities were not swept off the street just yet.

The nearest thing to a Mini was still the Fiat 600, which was revised in 1960 and now badged as the 600D. Mechanically this meant a bigger engine, a 767cc producing 29bhp. The front doors now had opening quarter lights and the boot lid new cooling vents. By 1964 the 600D finally got front-hinged doors, whilst the last changes in 1965 saw new headlights and a larger fuel tank. An astounding 2.7 million had been sold by the time the 600 was replaced in 1969. Before that happened, Fiat developed the new 850 out of it in 1964.

The Fiat 850, not as cute as a 500, but more practical.

Now the 850 was still a two door, rear-engined car retaining many 600 mechanicals, but apart from the roomier bodywork, there was also a new 843cc four-cylinder water-cooled unit. Two versions of the saloon were produced, the 'Normale' with 34bhp and the 'Super' with 37bhp. On a more practical note the Familiare replaced the 600 Multipla again with three rows of seats.

As for the 500, a 'Giardiniera' estate version was introduced for 1960 that rode on a stretched wheelbase and differed from the saloon with a horizontally mounted engine. Later that year the 500D arrived with a 499.5cc engine from the discontinued Sport model, but with a reduced power output of 17.5bhp. The 500D was replaced by the 500F in 1965 where the most noticeable changes were the overdue adoption of front-hinged doors and a revised transmission.

A very small picture of a very important car, the Autobianchi Primula.

It is all very well to list the various tinkering at Fiat HQ with their model line up, but elsewhere in the company arguably the most significant car built in the 1960s was Autobianchi Primula. Here was the true blueprint for the modern small car. Introduced in 1964 it was a small family vehicle with a transverse front engined driving the front wheels. Unlike the Mini, which had the gearbox in the sump, the Primula had the gearbox next to the 1100cc engine. Not only that, the suspension set up was MacPherson struts at the front that would become almost compulsory on all future hatches. Oh, didn't I mention that? At the back there was a tailgate instead of a lid. The neat two-box design became available with two and four doors.

My Mini Cooper it's part in my Breakdown

Oddly, contemporary descriptions of the car often failed to mention the tailgate or they might only allude to a 'top hinged rear door.' Sales were modest and restricted to Europe but the demand was strong as this was a unique car that would be the basis not just for future Fiats but all so called minis that would be deemed, super.

Meanwhile DAF uprated the 600 and struck on a new numbering system so that in 1963 it was replaced by the 31 and in 1965 the 32. The ultimate incarnation was the DAF 33 in 1967. The lines of the bodywork of the original DAF 600 were very much visible in this model, but it had grown more 'tighter' and angular over the years. The 33 still had the 746 cc two cylinder air-cooled boxer engine, but it now produced 32bhp. The tiny car weighed just 660 kg and still used rubber bands.

The Germans could still buy the Glas Goggomobil which limped on until 1967 when BMW bought the company and erased the last reminder of their micro car past but shutting them down the following year and using the factory space to build more BMWs.

The lovely little Messerschmitts didn't survive the economic miracle and by 1964 production had finished. NSU though had been steadily improving the Prinz. The Prinz 3 and 4 grew up and were finally proper four seaters rather than cramped little boxes. These models had wonderfully crisp styling and a brilliant view out that only old thin-pillared cars could provide. It thrived with a tiny two-cylinder 598cc engine. So the next logical addition to the range in 1964 was the 1000 with a four cylinder all alloy 996cc engine. It looked like a grown up Prinz with oblong glasses on, yes the headlamps were rectangular. NSU went even further with the 110 that not only added extra engine capacity, up to 1085cc, but also a useful 8 inches (20.3cm) in the wheelbase to boost legroom. The wheels were small, but not nearly as titchy as the Mini's, but the size still went up from 12 inches to 13 (30.4 to 33cm).

My Mini Cooper it's part in my Breakdown

**NSU Prinz, not a Zaporozhets, the badges were
different and so were the engines.**

Behind the iron curtain in Russia a curiously
similar vehicle to the Prinz was made by Zaporozhets in
1960. The small car had a V4 air-cooled engine mounted
in the boot. It stayed in production pretty much forever
and could still be ordered in the late 1980s.

Japan was not yet a threat to the European car
industry, but they were starting to build very credible
small cars. However, Daihatsu as a company and their
Compagno in particular have the distinction of being the
first Japanese company to export to many Western
markets in the '60s. The Compagno was also the first four-
wheeled Daihatsu to enter series production. The
company turned to Italian stylist Vignale for the design.
Consequently it looked neat without much of the clutter
and chrome that spoiled many Japanese contemporaries.

**First Japanese car in the UK and it's a small one too
the Daihatsu Compagno.**

The layout of the Compagno when launched was relatively simple. This two-door car had a water-cooled 797cc four-cylinder engine driving the rear wheels with all-synchromesh 4-speed gearboxes. The engine capacity rose to 958cc in 1965 and the saloon's power to 55bhp. The range expanded to include a four-door saloon and estate car based on that body

Rather more Mini sized was Daihatsu's charmingly named Little Fellow in 1966 with a tiny two stroke, two cylinder 356cc engine. Daihatsu became part of the Toyota empire in 1967, effectively becoming its small car division.

Honda's answer to the Mini. The N360 was very good indeed.

Honda embraced the small car first with a sports car, the S500 based on their own motorcycle technology and the later S600 was even better though not strictly a practical small car. Rather more relevant was the N360 in 1966, with a four stroke, twin cylinder, air-cooled 354cc engine that drove the front wheels. Like the Mini it was a two-box shape and quite significantly it was a teeny bit bigger than the British car as the tape measure reading was 122 inches (309.8cms).

Mazda's first car in 1960 was called the R-360 and it was called Coupe' but really apart from a slightly sloping rear window it is just a two door saloon. The R-360 had an unusual V-2 air-cooled engine and could also be ordered with an automatic gearbox.

Mitsubishi was a huge industrial conglomerate building planes, trains, ships and even automobiles. They returned to cars in 1960 with the pint sized A10. Another Japanese car that undercut the Mini by a couple of inches. Unlike the Mini though the engine was in the boot, a twin cylinder four stroke unit. The company moved fast though and by 1962 the Minica range became available as a small saloon or estate with a 359cc two-stroke twin cylinder air-cooled engine.

Toyota's own take on the economy car was the Publica in 1961. The twin cylinder 697cc air-cooled engine. For export the 1000 model not surprisingly had a bigger engine and estates, convertible and even a Sport models followed.

If the Japanese cars were maturing nicely and thankfully too far away from the UK to be any threat, there was still room for the gloriously oddball British car. Peel, from the Isle of Man. They made one of the weirdest examples of transportation anywhere with the Peel P50, which was effectively a Little Tikes kiddie car with a 49cc Anzani engine. Incredibly it was built from 1962 to '66.

The Bond Minicar would stay around until 1965 with its three tiny wheels and impressively long bonnet hiding a tiny motorcycle engine. In 1966 though the 875 came with a Hillman Imp engine, this time at the rear, but it still tottered around on three wheels. This was a direct rival to the Reliant Regal.

The Reliant Rebel. Not very rebellious is it?

By 1962 the Reliant 3/25 model had a more modern glass fibre bodywork but it could hardly be described as pretty. Indeed, realising the wheel shortfall put off a lot of buyers who didn't just rely on their motorcycle licence to get them through the winter without catching hypothermia, in came the Rebel in 1965. Well, I suppose it was a rebellion against the triangular wheeled layout of cheap Reliants. It even had the Regal's engine and a usefully spacious glass fibre body, which looked like a two box hatch. Except it wasn't, until the estate version came along. Quite basic and technically stone age compared to the Mini. Most importantly not nearly as cute, or small.

An honorary Brit Mini car was the Citroen Bijou. Plonking a weird 2-door glass fibre body on top of a 2CV and then calling it Bijou didn't help. By the time it was discontinued in 1962 just a few hundred had been sold, part of the problem was it was even heavier than a 2CV and genuinely ugly.

Hillman Imp. It could have been a Mini contender.

My Mini Cooper it's part in my Breakdown

By far the closest and most relevant rival to the Mini came from very close to home. The Rootes Group had actually decided to launch their own bubble car bashing vehicle way back in 1955. Long before those Mini orange crates were even nailed together.

Two clever development engineers were given a brief to look into the small car market and later one come up with a vehicle that could do 60mph and 60mpg whilst carrying two adults and two children. Given the unattractive code name of 'The Slug' probably because it had a tiny and crude small engine hidden in the boot. Presented to Sir Billy Rootes in 1957, he hated sight of it, but the basic principle of an economy car was accepted.

It was a difficult birth requiring a lightweight aluminium engine and more sophisticated suspension. It also needed a more appealing name and for the time being Apex would do. When the Apex was given the go ahead that's when it all got complicated.

Building an all-new car that was expected to sell in hundreds of thousands required lots of investment and ideally a new factory. Government policy had remained unchanged since the 1940s: build new factories in deprived areas. Companies that did this were rewarded with all sorts of grants and incentives. So Rootes had no alternative but to establish a new factory at Linwood, near Paisley in Scotland, just eight miles away from Glasgow. So the official announcement came in 1960 that Rootes would build 150,000 small cars in Scotland and export most of them. The government loaned the company £10,000,000 to make it all happen.

Progress was slow and the Hillman Imp, as it was finally christened, was introduced in May 1963. Unlike the Mini which had used an old engine, the Imp was completely new with crisp styling, lively and economical performance with a clever innovation on the saloon that allowed the rear window to be lifted up and the rear seat folded forward. Yes, the Imp was a hatchback too, how could it fail, even if it did cost £508, which was £61 more than the equivalent Mini?

Like the Mini, the Imp suffered from early teething troubles, but they proved to be rather more enduring and serious. The aluminium engine regularly overheated causing the head gasket to fail, which was never a good thing. Not only that, when garages needed to work on an Imp, usually to replace a head gasket, some were resistant to use the specialist tools needed to work on an aluminium engine which then caused damage. Also, whereas most cars used a throttle cable, the Imp used a clever pneumatic item, which sadly proved too troublesome in service. Lubrication was not required on the steering, but unfortunately on early models the whole system seized up because of, a lack of lubrication. Later cars got much better, but the reputation for breaking down at every unwelcome opportunity stuck.

Meanwhile, the Mini was proving that it's front engine, front wheel drive layout was the motoring future. So the Imp turned out to be the wrong car at the wrong time that at its very best sold 69,000 in 1964 and never got anywhere near the 150,000 capacity. Not only that, Rootes dealers had no experience selling small cars so they struggled.

Being Rootes there wasn't just the basic Hillman Imp, it came in all sorts of exciting flavours. There was the Husky estate, which was also available as a commercial van wearing a Commer badge. There were some sporty Sunbeams that you can read about later whilst the Singers were the posh ones, a bit like the Hornet and Elf. So a Chamois, had more chrome and wood veneer, and then there were the faster Chamois Sport and a Chamois coupe neither of which seriously bothered the Coopers. None of these models really helped matters. Here was a fundamentally good though slightly complicated car which, was built badly on borrowed money and sadly the ramifications for Rootes would prove terminal.

Mini Running Total 1959 19,749 • 1960 136,426 • 1961 293,485 • 1962 509,572 • 1963 746,285 • 1964 990,644 • 1965 1,212,618 • 1966 1,426,312 • 1967 1,663,539

Mini Driving Lessons. Well first of all that would be my sister being taught by Uncle Charlie in his Mini. She opted for Uncle Charlie because she thought it might be an easier than Dad telling her what to do. Big mistake. Uncle Charles and Aunt Flo had moved to Forest Gate by now, but would drive back to take her out. I tagged along because I thought I might learn something from the back seat. Actually what I learnt was how to swear. By this time the ex docker and now HGV driver, Uncle Charlie was perfectly qualified to pass on his skills and vocabulary. He didn't actually shout but could do low level menace very well. His patience level was non-existent, especially with himself and any other road users. It is only funny in retrospect. At the time it was truly terrifying.

It never did my sister any lasting damage and when it came to teaching me she never uttered anything remotely at expletive end of her vocabulary.

Technically the first car I drove was my father's Audi 100LS. After that though it was my sister's old Mini all the way. I think Dad didn't want his clutch mangled. As for the actual test. I've already covered this in The British Car Industry Our Part in its Downfall, but I won't spoil anything by telling you that I did pass, in the Mini, second go due to a condensation malfunction.

My Mini Cooper it's part in my Breakdown

I learnt to drive in this...

6. **The Mini is eight, gets renamed and bigger windows, but certainly not wind up ones. Yes it's a Mini makeover. Say hello to the Mark II and find out how the Autobianchi Primula pointed the way forward...**

Minutes before the press got to see the revised Mini for the first time, something vital was missing: the badges. They were being sourced from Ireland and the cardboard box containing them was sneaked past the waiting journalists and frantic BMC PRs had to rapidly press them into place.

Slightly better organised was the 1967 Earls Court Motor Show which was the public venue for the launch of the Mini Mark II. Marketing of the two Mini marques continued but with a further subtle name change as the Morris Mini-Minor simply became the Morris Mini.

For the first time in eight years the Mini received a facelift. The visual differences were obvious enough as the grille was squared-off with a much wider surround. The grille itself featured 11 bars on the Austin and 13 on the Morris with 7 vertical ones. At the back the saloon's rear window became larger and there were new shoe box sized square light clusters. On the road drivers would notice the difference when they tried to park. The turning circle had been reduced from 32ft to 28ft (9.75 to 8.53m) with modifications to the steering rack and arms. Stopping became less strenuous as increased bores in the brake cylinders meant smoother, yet lighter action. Performance was improved too because for the first time, the 998cc engine was made available in the standard Mini shell, having previously been fitted to the up market Riley Elf and Wolseley Hornet. This new 1000 model also benefited from the Cooper's remote gear change and a higher 3.44:1 final drive ratio. The AP automatic gearbox was improved and still available as an option with the higher compression 9:1 engine. Inside, a driver might have noticed safer bezels on the instruments and protective foam filled roll on the dashboard. In addition the switchgear had helpfully been located 3" (7.6cm) further forward.

Here's the rear view of a Mark 2 to show the larger rear window and big lights, and yes I know this is a Cooper S but this was the only period photo I could find that showed the back end. So please ignore the twin tanks and bigger ventilated wheels.

Long overdue instrument changes included the relocation of the floor mounted dip switch to the indicator stalk, which also housed a louder horn, whilst the flashing indicator warning light was transferred to the speedometer. And finally, those tiny windscreen wipers were taught to park themselves once switched off.

93

My Mini Cooper it's part in my Breakdown

The 848cc engined model, now badged as an 850 was still available in two levels of trim, basic and Super De Luxe (SDL), whilst the 1000 only came with the SDL trimmings. Like the Mark I these included, opening rear quarter lights, overriders but no corner bars, three-instrument binnacle, ergonomically effective seats, heater and carpets.

As far as the buying public were concerned the new Mini was more of the same successful formula. Sales were not going to be a problem. Motor journalists always on the look out for a reinvention of the wheel, were a little disappointed, especially after the exciting innovations delivered by the first Mini in 1959. Autocar certainly regarded the availability of the 1000cc engine across the range as important for this proven engine. They thought that the Cooper S final drive made a difference at high cruising speeds, whilst the remote control gear change, also from the Cooper was a very welcome update. A nice touch was the smaller turning circle and more effective handbrake. Then came the regrets. Heating and ventilation were just as poor as the old model. Despite the fact that new seats were fitted, they lacked support to the thighs. Visibility may have improved, but the rear view mirror was still the size of a post card. The view through the windscreen was not helped by the small windscreen wiper arc, which seemed biased towards the passenger. Overall Autocar were just a little disappointed, "We were expecting the new Mini to be announced with winding windows, like certain versions built in Australia. This must now be the only car without them, and they are sadly missed. It is also time such economies as cable release interior door handles were brought up to date; and some of the standards of fit and finish were disappointing. Carpets still do not lie snugly on the floor-a criticism we made in 1959." Nevertheless the magazine admitted that Mini was still in a class of its own. "When all is said and done, however, the Mini is a tremendously practical and dynamic little car that has few equals for town use, or as the second family transport.

My Mini Cooper it's part in my Breakdown

Here's the front end of an Austin Mini Mark II in Super De Luxe Trim.

Always difficult to please, Car Magazine in September 1968 compared the new Mini 1000 with the increasing number of rivals. There was the obviously outclassed Reliant Rebel 700, the obvious, but underachieving Hillman Imp and the exotic threat from the Far East in the shape of the Honda N600. It was the Honda, which came closest to trouncing the British car as it was faster, more economical and cheaper than the Mini 1000. However they found it, "Noisier and less comfortable with inferior handling. In so many ways it is so close to the Mini that as long as it holds its price at its present level it is bound to present a very considerable challenge." They weren't going to let the Mini off lightly after seeing the supermini future and the considerable far eastern threat. "Of the Mini itself, one is bound to say that some of the room for improvement which we have always said existed is still there. Rather than the restyled grille and rear lights with which we were regaled last year, we would have liked to see a lot more attention paid to driver comfort by way of supplement to vast improvements in ride and silence."

The short-lived Mark II was subjected to relatively few changes. In June 1968 the company replaced the convenient and ergonomically efficient door cables with fiddly door handles, possibly in response to Autocar's road test comments. The only big news was that from September 1968 an all-synchromesh four-speed gearbox first introduced on the Cooper S in '67 was standardised across the range.

Also in that year, as BMC merged with Leyland truck makers when production of the Mini was halted at Cowley and transferred to Longbridge. So the Leylandisation of the Mini had begun.

After the 'never had it so good' '50s the new car market entered the highly competitive '60s. This triggered a whole series of mergers, which overshadowed the industry during the decade. First in 1960 Jaguar acquired Daimler. The following year Standard-Triumph was bought by Lancashire based commercial vehicle makers Leyland. Meanwhile, BMC had benefited hugely from Issigonis's front wheel drive revolution which was led by the Mini and 1100 so output soared. Unfortunately profits didn't. BMC made a profit of £27 million on sales of £346 million, but by '67 although sales had risen to £467 million, it recorded a loss of £3 million. Virtually non-existent product planning and chronic under pricing were to blame and forced the company to merge with Jaguar in 1966 as British Motor Holdings (BMH). Then Leyland came back into the picture. As recent purchasers of Rover there was Labour government pressure to merge with BMH. On the 17th January 1967 the British Leyland Motor Corporation was born and became the world's fifth largest car company. Sir George Harriman was appointed Chairman and Sir Donald Stokes became Managing Director whilst ten board members were drawn equally from BMH and Leyland. Almost immediately there were problems as BMH was due to make a loss, but the merger went ahead anyway. Officially BLMC came into being on 14th May 1968.

What Stokes found was an overmanned, inefficient company. Profitability on the Mini was marginal and product planning was a haphazard affair with no clear model policy. The new management structure meant that Issigonis's influence was on the wane. Appointed Director of Research and Development, he was encouraged to innovate, though Stokes resented his dogmatic demeanour. Citing the Mini's sliding windows, Stokes claimed many years later that it was only pressure from the board, which brought in the winding variety in 1969. In fact, those Mark 3 changes were the last significant updates until the 1990s. The problem was that BLMC did not have any money to spend. The huge company had lots of other projects and lost causes and the Mini was the last priority. So until 1990s the Mini remained stranded in 1969.

The 9X from 1969 with its radical hatchback styling could have been the supermini quantum leap that Issigonis and British Leyland were looking for. Unfortunately they could not afford it.

Issigonis last complete project was the 9X a remarkable 6in (15.2 cm) shorter, but 2in (5cm) wider than the Mini. The suspension was conventional at the front were McPherson struts with trailing arms and coil springs. Power plants were overhead cam units developed by Downton Engineering with either four, or six cylinders allied to a hydrostatic transmission, a forerunner of the constantly variable transmissions CVTs of the 1980s. Best of all, the body style incorporated a tailgate. Hatchbacks may be common now, but it was a novelty then, especially on such a small car.

Researching through Issigonis files from this era I came across a very detailed MIRA vehicle analysis on a

1965 Autobianchi Primula. This is a model mentioned in the previous chapter. This was a Fiat based car that not only bore a strong physical resemblance to the 9X it had a front wheel drive layout and a tailgate. Clearly Issigonis had been strongly influenced by the Italian design.

Despite the existence of the Autobianchi, a marque little known outside Italy, the supermini had been born in the shape of the 9X and it was ready for approval in 1968. However, the new BLMC management knew how little money the original Mini was making and did not want to make the same mistake. Even so the 'BLMC Volume Passenger Division Proposal for a new 750-1000cc Mini' dated 9th August 1968 was very focused: "The objective is to provide a car with room for four adults and some luggage, within a competitive specification, at a price 5% below the current Mini, with the aim of major penetration into the world small car market, particularly in Europe...Briefly it comprises a new body shell 6in shorter and 2.5in wider than the current Mini, but with the interior dimensions identical. The engine is completely new 4 cylinder, with a maximum design capacity of 1000cc. Initially it would be offered in 750cc and 950cc forms opening up to 850cc and 1000cc two years after introduction. Six cylinder versions of 1200/1500cc can be developed of completely new design. The engine weight is 40% less than the current A series and it has a considerably narrower silhouette. Basic design is single overhead camshaft. Double OHC heads with hemispherical chambers are being developed.' Then there was a projection that would come to haunt the Metro: "Predicted production 360,000, 120,000 more than Mini with an 8 year design life. Introduction for the October 1971 Motor Show."

None of those things happened, but the production forecast was used to justify a huge investment for the Metro a decade later. At the time though, product planning were very enthusiastic about the 9X and wrote: "It is recommended that this programme be authorised at the earliest possible date."

Clearly Issigonis had proposed another truly innovative small car, so not surprisingly he was very bitter about the cancellation. Apparently he modified his views once the 'me too' Euroboxes arrived in the '70s when the 9X would have been indistinguishable. Surely the point would have been that the 9X was unique and hard to beat. Priced properly it could have made up for all those early losses and proved that a mini car could make a maxi profit. Sadly another opportunity had been missed.

Oh look, it's a mini hatchback. Well actually this is an Austin 1100 Countryman from 1966.

In 1962 BMC announced what could have been the Minis successor, the Austin/Morris 1100. This was a family saloon styled by Pininfarina. It came with the revolutionary Hydrolastic suspension system. Roomy and economical, only the small boot counted against it. Nevertheless between 1963 and 1971 it was Britain's best selling car. Not chic, or a motorsport natural it was a safe and sensible car with a very wide appeal. Once again BMC messed up the pricing. At £592 the sophisticated 1100 cost just £1 more than the conventional Ford Cortina. The 1100 showed up BMC's poor product planning as it sold against the Morris Minor and Austin A40, which shared the 1098cc A series engine.

What the 1100 did do was set a design philosophy whereby the Corporation aimed to produce technically advanced cars, which would enjoy long production runs and not incur large retooling costs. The Mini concept was stretched even further when in October 1964 the 1800 model was launched. This was a big car, which was even bigger on the inside, all the space utilisation lessons learnt on the Mini and 1100 were employed to roomy effect on this transverse engined, front wheel drive saloon. The execution though was less than successful. The styling was an unhappy combination of Issigonis and Pininfarina, with the Mini designer taking care of the centre section whilst Sergio Farina styled the front end. According to Issigonis the Italian "copied...Fiat headlamps which were the worst feature of the car."

The problem was that big cars are traditionally conservative in both styling and innovation. The novelty of a remarkable amount of practical and usable space was lost on most buyers. Structurally it was also one of the strongest monocoque hulls ever built, but the 1800 and its successors were always unkindly referred to as Landcrabs. Issigonis though always rated the 1800. "I still think it was our best car. I loved that car."

Less lovable was the Austin Maxi intended to slot between the 1100 and 1800. A lot of money had been spent on development by the time BLMC was formed and the decision was made to press ahead with production. Launched in April 1971 the hatchback styling should have been a sensation, but it looked a little dull. The new E series engine was flawed as was the five speed gearboxes. It was a missed opportunity as when finally sorted, it sold a consistent 30,000 units year until 1981.

The Allegro looked like the dumpy lovechild of a Mini and 1100, but it was no chip off either brilliant block. Awful.

Another cock-up was the Allegro, which was meant to replace the 1100/1300, which was still selling strongly into the '70s. Launched in May 1973 it had a bigger boot, similar interior room, but was a larger car overall. Worst of all the styling was blobby and bland. It's best sales were in 1975 at 63,339, which was half of the 1100/1300s peak.

The front wheel drive strategy should have worked. BLMC should have ruthlessly rationalised the range, repriced the models and as John Barber proposed at the time, reposition the company. "We could have moved Austin and Morris gradually up market; that would have kept volume down. It wouldn't have been a sudden change but each successive car would have been more expensive than its predecessor...We decided, in due course, that we would adopt the BMW/Mercedes-Benz approach rather than the Ford one. But we didn't have a hope in hell. We had too may different models made in too many different places."

In view of BMW's later acquisition of Rover these were prophetic words. You can clearly see where any potential development money went, squandered around the group rather than forging a new identity and innovative models.

Meanwhile the great grandfather of British front wheel drive, the Mark II Mini soldiered on, notching up bigger sales figures than ever.

My first Mini Car. My sister sold me her old Mini for £50. It was 1977 and she'd got a good few years used out of it.

My Mini Cooper it's part in my Breakdown

Mechanically it was fine, the bodywork though after fourteen salty winters was always going to be marginal.

My ongoing battle against rust was helped by the strongest weapon in my DIY armoury, glass fibre. A tube of Plastic Padding and a smaller one of hardener was fine for the little bits of rot on the gutter that you could rub down, dab with Kurust then paste over the cracks. However, for the serious outbreaks of rot on the wings and sills I needed industrial strength fibreglass matting and chemicals. Mixing it up and lashing it on was great fun and must have been a bit like working at Lotus. The downside was that the seams on top of the wing and round the lights got filled and smoothed off. For a while anyway. Soon they would crack, get a tinge of red and then flake off.

So I couldn't do much about the rot, but I did have some say when it came to colours. My first Mini was Surf Blue. It was a lovely bright and unusual colour, which by the '70s was starting to fade. I didn't mind that as faded denim was always a good look. I did fancy a contrasting roof though. White I thought would be far too difficult to pull off. Matt black though would look different and be a doddle. I bought a couple of tins of paint, put newspaper over the windows, rattled the cans, pressed the button and found that the paint covered just about a quarter of the roof. I was going to need more cans, but it was worth it.

Then there was the time I'd seen the 1971 film Two Lane Blacktop. I don't know if you are familiar with this work of art? Briefly it will bore anyone who doesn't like cars, or tortuously slow road movies with barely enough dialogue to cover the lack of plot. Obviously I loved it and the fact that it starred Warren Oates, plus a couple of musicians, James Taylor and Beach Boy Dennis Wilson having a go at acting. The real star though was the 1955 Chevrolet One Fifty, dechromed with a stark primer paint grey. I told Dad I was going to cover the Mini in grey and he thought I was mad. I don't think I could afford to buy twenty cans of primer. However, when I got a proper compressor my dream The Two Lane Blacktop colour scheme and no chrome look came true when I resprayed the Cooper. Photographic evidence will pop up later in the book.

That's not a vinyl roof but a matt black one from a spray can, well several cans, blame me for the late '70s hole in the ozone layer.

7. It's 1968 and there is revolution in the air, and while the Mini trundles on making feature films and cuddling up to the rich and famous, some very odd tots like the Bond Bug and Enfield were the weirder alternatives. Meanwhile there are some stirrings from the Far East which take us just a couple of years to the cusp of a new decade, and that would be 1970...
Minis Made in 1968 246,066 • 1969 254,957 • 1970 278,950

With the Mini upgraded for the first time in well, eight years, it has given everyone else time to play catch up and join the Mini car phenomenon, as it wasn't being called. Now all the micro cars were dead and buried, who constituted the opposition?

Fiat seemed to be continuing in the same vein with the 850, which just got some go faster models. Also the truly innovative Familiare was still around to little effect in the UK, but stayed in production until 1976, using a 903cc engine from 1970 onwards. In 1966 if changing gear was too much bother there was now the option of a semi-automatic transmission, which did without the clutch pedal.

Just like the Mini, the lovable 500 trundled on much as before and in 1968 the 500F was joined in production by the Lusso version, which offered several touches of big car luxury including reclining seats and even carpet. As well as the uprated interior trim there were external differences too, most noticeably the thin Miniature bull-bars adorning the front and rear bumpers.

Then of course there was the Autobianchi brand, or the experimental black ops arm of the Fiat Group. Pirelli withdrew from the company in 1968. As well as building the 500L new models were introduced for 1970. In particular the A112 with a 903cc engine was the small hatch that turned out to be the upmarket forerunner of the Fiat 128.

The most exciting three-wheeler to come out of Britain and Bond was the Bug in 1970. It actually had Reliant mechanicals but most importantly a groovy Tangerine coloured wedge body designed by Tom Karen.

Strictly a two seater it was primarily a fun mobile without proper doors. The whole front canopy swung upwards and

Autobianchi A112 from 1969. The world's first glance at the shape of superminis to come.

there was just flappy plastic where the doors should have been. With an extra wheel and indeed bigger wheels it could have been a contender. The Bug survived until 1974 when it looked to a bit too frivolous for what was such a tough and uncompromising decade.

The Bond Bug. Not enough buyers caught it.

DAF continued with the 44 and upped the ante with the 55 in 1968, which had a much bigger engine from a Renault 8 and front disc brakes. Also available as a coupe, which really meant the rear window sloped a bit, there was a stick on stripe down the flanks and black hubcaps that looked cooler than they sounded.

Although technically the Japanese were already here with Daihatsu that didn't really count. The most important Japanese car to land in the UK had a Honda badge and was clearly their answer to the Mini. There were two, 2 cylinder models, the N260 and N600, also available with a Hondamatic gearbox to make it the perfect City run-around. Rather more exciting was the stubby but interesting Z as a super economy model.

This tiddler is the Honda Z, which mever came to the UK. Had just 32bhp. Incredibly it seats four.

Daihatsu didn't bother to bring over their Fellow, or even the completely revamped Fellow Max, which now had front wheel drive and all-independent suspension, but still with a titchy 2-cylinder engine.

Subaru was equally stay at homes and redesigned the 360 model in 1970 and rebadged it the R-2. Suzuki also renewed their tiny tots. The Fronte LC 50 had a 3-cylinder 360cc engine driving the rear wheels.

Toyota's third outing in 1969 for the Publica eventually came to the UK as the 1000, though no one noticed, although it stayed in production until 1978. A smartly styled little car it formed the bedrock of Toyota's small car range and over 1.3 million were sold.

My Mini Cooper it's part in my Breakdown

A very short-lived British built, but Greek owned oddity was the Enfield in 1969. Backed by the Electricty Council and constructed on the Isle of Wight, it relied on batteries. While the Electricity Council snapped up 65, the remaining 43 struggled to find buyers stupid enough to pay £2800 when a Mini was comfortably under £1000. It looked like a cartoon car with aluminium bodywork by Hanna Barbera. Clearly the world wasn't ready for a silent car that could do 40 miles between charges. The company and its car ran out of juice in 1971.

Minis Running Total 1968 1,909,605 • 1969 2,164,562 • 1970 2,443,512

Mini Rock and indeed Roll. For a time my Mini was pretty much a Transit van, but much, much smaller. I did think that perhaps I could become a rock star. My motivation was the incontrovertible fact that girls seemed to like boys who played guitars, but it didn't work for me. Never mind, I had started a band with friends I'd met at 6th form college. We were The Sindicators and our strap line was, The Bastard Sons of the Blues. Which of course we were.

For a short while we played pubs on the East side of London for free and mostly in the easy key of E. Me Craig and a random drummer needed to be mobile which is where the Mini came in. Incredibly, with the rear seat foam squab removed I could get four bodies on board, two substantial speaker cabinets, plus a bass amplifier, a Watkins Rapier 22 guitar and a Teisco bass guitar. Not only that, the AC 50 Amplifier head unit would sit neatly in the boot. And no, we didn't put the drum kit on the roof that went in someone's Mini van. And yes, in a way it was a bit like Bruce Dickinson of Iron Maiden piloting his band and equipment around the world in a 757.

8. Flower power has gone, along with those 1950s sliding windows and to cope with the brutalist 1970s the Mini loses all its aliases, fancy bits of trim as the Hornet is swatted and Elf exterminated... yes it's 1969 and the Mark III is here to surprise and delight us...

Spot the difference. Wind up windows, new Mini badge and fixed door handles.

ADO 20. Not a very romantic model nomenclature. Why not call it simply the Mini? So they did, or more precisely BLMC did. To coincide with a number of important changes, the slate was wiped clean and from October 1969 the Mini was reborn and renamed.

Certainly, the Mini's parent company had gone through a name change crisis all its own, as the British Motor Corporation (BMC) merged with Jaguar to become British Motor Holdings and finally British Leyland Motor Corporation which consolidated all the independent British car manufacturers (Austin, Morris, Jaguar, Rover and Triumph). Rationalisation became the name of the game as the company realised that badge engineering was only marginalising and confusing customers. A single brand image was needed to market the car more effectively. No one really bought cars out of loyalty, only on performance, price and practicality. A tough lesson that BLMC only learnt when the Japanese invasion was in full mid '70s swing. For the moment though the company was gearing up for one of the most successful periods in the life of the Mini.

A glance at the new Mini Mark III involved a double take. Initially it did not look that different from the previous incarnation, despite simple Mini badging and blue Leyland postage stamp emblems on the A panels. In fact, the whole body shell had been comprehensively rejigged. The floor pan had been revised, along with the boot floor, windscreen surround, front parcel shelf and bonnet hinges. More obviously those external door hinges had finally been done away with, replaced by enclosed ones, which cleaned up the side of the car nicely. The doors were the focus of the most attention as they were now slightly larger and incorporated wind-up window mechanisms from the Elf and Hornet. In practical terms that meant a very large 5-inch reduction in width and sacrificing the cavernous door pockets. Many lamented the fact that the Mini was going soft and was not so spartan anymore. Even the trick, hinged rear number plate was bolted firmly to the boot lid in a deeper recess in recognition of the fact that few owners would actually bother to overload the inadequate boot anymore.

Under the skin was a fundamental rethink on the suspension front, with a return to the dry rubber-cone system first used in 1959. Although some drivers found hydrolastic a little bouncy, generally system worked well enough but was expensive to manufacture. Other uprates included negative earth electrics and a mechanical fuel pump.

On the model line-up front, the basic 850 remained just that, presumably Issigonis would have been delighted with this one. Single instrument, fixed rear quarter windows, optional heater and just the one visor, so if you still wanted to buy a spartan runabout in 1969, this was it, with no comfy Super De Luxe alternative. Even the magic wand gear lever remained. However, buyers could spoil themselves by specifying an automatic gearbox, but only up until 1971. Actually British Leyland were very good at building vehicles with standard extras and it was very difficult to buy an 850 without a heater, or seat belts although these were included in the price list from 1974.

Throughout '74 the 850 almost became luxurious. Never mind the inertia reel seat belts, a fresh air heater was finally standardised along with a heated rear window, a second sun visor for the passenger and a driver's door mirror. The general uprating of the 850 continued apace in the mid '70s with new seats and vinyl covers in 1975 complete with anti-tip catches and revised door pocket trim.

Mini City, the most basic form of Mini motoring with eye catching decals and even luxurious dog's tooth cloth trim on the inside. Otherwise it was poverty spec all the way with matt black bumpers, and the traditional single instrument binnacle.

Then there was a major interior facelift in 1976 as the instrumentation was uprated. The console now had rocker switches (hazards, heated rear window, brake circuit failure test, lights and heater controller plus the choke. At the driver's feet were larger pedals donated from the Allegro. However, owners still wrestled with a

My Mini Cooper it's part in my Breakdown

Routemaster bus sized steering wheel, but there was a new ignition lock on the column and two control stalks. By '77 there was even a vanity mirror, padded steering wheel and hand brake grip, which had first seen service in the Allegro.

Apart from the cosmetics there were subtle range changes, which made the Mini more drivable. Improved synchromesh, an alternator and remote gear change in '72 and radial ply tyres a year later. For '74 a new carburettor, revised manifolds, air cleaner and twin silencer exhaust made a slight performance/economy improvement followed by softened rear suspension in '76. On the outside there were few changes, only a matt black grille in 1977 made a real difference.

Although the 850 slipped quietly from the price lists in 1980 just as the Mini Metro arrived, there were a couple of swan song models at the two extremes of the specification spectrum. In 1979 the City embraced the original Austin Se7en's spartan spec with colour keyed black bumpers, roof gutter, wheel arches and City decal on each front wing and the boot complete with a three band coach line. Inside there was dog's tooth check upholstery. The antidote to that poverty spec model was a Super De Luxe that mirrored the 1000 which meant three instrument binnacle, striped seats, fitted carpets and decent roll ball ventilation. In the 850's last year it even benefited from the last few range benefits over the closing months. So a 7.5-gallon fuel tank to boost the range and much trumpeted sound deadening made those longer journeys even quieter.

The Mini 1000 effectively took over from where the Mark II Super De Luxe left off. So it was a case of better trim, opening rear windows, heater, two sun visors, three-instrument binnacle and full width wheel trims. Most of the mechanical changes were as the 850, although the trim was repeatedly uprated. Better carpets in 1974, eyeball fresh air vents in 1976 and from 1977 reclining seats. These new seats were covered in two-tone nylon. Everyone now knew that the Mini was backing in their direction as reversing lights were standardised. Door map pockets at the front came in useful, as did the dipping rear view mirror.

Inside the City it was very black and basic, although there is also a radio/cassette in there plus some very untidy wiring.

Car magazine were not that impressed by the Mini 1000 when they tested it in February 1975 as a response the rapidly rising price of petrol and citing the fact that 40mpg would be the only acceptable consumption figure for the contemporary car, they pitched the Mini against a Fiat 127 and Toyota 1000 (Publica). "The elaborate fittings of the Toyota are attractive, and so is its smooth, happy engine, but it falls down by being short on interior space and having only mediocre handling and road holding...The Mini is an embarrassment. It's painfully out of date in just about every respect except price, but will continue to find adherents regardless; it may not be a good car any more, but it is a convenient one that the vast majority of people understand...Of course the Fiat is by far the best value. The very fact that its interior can be converted into a sort of estate car is a tremendous point in its favour."

Despite criticism the Mini not only stayed in production, but prospered. As the car reached it's 20th birthday, Autocar celebrated with a pretty positive road test in August 1979 and came up with some useful explanations as to why the Mini had survived. "It is not in the least surprising to hear recently that Mini sales were shooting up again. A car like this which offers a near certain 40mpg to the normal owner - provided he or she does not drive flat out all of the time - is vital to many pockets these days...On the open road, the limitations of the performance become more obvious...Those who appreciate the cardinal virtues of driving - good steering, road holding, responsiveness, stability are the ones that apply here - have confessed at one time or another to an unavoidable affection for the Mini...The immediate unthinking reaction today on some people's part is that the Mini has been overtaken by the competition. This is only half true - for the simple reason, which torpedoes most of the argument right at the start, that the Mini has few competitors. Such critics are thinking of Fiat' 127, Renault's 5, Volkswagen's Polo, Ford's Fiesta - but these are all very much bigger cars. Of the ten breeds of under one litre car which in any way compete with the Mini, none are just a quarter inch over 10 feet long - the Fiat 126 is the nearest at 10ft 3ins - and the rest are none less than a foot longer; and of those only four have appreciably better overall inside space. If you really want the Minimum of car there isn't much other than the Mini".

ADO74, a Harris Mann solution to the problem of designing a Mini successor. His brief was to come up with something bigger and more profitable. This was one of several similar proposals.

Three Mini replacements were seriously considered in 1972 and were given insect project names. There was the Ant, a dimensionally identical car to the Mini, which although it reached the clay model stage was deemed too close to the original to be worth developing.

Then there was the Dragonfly (a code name that surfaced yet again in the Mini's history a booted saloon that was rejected fairly quickly. Finally the Ladybird, which was 1.5 feet longer than a Mini and featured a hatch-backed rear, received approval quite rapidly. Code named ADO74 it went from clay model to full sized buck in record time. Harris Mann, stylist of the Allegro, TR7 and Princess was briefed to come up with a larger and more profitable model and at 11ft 6in (3.5m) by 5ft 1.5in (1.65m) it was just that. Its £130 million development mirrored the work being done at Ford on the Fiesta and the ADO 74 could have been launched at the same time. There was even MacPherson strut suspension on the BL car, which mechanically could have featured an early version of the remarkable K series engine, which later went on to power the Rover Metro. Another victim of market research ADO 74 was killed off for not being distinctive, or a direct Mini replacement.

Minissima arguably one of the most innovative Mini reskins, pictured with designer William Towns.

My Mini Cooper it's part in my Breakdown

Designer William Towns, famous for styling Aston Martins made a big impact at the 1973 London Motor Show. Incredibly it was even smaller than the Mini at a stunted 7ft 6 inches (2.28m) in length. The track, height and width were all identical on this motorised cube, which was powered by a Mini engine and automatic gearbox. There was just one door, at the back and the idea was that it could park at right angles to the kerb so that everyone could exit safely from the rear. There was conventional seating up front, whilst those at the back sat opposite each other. It was such an interesting basis that BL bought the rights and used it as a promotional vehicle and then stuck it in the Heritage museum. It was an interesting concept and should have been developed into what could have been the very first Smart.

ADO 88 caught on the move and in disguise. Designed as a successor to the Mini, it looked slightly like the Metro.

BLMC ceased to exist on 27th June 1975 when it was renamed British Leyland Ltd. The company had been nationalised after a steady slide towards insolvency. Sir Don Ryder had been commissioned to make a report about the state of the company and recommended that BL should stay as a producer of volume and specialist cars aided by huge injections of public money. Arguably the most damaging recommendation was amalgamating all of BL's car divisions into one. It did not work and BL lurched to another cash crisis in 1977.

My Mini Cooper it's part in my Breakdown

Ford became the nation's biggest builder of cars, largely by importing hundreds of thousands from its plants in Europe. As Michael Edwardes took over as chairman it all looked pretty bleak with union militancy, plant closures and an incoherent model policy. Probably the bleakest thing on the horizon was ADO 88, the Mini's replacement. It was BL's most advanced new project having cost £300m to develop, yet within a couple of months, Edwardes had canned it. He was quoted as saying that the car had looked "Like turning into a national disaster." Customer clinics were held around Britain and Europe and on one occasion a mere 3 per cent of the 500 question expressed a preference for the proposed new Mini, whereas 40 per cent responded very favourably to the all new Ford Fiesta. Part of the problem may have been that the ADO 88 was not the radical quantum leap that the original Mini had been.

ADO 88 had been accepted for production until Michael Edwardes indicated otherwise. It was due to make its debut at the first International Motor Show to be held at the National Exhibition Centre in Birmingham in 1978. In overall charge of the project was Technical Director Charles Griffin who was aiming to address the old Mini's shortcomings of too much noise and not enough refinement whilst boosting the interior space by making it bigger. Harris Mann did the styling and there was a hint of Princess 'wedge' about it all. The length was 10 ft 6in (3.2m), the track at the rear was now the same as the front and an extra two inches (5cm) in width was accommodated by curved body sides. Mechanically there did not seem to be any power unit better suited to the job than the old A series. So a £30m programmes to update it as the A plus was initiated. Like the original Mini the suspension was to be a critical factor in the car's success. So to keep the interior packaging neat and the floor usefully flat, Hydragas suspension, as later used on the Metro, was proposed.

However, the bodywork seemed to be the big problem area. Pininfarina were even asked to chip in with their interpretation on the small hatchback theme in 1976, which was deemed just too pretentious. In the cold light of the Europe wide customer clinics the reaction was far from favourable. The decision was taken to upgrade the model to supermini specification and dimensions if it was to stand any chance against the Fiesta, Volkswagen Polo, or Fiat 127. The new project was code named LC8, but underpinning it all was ADO88.

Market research indicated that the new car would not immediately replace the Mini. It was still useful to BL dealers as a second car proposition for two car families. So the Mini was saved yet again. In June 1979 the ADO 88 became the Metro after the ballot of the work force put that name ahead of Maestro.

So the Mini entered the '70s in very rude health as the unassailable small car. The absolute peak was reached in 1971 as combined production of Minis and Clubmans topped 320,000. It was the 4th best selling car in 1970, moved up to second behind the 1100/1300 a year later then 6th in '72, 5th in '73 rising to 3rd a year later and even entered the '80s in 4th spot.

Although the Mini missed the Suez crisis fuel restriction measures that inspired it, the Mini was in the right place at the right time in 1973. Firstly there was the Arab-Israeli War, which seriously affected Britain's oil supplies, as Arab oil exporting countries used the commodity as a political weapon. Consequently the priced quadrupled and to counter the effects Edward Heath's Conservative government introduced the three-day working week from 1st January 1974 and imposed a national 50mph speed limit. Trade union opposition to the government's counter inflation measures resulted in the miner's strike.

Not surprisingly the car that the nervous, frightened and frugal buyer turned to was the Mini. Much to British Leyland's annoyance the loss-making Mini overtook the relatively new Morris Marina as their top seller for 1974. The same thing happened again in 1979 when petrol prices soared after the Iranian revolution. The marginally profitable Mini led the way for BL's products, with the Marina and Allegro bringing up the rear.

Interviewed in Michael Wood's brilliant book Wheels of Misfortune Lord Stokes summed up the situation perfectly, *'Everyone stopped buying expensive cars in order to buy the ruddy Mini again'.*

The Mini was clearly the car you bought in a crisis. The model that you could rely on to be economical, reliable and practical, it appeared to be irreplaceable. However, the era of the supermini was dawning. After being unchallenged for so long, with just a few pesky imports to deal with the biggest threat to the Mini was to come from another UK built baby. Ford who had wisely avoided the small car market by finding out first hand with spanners that 'Mini cars make Mini profits' came up with their own interpretation. The Fiesta. This hatchback announced in July 1976 and costing one billion dollars to develop, finally overhauled the Minis sales figures in 1980 shifting 91,661 compared to the Minis 61,129, still pretty impressive for a 21 year old.

British Leyland had to do something. That something was the Metro, but that was different model and another decade.

Reliable Mini. The great thing about Minis is that they would just keep going. When the starter motor failed once, I didn't have the spare cash to pay for an exchange unit. So for about two weeks I simply jump-started it. Have incline, would travel. Actually with or without an incline, Minis are light enough to push start first time, every time. I just dumped the clutch and we had power. I got quite used to doing it and have probably never been fitter.

Yes my Mini never, ever let me down. I can remember it overheating in Essex at one point, but once cooled down and topped up with water we were off on another adventure. A reconditioned radiator from an engineering shop in Leyton helped even more and introduced me to the utter inaccessibility of the bottom hose. I remade the bracket so that it was easier to undo and even sent a picture and details to Car Mechanics magazine that would pay a fiver for published tips. I never heard a word from them. Relying on my Technical Drawing O Level I produced fairly detailed plans for a hinged rear seat and a rear seat bulkhead cut to allow awkward loads. That didn't impress anyone either. It would have made a great **Rüpp***Speed*® product and was a step up from pimping Corgi model cars.

My Mini that had previously been my sister's Mini finally became Uncle Charlie and Aunt Flo's in 1979. The irony was that it replaced a much newer and really quite awful Austin Allegro, complete with quartic steering wheel which had failed to live up to expectations, certainly as far as reliability was concerned. I delivered the Mini to Great Yarmouth and they ran it until the coastal weather bit right through the floorpan. At that point I went back to the seaside and unbolted all the big oily bits to bring home.

9. **Join the Club, man. After a decade of having the same happy face, BL bring in the bloke behind the Cortina to attach a blunt front and effectively create the Ford Clubman. At least there is now more room to change the fan belt...**

The Mini was perfect. So why tamper with perfection? Why indeed. Result: Mini Clubman. If anything looked as though it had been designed by a committee then the Clubman had to be a strong candidate. British Leyland needed to make more money from their small car and ideally replace it. The Wolseley and Riley derivatives proved that you could charge more for a tarted up car, if there was enough chrome and equipment to justify a price hike.

"First of all they have ruined the appearance, which is a great pity because the original car was completely functional and well proportioned. That awful Clubman bonnet would look very well on a Japanese car, but it clashes hopelessly with the shape of the rest of the body. In any case it's less efficient aerodynamically than the original bonnet and probably takes a mile or two off the top speed. They have also stuck boy racer stripes along the sides: just the thing to attract the attention of the police." So wrote a very disappointed John Bolster for Autosport about his 1275GT.

The Mini Clubman. Blunt fronted and fabulous to some.

My Mini Cooper it's part in my Breakdown

Roy Haynes a designer previously with Ford as head of Car and Truck styling and British Motor Holdings shell making subsidiary, Pressed Steel Fisher was given a brief to come up with a restyled body for the Mini and essentially created the Ford Clubman. With the Cortina Mark 2 to his credit maybe it was not surprising that Haynes should come up with a squared off bonnet just like contemporary Cortinas. Not only that, he tacked on a sizable rear end with huge C pillars with no suggestion initially that it could accommodate a third door. Although the rear flange gave a natural break for a hatchback, the actual hump itself still looked very unnatural indeed. Another route explored by Haynes in his search for extra luggage space was to utilise the Elf/Hornet, winged rear end. It got as far as a mock up before being rejected. So Leyland ended up only using the front end. This made the Clubman 4" (1.21m) longer, a tad heavier at 1406 lbs (637 kilos) and less economical too at 34mpg instead of the Mini 1000s 35mpg. And then there was the 1275GT. It had the impossible job of taking over from the much-loved Mini Cooper. It had three years to establish a reputation before the Cooper was phased out, but dismally failed to leave any lasting impression. There was more Ford influence too with the smallest Rostyle wheels yet, also used on the Cortina 1600E. Even the 1275GT decals aped those running down the side of the Le Mans winning Ford GT40.

Despite all these obvious objections the Clubman never suffered that badly in the marketplace. The buying public simply lapped up any new version of the Mini even though at £720 the saloon cost £45 more than the standard 1000. The flat, square, bonnet was relieved by just a few ridges leading down to a snub front which housed a full width grille with round headlamps at either end and a chrome trimmed grille. The bumper was much higher and the new grille badge formed a narrow centrepiece. To some it was like seeing an old and handsome friend after some ill advised plastic surgery. Others, like 1275GT owner Kate Perrins, did not have a problem with the nose when I interviewed her in 1996. "There is four inches more room under the bonnet, it makes all the jobs under there easier. My engine, which is

The Clubman could have looked like this with the Elf/Hornet tail to boost luggage space, like it did in South Africa.

prepared to concours standard, would not be as good if it was in the tight bay of a Cooper. For me, the Clubman is much more practical and easier to look after."

Essentially the Clubman came with the same level of trim as the Super De Luxe Mini, but was distinguished by the door trims and unique, for a Mini anyway, instrument binnacle which sighted the two dials directly in front of the driver: speedometer on the left and a combined fuel and temperature gauge on the right. A three-spoke steering wheel with Clubman on the boss was another original feature. The thickly padded seats were more comfortable too, so it was not all bad news. Another giant leap forward was fresh air ventilation provided by the extremely efficient and brilliantly simple eyeball type vents so popular in the '60s. Overall the interior had a distinctly Ford aura, not least because another ex-Ford stylist Paul Hughes designed them. In particular those air vents were just like the Cortina's 'Aeroflow' system. And atop the now padded dashboard, a D shaped revolving ashtray was very similar to that enjoyed by the Ford Anglias rear seat passengers. Then there was the three spoke deep-dished steering wheel of the 1275GT, all very

Cortina. BL weren't bothered as they signed off the AD020 and set about reorganising the company. Haynes left amid the chaos when his dream of streamlined model ranges was unlikely to happen.

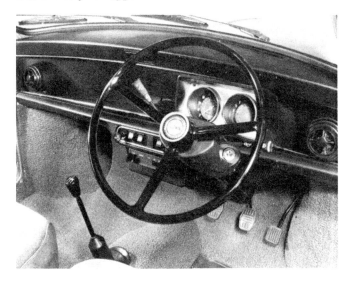

Inside, the Clubman driver got the instrumentation directly in front of the steering wheel in a little plastic box. A radical break with the centrist Mini instrument tradition of the previous decade. This is a '76 interior with new column stalks.

Whilst the standard Minis had switched back to rubber cone suspension, the Clubman retained the expensive Hydrolastic system until 1971. Under the bonnet was the 998cc engine and like the standard Mini, automatic transmission was extra. Across the range an estate version directly replaced the Countryman and Traveller, whilst the 1275GT was seen as the logical successor to the current Cooper.

A 1275GT, which looks very cool.

The press reaction to the first and so far, only major stylistic change to the Mini was generally enthusiastic. Custom Car wrote colourfully about the new model. They reckoned that the Elf and Hornet were wrong turns which deviated too far from the spartan original, but "All they needed to do was refine the basic formula to pamper to the buyers who feel they've got something a bit better than Glad and Bert's six year old 850...and pull back some of the doubters who maybe thought that buying a ten year old design did not adequately reflect their automotive trendiness." Consequently they liked the wind up windows, new dashboard and extra elbow room under the bonnet. "Not, then a truly memorable little car, but not half as bad as some pundits would have us believe."

Motor also liked the new package and tested all versions in October 1969, "Many of our criticisms have been answered in one go with the introduction of the long nosed variants which are a lot more civilised and habitable than any previous Mini. The much improved seats point to a growing awareness within the Austin Morris division of British Leyland that seating comfort really matters. Add to this the significant changes in the ventilation, furnishings and instrument layout, not to mention the all-synchromesh gearbox introduced earlier and a gear change that feels much better than before, and the result is a dramatic overall improvement in both creature comforts and drivability. No longer is a long Mini journey something of an endurance test, even though the noise level is still high (particularly so in the 1275GT) when the engine is extended and the ride on poor roads as bouncy as ever."

1976 Facelift, but little more than a new grille and some minor interior updates.

The Clubman during its eleven-year production run changed very little. Like the standard Mini there was not much money to throw around on the development during the '70s. Broadly the mechanical modifications were as the Mini. June 1971 must count as one of the most significant dates when suspension on the saloon was switched to rubber cones. In '72, improved synchromesh made gear changing easier and an alternator did the same for battery charging. Radial ply tyres arrived in 1973 along with rod shift gear change. For '74 it was inertia reel seat belts, heated rear window and twin silencer exhaust. An important adoption in 1975 was the 1098cc engine for the manual gearbox saloon a unit first fitted to the 1100 series back in 1962. Consequently the manual 998cc unit was deleted and available only with an automatic gearbox.

Cloth and reclining seats were also standardised. 1976 turned out to be the Clubmans' one and only major facelift and it amounted to little more than a new grille with two chrome horizontal bars and the word Mini, plus BL logo in the middle. Inside there were instrumentation updates which affected the whole range including column mounted stalks, rocker switches and larger pedals. Apart from moulded carpets, the rear suspension was softened up. The last round of changes occurred a year later in 1977 with new wheel trims, locking petrol cap, reversing lights tinted glass and a leather-rimmed steering wheel.

For a while the Clubman really was the least loved Mini, even if there was a bit more room to fiddle under the bonnet. The more experimental owners found it easier not just to install bigger engines, but even smaller motorcycle ones too. In time the '70s became cool and suddenly the Clubman didn't look so out of place. The 1275GT in particular came in for some overdue re-evaluation. The Clubman was a product of its time and that was the only time the Mini looked truly different. I think that's why people like them now.

Our Mini Clubman 1977 – 1982. In 1977 Dad bought a Mini Clubman and it always smelt of WD40. It was a jerky little automatic bought so that Mum could drive, which she never did. She tried, but driving really wasn't her thing. My sister took her out once, but the experience was very traumatic, with Mum literally cutting corners. A good job no one was standing on them at the time.

On that face of it an automatic Mini Clubman wasn't a very exciting prospect except that it was a Wood & Pickett one. Well actually it wasn't, but it did have that company's nudge bars front and rear. The BL dealer offered them and Dad ticked the box to buy them, which was great. It looked fantastically cool and I would borrow it when I could. The three-speed automatic was noisy and stuttered around in a very lovable way.

It was also pumped full of Ziebart which explained the lubrication related aroma. Zeibart was a popular preparation, which stopped rust. A hot waxy injection that would certainly help a Mini resist the ravages of time. Indeed the Clubman knocked about within the family for many years. My sister had it for a while, so did Uncle Charlie and when Uncle Joe retired from being a chauffeur, the Clubman was his next limousine.

**Mum and Aunt Flo next to the Clubman.
I miss them all.**

10. **It's 1971 and small shopping cars now have an extra door, except for the Mini and by the time that Britain was baking in the great big giant heatwave of 1976 even Ford had joined the hatchback party, so BL were clearly having a siesta at the time.**
Minis made in 1971 318,475 • 1972 306,937 • 1973 295,186 • 1974 255,336 • 1975 200,293 • 1976 203,575

Remarkably the Mini was still at the top of its game as it went into its third iteration and still nothing really new was challenging it, but surely an exciting new decade would mark significant technological leap in the way small cars were designed and built?

Well Fiat were still pumping out the 500 and the final version emerged in 1972 as the 500R which used a new 594cc engine from the 126, with a reduced output of 18bhp. The R also had the floorpan from its successor and adopted the new Fiat logo, with different wheels and a few other changes. Some things never changed though because the only items stopping the 500 were basic drum brakes whilst the 'crash' non-synchromesh gearbox provided lots of noisy entertainment.

Here's a late model Fiat 127, say a proper hello to the modern supermini.

Luckily Fiat did have a car up their corporate sleeves, which was genuinely new and exciting, the 127. Voted 'Car of the Year' in 1971. This was the model that brought Fiat into the modern era, adopting the front-wheel drive layout from the 128 although the model was one size smaller. Most of the mechanicals were based on the 128, although the 903cc engine was a derivative of the 850 Sport unit. Performance was perky and the handling was very sharp. Initially launched in 2-door form, it only really made sense as a 3-door hatchback. So here was the official arrival of the supermini into the automotive community, even though the Autobianchi Primula (but still Fiat) got there first. Combining a brilliantly packed drivetrain with the convenience and practicality of a tailgate in a neat two-box design. Small cars would never be the same again.

Fiat 126, not a cuddly and lovable as the 500.

Then there was the Fiat 126, which was first seen at the 1972 Turin Motorshow and proved to be a logical, if not so endearing successor to the legendary 500. Using an enlarged engine of 594cc it still retained the familiar running gear of its predecessor, what differed was the all new body shell. Styled with '70 straight edges and not so cute as the rounded 500, but at least it soon became available with a canvas rollback roof like the old 500. It was a buzzy little thing, which could get to 60-60mph tops and was built down to and offered at a low price. For some odd reason the largely identical but completely forgotten, 133 with a bigger 843cc water-cooled engine was imported from Spain, where it was badged as a SEAT.

Still in Italy Innocenti were making the their own Bertone styled version of the Mini as a 90 and 120 model, but you can read about that elsewhere. Whether British Leyland should have imported it is another debate as they had problems of their own which led to them severing all connections in 1975.

The Renault 5 in its brilliantly original form.

If there was innovation over at Fiat, something was also going on at Renault. The 16 had been the first front wheel drive hatchback, but this had been a full sized family affair. Downsizing it to create the Renault 5 was a clever thing to do. The gearbox sat in front of the engine and the torsion bar independent suspension meant a superbly smooth ride. Cleverly packaged with lots of room inside and useful boot, suddenly the Mini's days looked numbered as market leader. Not only that this new rival had genuinely chic styling and equally impressive handling. The Renault 5 had huge appeal throughout Europe and would sell in very large numbers.

The Peugeot 104 in 1973 was another capable supermini, which had a shortened wheelbase and three doors. The light alloy engine and all coil, all independent suspension meant it was fun to drive. Not nearly as cute as the Renault 5 though with rather dull right angle styling which didn't help sales. It also troubled Citroen's showrooms badged as the LNA for no apparent reason.

DAF replaced the 55 with the rather more bland 66 in 1972. Volvo though took a controlling interest and for a while brought back the smaller engined 46, before renaming the 66 as the Volvo 66 in 1976. A lot of ominous sixes there as the time for exclusively Dutch small cars propelled by rubber bands came to an end.

Reliant Kitten. A slightly pointless but rust free small car.

By now the Japanese were in full invasion mode sending their cars all over the world, but most of the tiniest models stayed at home to comply with their complex parking and engine size regulations. Daihatsu took the Fellow Max beyond its logical conclusion and came up with the nicely proportioned 2 cylinder Cuore in 1976. Mazda had the Chantez, a slightly glitzy offering with a 359cc water-cooled two-stroke engine. Mitsubishi continued with the Minica series as Toyota did with the Publica. Datsun had the Cherry, which wasn't really that Mini. Subaru meanwhile changed the R-2 into the friendlier Rex, although adding D-2 in 1977 might have helped sales to Star Wars fans.

We haven't mentioned the Imp for a while which soldiered on to the complete indifference of Hillman's new owners, Chrysler. Along with the better-trimmed and more powerful Sunbeams they lasted until 1976. The posh Singer version had already passed away in 1970.

The Reliant Kittens had the huge advantage of a wheel at each corner layout over the rather less stable

Robin product range. The Kitten wasn't that cute and just looked like a glass fibre van with windows, oh and Mini hubcaps. However, more buyers, or wintering bikers went for the three wheelers. Introduced in 1975 it was up against tough opposition. The main advantages over the Mini was a body that didn't rust otherwise it was hard to fathom why anyone would bother (but 4075 buyers did) and it was put down at the vets in 1982

Audi 50, a classy package that hit the big time when it became a Polo.

In Germany the NSU Prinz models came to the end of their production run in 1972 and 1973. Meanwhile the Ro80 continued to cause problems with its tricky Wankel Rotary engine whilst owner Volkswagen wanted to kill off the smaller models and replace it with it's own. Except that Volkswagen didn't have any. Until that is the Audi 50 arrived. This had a 50bhp engine, hence its name and was suitably compact too. The 50 also had crumple zones, a decent amount of room inside and the all-important hatched back. Launched in 1974 and built in Wolfsburg on the Volkswagen lines, the Audi badges were replaced by VW ones in 1975. That's when the specification was stripped back to the bare bones. It's also when sales of the new Polo went through the roof finally reaching the UK in October 1976.

Ford finally shrink a car to create the Fiesta.

Actually the most important thing to happen in 1976 came from Ford. They had been watching carefully as cars had been getting smaller and possibly just a bit more profitable than the original Mini had been. So their first supermini was badged the Fiesta and came with all the usual transverse engine and front wheel drive mod cons. The styling was contemporary and neat by a chap called Tom Tjaarda who worked in Ford's own Ghia styling studio. With immaculate timing the Fiesta was able to take advantage of the post-oil crisis demand for decent fuel consumption.

My Mini Cooper it's part in my Breakdown

Fiesta Ghia from the rear, where there is a great big boot, and tailgate.

Fiesta buyers could get a really basic 950, which had black bumpers, which Henry Ford would have approved of, plus, rubber mats, 2 spoke steering wheel, and the option of either a low or high compression 957cc engine. Those after real luxury could splash out on an 1100 L, which came fitted with show off chrome bumpers, teasingly erotic reclining seats, deeply indulgent door pockets, extensive carpeting and a rear parcel shelf.
So when Ford jumped aboard here was confirmation that the hatchback was the everyone's new favourite type of car.

Mini Running Total 1971 2,761,987 · 1972 3,068,924 · 1973 3,364,110 1974 3,619,446 · 1975 3,819,739 · 1976 4,023,314

Date: October 1979 Mileage: 96,684 Amount spent: £200 and a bottle of wine. Minis in my Life: 1964 Mini Cooper MOT: Yes. Expires June 1980.

What I always wanted was a Mini Cooper. I'd spent years looking in the Exchange and Mart, which still had dozen or so every week back in the 1970s. Luckily my dad always knew the right or sometime wrong people and there was this slightly dodgy bloke in Berkshire who often had one or two in circulation. He offered to drive it over on trade plates and £200 seemed about right. Dad had some odd German Rieseling in comedy sized giant bottles as a distraction from the iffy contents. So we gave him one of these for his trouble. In retrospect a bargain and also one of the smallest sums of money I've ever spent on the Mini Cooper.

Parked on the drive, the Cooper looked beautiful, if a little bit tired as clearly it had led a very hard life. The paintwork was decidedly patchy. There weren't so much touch ups as major hand held aerosol bodge ups which were probably visible from the moon. Inside, the trim wasn't exactly complete. The driver's seat had become unstitched and was only held in place with a black plastic padded and well bolstered seat cover. It was actually a cool looking cover that did a better of keeping you in the cockpit than the standard seat.

The driver's door card was missing and in it's place was some dirty matted sound proofing which looked more like old lagging a loft. Most of the chrome was pitted and tinged with red. The brightwork around the wheel arches wasn't all there. Mechanically it seemed extremely tired, the brakes were not happy and the engine seemed like it needed more than just a simple service. Perhaps the most exciting thing about the Cooper is that a previous owner had sourced Cooper S reverse rims. Not all the hubcaps were there, but for me that made it look even better. According to the documentation and that included the registration document, it was a 1964 Austin Mini Cooper with the 997cc engine. That made it fairly rare at the time as many owners had found that engine lacklustre and so would have replaced it with a livelier lump.

I couldn't afford to run and restore at the same time as I was poised to become a full time student again. So I pushed it into the garage and spent the next three years mainly sorting out the bodywork.

My Mini Cooper it's part in my Breakdown

11. **Minis that sounded like they belonged in the Hobbit, Elfs, Hornets, Mokes and Vans were all jolly good, some could take sacks of spuds on board with ease, whilst others had rather a lot of chintzy chrome and walnut, whilst one didn't even have a proper roof.**

If any production car lent itself to being adapted, developed and derived, it had to be the Mini. With the drive train neatly packaged at the front in its own sub frame the Mini could be stretched, adorned and stripped, hence the vans, pick-ups, estates, Elfs, Hornets and Mokes which took the Mini concept to the outside edge of usefulness and frippery. It did not take long for there to be a Mini for every job and eventuality. So here they are.

The GPO put thousands of these to work and simply beefed up the rear doors to keep thieves at bay.

In the beginning (1960) there was the Mini Van. This model was a pretty crucial element in the success of the Mini, which traditionally had formed the bedrock of mainstream BMC models. Previous big hits in the light commercial vehicle (LCV) market were 210,000 Austin A30/35 vans and more than 325,000 Morris Minor vans and pick ups. That was profitable business, so Leonard Lord wasted no time introducing a Mini LCV. A mere five months after the launch of the saloon, BMC revealed its first commercial derivative in January 1960. Based on the saloon floor pan, this 1/4-ton van was stretched by 4 inches (10cm) and the total length of the Mini grew to 10ft and 3/4 inches (3.27m). Up to the B pillars it was standard Mini, beyond that it was pure panel van. A raised load platform in the floor added the necessary structural rigidity, which also housed both the spare wheel and battery in a gap immediately behind the front seats. Right at the back, adjacent to the axle was a specially designed oblong fuel tank, which held 6 gallons (27 litres).

Underneath it all the rear suspension was modified with longer turrets, which both stiffened and raised the ride and lifted the rear end. What all this added up to was a usefully low loading height of just over 17 inches (43cm) and 46 cu ft (1.3 cu cm) of load space. Turf out the passenger and remove their seat (which was an optional extra anyway) and it suddenly increased to 58 cu ft (1.64 cu cm). There was a lengthy 55 inches (139cm) of space from doors to seats and almost 54 inches (137 cm) width to play with, so it could accommodate some surprisingly large objects. The payload was officially 5cwt, but users soon exceeded that weight on a regular basis.

The Mini Van. Ready for work.

My Mini Cooper it's part in my Breakdown

Specification was kept to the bare minimum. At the front, the grille was simply stamped out of the front panel (which Issigonis had originally envisaged for the no-frills Minor and Seven) restricting maintenance access. At the back there were quarter bumpers, which at least did not get in the way when loading. Inside was the minimum of trim with lots of metalwork on show and heavy duty floor covering. Even a rear view mirror was an option as the wing mirrors satisfied the minimum legal requirement.

Despite the spartan specification, the Mini Van proved to be very popular with private customers, not least because the price was £360 as opposed to the saloon's £497. The difference was purchase tax, which was not payable on commercial vehicles. All the owners had to do was refrain from cutting out windows in the side panels, so that the van still qualified as commercial and for tax purposes as a business tool. Oh and owners had to keep their top speed to 30 mph at all times except on the new fangled M1 motorway where they could speed up to 40mph.

Mini Vans proved to be very popular with mods (as in Mods 'n' Rockers) in the early '60s. They regarded the car as modern and smart with a useful amount of rear space for a dead Lambretta, or just to crash out in after a hectic weekend in Brighton. A Mini Van was certainly a lot less draughty and more reliable than a scooter. Not surprisingly for owners who wanted to carry two extra passengers in some degree of comfort, after market conversion kits quickly became available. BMC marketed their own kit, which retailed at £15 10s, which used parts from the estate car. A contemporary advertisement showed how easy it was for the DIY motorist to install. Firstly a section of the false floor was cut away and the seat filled the gap between the rear wheel arches. The only problem was that rear passengers rubbed shoulders with the relocated battery and spare wheel. Nevertheless, with the rear seats folded flat the load bay was just as big and flat as before unlike many modern hatchbacks with split fold seating arrangements. Oh yes and if you wanted passengers to luxuriate in carpeted comfort, the PVC bound item cost £3 7s 6d extra.

Mini pick-up, even more versatile with room for more stuff and a ladder.

Of course the best customers were those who were going to put them to work and the country's biggest LCV fleets took the little vans to the hearts, proving to be very useful for the Post Office and Police, whilst AA patrolmen everywhere breathed a sigh of relief at getting a proper, weatherproof car instead of an uncomfortable motorcycle and sidecar combination.

At the launch in 1960 there were two models, the Austin Se7en Van and the Morris Minivan, distinguished only by their badging. To some extent these models existed in their own time warp, almost untouched by saloon developments. In 1962 when the clumsy Se7en designation was dropped to become simply the Austin Mini Van, such luxuries as windscreen washers, an interior light and bumper overriders were standardised. By 1967 the 998cc engine became a not especially popular option with 3.44:1 final drive. In 1969 a range name change turned all the models simply into Mini Vans. This coincided with the adoption of negative earth electrics and a mechanical fuel pump. Into the '70s and synchromesh was improved, rod operated gear change introduced, the interior was uprated with rocker switches and column stalks. In late '78 'Mini 95' badges showed the designated gross weight of the van. A year later a touch of luxury courtesy of the 'L' pack brought cloth faced seats, carpets, passenger sun visor and extra sound deadening as standard to the 1000 and optional on the 850. In 1983 the Mini Van was directly replaced by the roomier, but unlovable Metro Van.

The next logical commercial development after the Mini Van, had to be the Mini Pick-up, which arrived a year later in 1961. It was largely identical to the van except for the missing roof and side panels. Adding strength to the structure was a bulkhead directly behind the front seats with a flat rear window. The flat deck led to a tailgate, which was secured by two hinged arms, and like the saloon there was a hinged number plate, which allowed full-length loads to be carried, completely legally. It also had van like versatility because an optional, later standard, canvas cover could be erected over two steel hoops and then tailed off with a transparent plastic rear screen. Laurence Pomeroy memorably compared the styling of this new light commercial vehicle as "Curiously prophetic of the 1963 Ferrari LM."

Development mirrored updates to the van. The 850 version was the first to be discontinued in 1980 whilst the 1000 model lived as long as the Van. In May 1983 it left the price lists forever, never to be replaced.

The commercials inhabited a stubbornly Mark 1 body that never grew up. Neither the Van, or Pick-up ever flirted with Hydrolastic suspension, or faddish, Clubman style updates. External door hinges, door levers, sliding windows, door bins and shoe print rear lights survived on the commercials until they were discontinued in the '80s. A fabulous throwback to a simpler automotive era and arguably the models that remained closest to Issigonis' ideal.

Having successfully extended the Mini floor pan to accommodate Van bodywork it was only a matter of time before windows were officially installed to mark the arrival of the estate versions. The Austin Se7en Countryman and Morris Mini-Traveller were launched in September 1960. These new vehicles were obviously based on the wheelbase of the van, but there the similarity ended. The estates weighed around 1 cwt (50kg) more than the van as a result of the fixtures and fittings. The luxurious touches included a trimmed fuel tank, headlining, carpets and hardly a bare piece of metal on show.

Outside, the most notable difference was the extensive exterior woodwork, which the marketing department had deemed necessary to cultivate an upmarket gentrified image. This was an indulgence that Issigonis was violently opposed to, but he was not successful in getting it removed. This mock Tudor beam work did however connect the models with other BMC estates, principally the Morris Minor Traveller, although that estate actually needed the wood to hold the rear of the car together whereas on the Mini Countryman and Traveller it was entirely non-structural. The timber was simply glued onto the rear side panels behind the B panel and on the twin rear doors. Also adding to the weight were rear seats and the De Luxe level of trim, although like the van, a rear view mirror was on the options list. The rear windows were positively panoramic and also offered plenty of welcome ventilation because like the ones at the front, they were sliding affairs.

A 'woody' Mini Estate down on the farm.

Compared to the paltry boot space of the saloon (5.5 cu ft, 0.15 cu m), the estates offered cavernous

144

accommodation. With the rear seats folded it was 35.3cu ft (0.99 cu m) and if there was four up, then there was still room for 18.5 cu ft (0.52 cu m). To cope it had stiffer van suspension and weight distribution biased more to the rear than the saloon. At the back there was no room for the spare wheel and battery so they were positioned under the floor where the van's petrol tank had been. That meant that the estates used the saloon's tank which was positioned bulkily at the rear offside of the load area. Power was provided by the standard 848cc unit. So these vehicles struggled to 70 mph, were slightly slower off the mark and suffered by around 2 mpg. But they more than made up for these deficiencies with considerable practicality.

Autocar seemed to like the package when they tested one in September 1960. " Already holding a reputation of being a great little car, this latest version will certainly enhance this assessment. For town use it remains easy to park, and is fast through traffic because of its compact dimensions. On the open road its performance is adequate to transport four people and luggage with considerable economy and ease."

Motor tested an untimbered Mini Countryman for 1734 miles. The magazine pronounced, "Having long put up with the difficulty of wedging articles on the back seat, the shopping housewife will find the low loading ease of the Countryman a big attraction, for the Mini is the lowest of all; dog and carry-cot are both so much more easily catered for. Just as comfortable and acceptable as the Jones's four door saloon, estate cars no longer carry the stigma of a 'trade' vehicle." They also undertook a slightly bizarre test to see how many lions they could pack into the back of their Countryman, 1,764 to be precise. But only with the distinctive lion logo for the egg marketing board is stamped on them of course. That translated into four large boxes of eggs, plus 18 further packs, containing six eggs each. There was room for many more if rearward vision was not to be a priority. On their performance tables Motor compared the Mini statistically with its rivals, a long time before the comparison road tests became commonplace. The Mini lost out slightly to the Austin A40 on maximum speed, but was by far the most impressive in acceleration terms. The otherwise unremarkable Fiat Giardiniera beat the Minis mpg. Overall though the A40, Fiat, Ford Anglia Estate and Hillman Husky were also rans compared to the thoroughly modern Mini.

**Metal bodied Mark 2 Mini estate,
this is an Austin Countryman.**

Consistent Mini fan, John Bolster in Autosport made a convincing case for the mock Tudor timber. "The shooting brake, station wagon, utility, call it what you will, is an extremely popular type of dual purpose vehicle. When I was a boy, a certain aura surrounded these machines, and I don't mean just the scent of varnished timber of which they were constructed. Chauffeur driven, they whispered down the long gravel drives of the big houses, taking beaters to the shoot or collecting guests from the train. One kept the chassis of last year's Rolls and sent it to the coach builders for such a conversion, after which it became the most useful form of transport that any family could possess. There has been a revolution and the spacious days are no more." Even so the Mini did not disappoint. "The Traveller which I took over was resplendent in white paint and varnished wood and I had to admit that it was monstrously handsome. I purposely drove to fetch it in my own Mini, so that a comparison would be immediate, and I at once admired the better quality of the carpets, upholstery and interior trim. I found that the little brake had a slightly better gear change with rather more effective synchromesh."

1962 proved to be an interesting year for these models. Firstly the clumsy Se7en name was dropped and BMC also marketed an all steel version of the estate. First produced for export purposes only a year earlier, this unadorned model represented a saving of £19 and quite a few planks of wood. In all other respects the models were identical with De Luxe specifications. Development thereafter followed the saloon. Like the van there was no experimentation with Hydrolastic suspension and an automatic gearbox was never an option.

When the Mark II Countryman and Traveller were introduced in October 1967 the big news was the adoption of the 998cc engine. At last the little estate to lug heavier loads without getting left behind. Apart from the face-lift front end the model remained largely as before. Both woody and plain Jane metal versions were on sale, the price differential remained £19. There were rear-sliding windows as before and the foot print rear light clusters were not replaced by the saloon's shoeboxes.

Mini Clubman estate complete with unmissable vinyl coated, wood effect, steel battens on the flanks and rear doors.

At a stroke, British Leyland rationalised their range of small estate cars. At a stroke they also horrified traditionalists by repackaging these models in Clubman clothing. Out went the cuddly old woodies and in came the cubed Clubman with vinyl coated steel side trims, which looked like a particularly narrow Formica sideboard. To be fair though, the square front looked much more at home on the longer estate bodywork. It is just that those stick on fake wood trims, which ran down the flanks, and around to the rear doors took a bit of getting used to.

Generally the press welcomed the new range. Autocar went and bought one to run as a long termer and were a little disappointed when they reported to their readers after 10,000 miles. Build quality on collection was hardly inspiring and with just 22 miles on the clock, there was no handbook, both rear ashtrays were missing, the rear number plate lamp glass was cracked, and all the carpets were unclipped and badly fitted. Mechanically things were not much better as there were noisy tappets, an exhaust popping on the over run, squeaky pedals and heavy fuel consumption. Not only those, the speedometer, universal joints and carburettor needles were replaced during this period.

By 1977 the mock wood had gone, replaced by stick on vinyl stripes.

Developments over the years were as the Clubman saloon. A single door mirror replaced the wing variety in 1973 and most significantly in 1975, the 1098cc engine became the standard manual gearbox power unit, whilst 998cc engined models were automatic only. In 1977 the BL admitted that the mock wood was pretty risible and replaced them with cheaper side stripes. Significantly, the Clubman estate was not killed off immediately by the arrival of the all-new Metro, after all there were surplus stocks to be sold. Technically it could be called a hatchback, certainly it was no bigger than the more modern superminis, but by comparison it was hopelessly outclassed.

In June 1973 Motor cottoned onto the emerging trend for so called superminis, although they called them 'Budget Holdalls'. "The starting point...was the Renault 5, a car which embodies no technical innovation - indeed it was built up largely from existing components - but which does, we believe, represent a landmark in packaging and styling with its roomy and versatile three door body...It brings to the small car class the rear door and the estate form of bodywork which we anticipate will eventually become almost universal for saloons of all sizes." Their first choice as a rival was in their view the archetypal compact car, the Mini in Clubman estate form. This was joined by the Fiat 127, a Datsun 100A estate and a Sunbeam Sport, the performance variant of the Hillman Imp. In their summing up, Motor were painfully accurate in their assessment. "Regrettably, the Mini Clubman estate is easily disposed of. As a package, it is still unrivalled. It is easily the most compact car of the five, yet has plenty of interior space, so if you have a particularly small garage or the constant need to park in confined spaces then the Mini is for you, especially as it is one of the cheapest cars in the group. Unfortunately in most other respects it is also the worst car in the group, with the poorest performance, gear change, ride and road holding. It's the sad result of some 10 years of neglect."

Two years later in 1975 What Car? had what they believed were the answers to the energy crisis as cheap and basic transportation. The Clubman was pitted against the cheap and cheerless Lada 1200 estate and the Renault 4DL. The magazine believed that there was a market for these cars despite the popularity of the hatchback. The Clubman did not impress, "The Mini Clubman's carrying capacity will satisfy those people whose demands are not excessive. It is a light, easy to drive, economical car that

provides basic transport at an inflated price (£1248)."
The winner turned out to be the Renault, which the
magazine admitted, was an emotional as well as a
practical decision. Outclassed by a Renault and a Lada,
what a sad state of affairs.

**Original Riley Elf had rear wings, a fancy grille and lots
of chrome. Wolseley Hornet identical on the outside.
Within months both models had bumper overriders and
a diagonal seam on the front wing like all other Minis.**

Given the continuing success of the Mini and the
benefit of hindsight, maybe BL should have retro fitted the
Mark 3 front end, dusted off their woodwork tools and
carried on marketing the smallest estate. It could have
been a contender well into the '90s and as retro popular as
the Cooper.

Badge engineering. Almost a religion amongst car
manufacturers in the '50s and '60s. As marques merged
and models were rationalised, it still seemed sensible to
cultivate marque loyalty. Certainly plenty of customers

would buy a car simply because it had a certain badge on the bonnet. Many years ago I spoke to Bill Preston Sales

Wolseley Hornet rear end, with its little fins.

Director at G. Kingsbury, BMC dealers in Hampton Middlesex about his early salesman years. "Wolseley was the popular choice around here. The only car with its name in lights our affluent, upper middle class customers preferred to be seen in a Wolseley. So for us badge engineering was a very good thing."

BMC were delighted that the spin offs from the original ADO15 had all been incredibly successful. Austin and Morris Minis now dominated the small commercial sector with the van and pick-up then gone on to create huge demand for a sports saloon courtesy of the Cooper, so the only way was up. Hence the pocket Rollers in the shape of the Riley Elf and Wolseley Hornet. And what shapes they were too, not content with an interior, which resembled the smallest room in a stately home, BMC also made an effort to give the cars highly distinctive body styles. These models were not just cynical badge engineering exercises, they were very different, often embracing developments, which would eventually filter down through the rest of the range.

The man behind the restyle was Dick Burzi, who had worked on many of the '50s Austins. Consequently the styling was a retrograde step. The clean, simple lines of the original car had been seriously compromised in the interests of gentrification. At the back there were little fins, which were rapidly going out of fashion. The intention was to add authority to the rear end and provide a better frame for the more traditional boot. Actually the 6 cu ft (0.16 cu m) of space only amounted to a 0.5 cu ft (0.01 cu m) increase capacity over the standard saloon. Although it could accommodate marginally more bulky items the fact that it was hinged at the top and the number plate was not hinged at all, meant that any luggage over spill could not be piled conveniently on top.

Parking was also more of a problem as this fancy tail added 8.5 inches (21.5cm) to the overall length. Never mind. At the front there was an equally pretentious upright grille arrangement, which amounted to a '30s throwback, with exaggerated moustache chrome addenda at either side. Worst of all the grille was attached to the bonnet. Access to the engine was always limited at the best of times, but this great big chrome tooth just got in the way. Practicality was not the models strong points, but according to the BMC research, owners of Elfs and Hornets were the least likely to tinker, or over load their little limousines. They also did not plan on going anywhere too fast, the extra few pounds of weight and reduced aerodynamics meant that the 848cc engine had a slightly harder and slower time of it.

As a triumph of snobby style over practical content, the Elf and Hornet were completely successful. Arriving in October 1961 the differences between the standard and these swish Minis was obvious. Apart from the revised face and tail, the join between the A panel and front wing was missing. There was a smooth line from headlight to door hinge, which would not last for long. The bumpers were different too, no overriders and at the back they were a full wraparound design. The grilles were in keeping with the marque identities as the more upmarket and slightly more expensive Riley had a peaked and blue-badged affair, whilst the Wolseley featured its illuminated name. Chrome trim also decorated the windscreen and bonnet join and ran around the side on to the door and

**Inside an Elf. This is the full width view in a wind up
window Mark III with
two lockable glove compartments.**

finished at the C pillar. Cooper style surrounds also perked
up the side windows and there were of course full De Luxe
wheel trims, with the option of whitewall tyres. Colours
were unique to the range and often featured a contrasting
roof.

Inside, the Elf and Hornet were a class apart from
the bog standard Mini and even maintained a little
respectful distance between themselves. The Elf was
regarded as the hierarchical leader so it had a full width
walnut dashboard with two lockable glove compartments
on either side of the three instrument dials. By contrast
the Hornet had the standard oval three-instrument
binnacle with a wood veneer finish. Otherwise both cars
had increased seat padding, the facings being leather cloth
and extensive carpeting.

The late and very great George Bishop, editor of
Small Car magazine had some reservations when he first
tested a Riley Elf in September 1962. "Heads turn when
you drive an Elf. People recognise it as some rich relation
of the BMC twins, but are puzzled by the boot at the back,
the chrome waistband and the cloud of cigar smoke

around it...the traditional Riley radiator shell that lifts up with the bonnet, all ready to bang your head on...at the rear it has a boot with six cubic feet capacity which will take many odds and ends or one large suitcase and fewer odds and ends...The Elf, a creature which surely should be

The Mark III Hornet is almost stark with a Minimal amount of burr walnut surrounding the familiar three-instrument binnacle.

light and airy, is in fact 190lb heavier than a standard Mini...the boot lid is decidedly heavy to lift and, by the way, ready to snap down like a Zambesi crocodile on the unwary." Even so Bishop was not put off completely, "I liked the Riley, and had a great deal of fun driving it...The finish is better than on the cheaper Mini versions, and the interior with better seats, carpets and all that wood and leather like stuff, is cosier."

Development of these luxury cars was rapid. BMC quickly realised that nothing, but leather trim would do, so this was standardised in 1962. The prominent body seams, which had been expensive to engineer out of the original model, were now an integral part of the structure, whilst the bumpers were beefed up with overriders. They also addressed the sluggish performance the following year with the launch of the Mark II model, which featured a new 998cc engine. It consisted of an Austin/Morris 1100 block and the shorter stroke crankshaft from the Morris

Wolseley Hornet Mark II, identical except for Hydrolastic suspension and a 998cc engine under the bonnet.

Minor. The extra 4 bhp made a difference to both the speed and economy, whilst wider front brake and twin leading shoes made stopping a formality.

Motor were pleased to see the improvements featured on a Wolseley Hornet and pronounced that although it "costs over £100 more than the basic Mini...the trappings of luxury...put it in a small but useful market of its own."

Like most of the Mini range, Hydrolastic suspension was fitted in 1964. Small Car, which had become Car Magazine with Doug Blain at the helm still had plenty against the upmarket version of the Mini. Given a Hydrolastic Wolseley to play with this is what he said: "Pitch free ride on wavy and bumpy surfaces is supposed to be Hydrolastic's forte, and certainly in the BMC 1100 range and even more in the 1800 there's an astonishing freedom from vertical movement even on the most frightful farm tracks. The Hornet's short wheelbase doesn't really make such an ideal platform, and at the fairly high cruising speeds of which the car is capable a sensitive driver gets the feeling that there isn't really time for the front end to warn the tail accurately about what's coming...The less said about the Wolseley part of the specification the better; the hideous grille on the front is a mere mockery (it is more than two feet away from the radiator proper anyway) and the ungainly bustle at the back makes just enough difference to the overall length to keep the car out of the special little parking spaces which so often seem to open up for an ordinary Mini."

Just in case their readers did not get the message, the magazine returned to the same theme in June 1966 when they compared the Hornet to a Hillman Super Imp. In the all-important areas of handling and performance the Hornet came out decidedly on top. Otherwise the car's styling and the fact that there was no synchromesh on first gear counted against it. Obviously Car lost no opportunity to rubbish the Hornet's pretensions. "Both the Wolseley and the Hillman are wrong insofar as they pretend to be luxury cars. They are too small to be truly luxurious and still hold four people. With this in mind, we prefer the Hillman because it is much less false: it lacks the Hornet's silly associations with a long-dead marque, and it offers a few more genuine features such as sound deadening. The other things are valuable only when they help to disguise any economy car's bargain basement origins. In fact the only luxury to which either aspire is psychological."

In October 1966 the model entered its final Mark III phase and some important Mini firsts. The most immediately apparent change was that the door hinges were now internal. Inside, both driver and passenger could gracefully wind down the windows, rather than crudely slide them open. If that was not enough ventilation entered a new era with eyeball type vents mounted at either end of the dashboard. Even changing gear became a pleasure thanks to the Cooper remote gear change.

My Mini Cooper it's part in my Breakdown

**Mark III Elf meant major revisions as the door hinges
went internal and the window wound down sedately
into the door.**

However, the Mini Limos days were numbered
although there was continuing subtle changes to the
specification. More comfortable restyled seats along with
another Mini first, in the shape of a combined stalk switch
on the steering column, was introduced in 1967. This was
a year when an automatic gearbox finally became
available as an option, surely the extra that all those
retired Colonels and Women's Institute members had been
waiting for. Nevertheless, rational Leyland saw no room
for these most niche of niche products. Yet surely keeping
at least one upmarket version in production would have
been one way to claw back some profit on the Mini? A
premium model always makes premium profits and the
Hornet/Elf was a consistent seller, so it seems odd that the
model was dropped, but then Leyland spiked the Cooper
too.

The Mini Moke episode is a confusing and
ultimately disappointing tale. Officially sold as part of the
1/4 ton Mini Commercial range throughout its production
life in Britain it was never that commercial, or even that
practical especially when it came to making its mark in
the UK. It was destined to flourish elsewhere. On the face

of it though it seems to been incredibly optimistic of BMC to think that they could build a military vehicle based on the Mini.

Mini Moke. Less is more, Moke.

However, a glance at the Alec Issigonis CV gives an important clue to the sequence of events. During the war at Morris he had designed a 'Mini' tank. The Salamander was a scout car of monocoque construction, its torsion bar suspension was later used on the Morris Minor whilst the front wheel drive and wishbone suspension would surface many years later on the Mini and indeed the Moke. Not only that, Issigonis had been involved in the development of the Austin Champ, a Rolls Royce powered 4 x 4 that never came close to rivalling the Army's abiding Land Rover preference. Certainly Issigonis had been doodling an open type vehicle for some time during the development of the Mini and had prototypes running at the same time. Certainly, BMC liked the idea of a big juicy War office contract. There was a need for a small light vehicle much like the original Willys Jeep, which could be parachuted, packed flat and generally abused. Indeed, the Royal Navy had been using Citroen 2CV pick ups, built in Slough specifically for the Admiralty. These pick-ups were literally picked up by helicopters and dropped ashore for operation over rough

terrain. Production was coming to an end so there was
potentially a large military market.

Unfortunately the prototypes prepared by BMC
did not quite measure up. They were incredibly light at
under 3 cwt (152 kilos), hardly surprising as they were
made from buckboard with Mini suspension and a 948cc A
series engine. These Mokes passed the stacking test with
flying colours, but were otherwise when it came to
anything approaching off road work. Tiny ground
clearance hampered the Moke's terrain hopping abilities.
Gradients were a problem and the buckboard was hardly
tough enough. Back to the drawing board. What Issigonis
came up with in 1962 was a shorter wheelbase at 72.5in
(184cm), raised the suspension and stuck a sump guard
under the engine in an attempt to tackle the lack of
ground clearance. It now had the name 'Moke' which
according to the Concise Oxford Dictionary is Australian
slang for a donkey, but that didn't help either.

You certainly can't accuse BMC of giving up easily
as Issigonis proposed going the whole four-wheel drive hog
by installing an 848cc A series engine at the rear of the
vehicle. This was quickly referred to as the 'Twini' Moke
and dramatically overcame the traction and performance
problems suffered by the original prototype. Novel as this
solution was, it failed to impress the authorities.

After getting the thumbs down from the military,
BMC now tried their luck with the civilian population.
Having invested so much time and effort to get this far,
the next stop as the home market and some subtle
changes to make it saleable. They reverted to the standard
Mini wheelbase, 848cc A series engine, sub frames,
steering, suspension and brakes. Using those components
as the basis they built a simple steel body at Longbridge.
This unitary construction vehicle succeeded in looking
like the utility vehicle it was intended to be and
resplendent in military Spruce Green paint work. The
front end was flat featuring a stamped out grille with
headlamps and large indicators. The bumper comprised a
simple steel bar. At the side were boxy sills almost like
raised running boards, which contained extra storage
space as well as the battery and fuel tank. At each end of
these sills were substantial, flat mudguards. The equally

flat screen could fold flat and be detached, just like the bonnet, the most curved item of metalwork anywhere on the vehicle. At the back was more flat steel and in traditional off roader style a spare wheel was mounted on the panel. Inside there was a single driver's seat, any others were optional extras. Like the saloon, it had a single central instrument pack, but there the similarities ended. The speedometer was mounted into a bulkhead mounted pod with switches and ignition sited at each corner. A switch operated just one windscreen wiper, a second being an optional extra. At least the occupants could stay dry thanks to a vinyl treated fabric hood, which was supported by poles placed around the deck, side screens and heater though were on the extras list.

When launched in January 1964 as the Austin Mini Moke was effectively an open top Mini. The only significant mechanical difference from its hardtop cousin was a higher 3.44:1 final drive, revised gear ratio and ignition timing designed to cope with poor grade petrol. The Morris version arrived six months later and badging was the only difference. The most attractive thing about this new vehicle was its price. As a commercial vehicle there was no purchase tax and bottom line price of £405. Hardly surprising then that the reclassification of this vehicle in 1967 as just another passenger car, added £78 and killed off the plucky little Moke. In truth it was the poor relation of the range never updated, revised, or deemed appropriate for Hydrolastic conversion. As the army discovered, the Moke never fitted easily into the work sphere because of the low power and negligible ground clearance. It stood more of a chance as a purely recreational vehicle, but the British climate was hardly ideal to experience completely open air motoring as a result the bulk of production went abroad.

The Moke was largely ignored by the British Press. Motoring Which? best summed up the general apathy surrounding this unusual vehicle. "You have to accept the fact that the Moke is not a car for long journeys. Once you have accepted that, the Moke is fine if it's fine, and not if it's not. Unfortunately, it suffers by not being as cheap as it looks. If you want a cheap country workhorse, the basic Renault 4 at £544 seems a much

160

better bet. And in town, unless you are very optimistic about the weather, it does seem slightly eccentric to pay nearly as much as a Mini for a car which gives you such an unpleasant time in bad weather. If you can afford to keep a Moke tucked away to enjoy the fine weather when it comes, well and good. Otherwise we would think that you are likely to spend more time being miserable in the Moke than being happy. But we hope that BMC are making a fortune exporting it to San Francisco."

Mini Moke as made in Portugal in the 1990s with alloy wheels, sump guard and a bull bar.

What the Moke did provide was an excuse for magazines to do pseudo swinging London photo spreads. Car Magazine sent their 'Kinkiest staffer' Jan Condel to try the Moke for size and found that "It mayn't be much in the mud - but in Chelsea it's fab, gear, rave."

Despite all the practical criticism conversion specialists Crayford nevertheless saw the trendy potential and produced a Surrey version with a stripy roof and trim. Picked up by the producers of The Prisoner TV series it made quite an impact. It's film career also included guest appearances in the Beatles film Help and a James

Bond: The Man with a Golden Gun. So maybe more savvy marketing at the time would have helped the car's fortunes. The Moke story did not end in 1968 when production had topped 14,500, although only 1,500 had been sold in the UK. Subsequent chapters were set in Australia, Portugal and Italy. It has also made several comebacks to Britain over the years.

Runamoke, obviously Moke specialists based in Battersea London, imported Australian built Mokes in the late '60s and '70s complete with huge bedstead like Kangaroo bars. In 1983 Austin Rover asked for tenders for the UK Moke franchise and Dutton Cars won. These 998cc models with an Australian Californian specification included 13" (33cm) spoked wheels, roll cage, additional bumper bars, high back seats and hood. Due to import restrictions and other difficulties only around a dozen examples were actually sold. Things went a little more smoothly for the Duncan Hamilton group, which successfully imported Mokes from 1988 until Portuguese production ceased in 1993.

The Moke may be dead at the moment, but it has a habit of bouncing back.

Date: 1979 – 1984 Mileage: 98,712. Amount spent: £327.81 Minis in my Life: 1964 Mini Cooper. MOT: Yes. Expires October 1984.

My Mini Cooper it's part in my Breakdown

I might be sad individual but the years I spent sort of restoring my Mini Cooper were probably my happiest. I managed without a welding kit relying on pop rivets to attach the wings. I actually made a pretty good job of it and it was never an MOT fail point.

Dad and me went to Ilford and the heart of the used car universe, the Romford Road and bought a compressor and all the bits and bobs you need to spray a car, including the paint. I rather enjoyed the whole process of mixing the paint. It was cellulose in those days and I dread to think how much I ingested despite the mask and goggles. Indeed, I remember spraying deep into the night and emerging from the garage in a haze of fumes backlit by the bulb behind me. This apparition was enough to stop a midnight dog walker in his tracks.

I should have concentrated on the details as the MOT fail sheet didn't make very good reading. First of all the headlamp aim was too high. The nearside indicator and brake warning light wasn't working. The offside front wheel bearing had excess play. Rather more seriously the front brakes had 70% and 80% effectiveness, but no reading on the rear brake at all. The local garage, were confused by a lack of seat belts in the rear. Oh yes and the wiper blades were worn and the horn did not work either.

I ended up spending a whopping £327.81. In that the MOT cost £9, those were the days and the garage, I & K Brown (Automotive) Limited even had to put £2 worth of petrol in. Looking at the old bill, the list of replacement parts is as long as time I spent in the garage, doing what exactly?

Mini Cooper in Primer, family Clubman bumper bars just visible.

12. **Take a Mini and add a Formula One constructor
and the result is something that is utterly amazing, yes
it is time to talk Cooper.**

Just as one man, Issigonis, was responsible for
the Mini, then the blame for the performance version can
be attributed solely to one man: John Cooper. Since 1961
his name has been inextricably linked to the smallest,
fastest and most charismatic car. Hardly surprising really
as locating the engine behind the driver was an inspired
development which won Cooper's team the Formula 1
World Championships in 1959 and 1960 ushering in a
racing car revolution whose effects are still being felt
today. A chance meeting between the two great men back
in 1946 led to a life long friendship. Cooper had taken his
prototype 500 Special to compete in the 500cc and 750cc
classes at the Brighton Speed Trials. Running against him
was Issigonis in his pre-war, rubber suspended
Lightweight Special.

**A German registered Cooper. The 997 Cooper is
indistinguishable from a Super De Luxe,
apart from the badging.**

Issigonis always resisted any attempts to tart up, market and generally interfere with the brilliantly simple original concept. When it came to the go faster Mini, initially he was sceptical and took some convincing. However, the Mini Cooper proved to be the most significant model of the '60s, let alone the century. Another Mini sized legend was born.

Just as Issigonis and Cooper had crossed paths as adversaries, the former in his Lightweight Special and the latter in a 500, they also dealt professionally: Cooper was also a customer of Morris engines which were used in Formula Junior cars. As technical director, Issigonis would regularly liaise with Cooper on engineering matters. The successful combination of BMC A series engines in Formula Junior, led to Cooper running the works team and ultimately access to prototype ADO 15s. He took one to the 1959 Italian Grand Prix with driver Roy Salvadori, beating fellow Formula One star Reg Parnell in an Aston Martin DB4GT. At the circuit Ferrari's chief designer Aurelio Lampredi asked for a drive and was suitably impressed, "If it were not for the fact that it is so ugly, I'd shoot myself if that isn't the car of the future."

The heart of the 997cc clearly showing the excellent remote control linkage for the gearbox, the power promoting twin SU carburettors and the innovative, but less than effective disc brakes.

My Mini Cooper it's part in my Breakdown

Cooper was equally bowled over. He had been searching for a decent model as a sporting saloon. He believed that there was a market for a four seater, which could match the handling and performance of the benchmark Lotus Elite. Experiments with a Renault Dauphine fitted with a Coventry Climax engine and ZF gearbox were disappointing. It was quick, but the handling of the rear engined car left a lot to be desired. Cooper though tinkered with an 850cc (fitting an 1100cc Formula Junior unit) and realised that the potential for a sports version was overwhelming. Both of his contracted Formula One drivers, Jack Brabham and Bruce McLaren enjoyed their new toys, so Cooper reckoned that a proper production version with disc brakes and a remote gear change would be an obvious new product for BMC. Issigonis remained distinctly under whelmed, preferring to see his creation as a simple 'people's car', despite the obvious success that some rally privateers were having. As a compromise, Issigonis said: "let's go and see the headmaster". The BMC boss George Harriman listened to Cooper's proposal for a homologation run of 1000 specially tuned Minis to qualify for touring car racing. "Take one away and do it" was Harriman's response even though he had doubts that 1000 could be sold. Just two weeks later he was taken for a spin in a performance Mini prototype that contained the constituent parts of a Formula Junior engine. ADO 50 was born.

There was not much wrong with the standard cooking Mini. Remember that at the prototype stage the original A series installation was a 948cc, which resulted in an astonishing 90 mph speed from a mere 37 bhp. Cooper was at the time extracting over 80 bhp for Formula Junior in competition, which might have been considered a little excessive in a road going Mini. Even so a racing engine would not be refined, or durable enough to cope with the demands of everyday motoring. What they did was stroke the 848cc to 81.28mm and reduce the bore to 62.43 and produce the first 997cc Cooper engine. Twin 1.25in SU carburettors helped to pump the power up to 55 bhp at 6000 rpm. Internally the piston tops were domed which increased the compression ratio to 9:1. The inlet valves were enlarged, as were the exhaust bores and double valve springs were fitted to create a high lift camshaft, whilst a three way manifold got rid of the exhaust gases. To cope with the extra power the bottom of the engine was strengthened, a damper reduced the vibrational wear and an oil way was created to feed the crank and bearings. To reduce noise a sixteen blade cooling fan made a big difference and was not surprisingly fitted to the rest of the range in due course. This new engine made much more of a din so the amount of sound deadening material was increased on the bodywork especially around the wheel arches.

Morris Cooper. As the Austin, but with a seven slat grille.

A remote gear change was regarded as essential and this was allied to longer gear ratios, whilst the final drive was raised to 3.765:1. To make the whole thing stop Lockheed specially developed the smallest set of brake discs then produced. At seven inches (17cm) they managed to stop the ten-inch (25.4 cm) wheels spinning very effectively for the time although they would ultimately come in for criticism. Cooper himself was instrumental in persuading the company to produce them. Even the otherwise standard rear drums were modified with a pressure-limiting valve. Plus the wheels were shod with wider Dunlop SP3 5.2" x 10" radial ply tyres.

My Mini Cooper it's part in my Breakdown

Launched first privately to the press on July 17th 1961 the venue was once again the army proving ground in Chobham. At least ten cars were required, but by July 10th all that existed were piles of unassembled parts. Of course BMC met the deadline and the Coopers were put at the disposal of several Formula One drivers as ultimate proof of the car's capabilities. Everyone was impressed. However, production delays meant that the Cooper was only revealed to the public in September. What they saw were top specification Minis badged as the Austin Se7en and Morris Mini Cooper. Like the Super models with the standard 848cc unit, which were launched at the same time, the trim was almost identical. On the outside the obvious difference were the unique grilles as the Austin had 11 thin horizontal bars and the Morris 7 chunkier Venetian blind style slats. Both sets of bumpers featured corner bars and chrome surrounded the door window frames.

Perhaps the most distinctive clue that these cars were something special was the famous two-tone colour scheme. The natural break for the roof panel caused by the gutters meant that a contrasting colour looked perfect. In most cases the roof was finished in Snowberry White (including the steel wheels) when the main body colour was either blue, green, grey, or yellow. The exception was Tartan Red bodywork, which was contrasted by a black roof. Inside, it was essentially Super trim. This meant full carpeting, including a boot board, which formed a platform over the spare wheel. The seats were covered in two-tone leather cloth material whilst the dashboard and top rail had black vinyl on them. In the centre of that rail was a chrome-lidded ashtray, but more important was the oval instrument binnacle featuring three Smiths dials. Water temperature on the left, oil pressure on the right and in the middle a very different speedometer, which was optimistically calibrated up to 100mph.

Despite the fact that the car was priced at £679. 7s. 3d, effectively £25 4s 6d more than the most expensive Mini, the Riley Elf, BMC were overwhelmed with orders. The press reception which greeted the Cooper was rapturous. Confirmed Mini fan John Bolster writing in

My Mini Cooper it's part in my Breakdown

Autosport accepted that the time was right for a Grand Touring version of the Mini. All the correct ingredients were in place including Formula Junior experience, remote-control gear lever and specially developed brakes. Underpinning it all though was the brilliant original concept. "When Alec Issigonis designed his revolutionary BMC baby car, it was intended to be a better form of transport for the masses. He tried to make it as safe as possible in the hands of indifferent drivers, but in achieving this he also gained an entirely unexpected result. The road holding and stability were such that the Mini and the Seven could safely out distance more powerful cars on winding roads." Road testing it for the magazine a few months later Bolster was still entranced by the handling qualities. "It is the celebrated road holding which contributes most to the overall performance. We have all seen Minis in saloon car races demonstrating their high cornering power against more conventional cars. This cornering speed is certainly a little greater than that of most of their competitors. What is so remarkable though, is the phenomenal 'dicing margin' that is available."

Sports Car Graphic used the headline Mini-Minor becomes Maxi-Major. They got a sneak preview of a prototype and raved. "There was no time for any real road test but a couple of hours on the highway convinced me that Austin is coming out with a winner, not only because this car should be quite unbeatable in its class but also because it gives you such a tremendous driving pleasure as well as confidence." When they finally nabbed the first Austin-Cooper to arrive in California, "We found it difficult to drive without grinning from ear to ear. The performance is so startling for the overall size and appearance that it's ridiculous." They even took the car on a weekend camping trip to the Joshua Tree National Monument. 133 miles from Los Angeles to Indio on freeways and highways, then a further 90 miles to Twenty-nine Palms on desert and often unpaved roads, before travelling another 153 miles back to L.A. Not only were our American friends amazed at the performance from 'the flying shoe box', but also the amount of usable interior space. "Into the apparently minute trunk went a tent, sleeping bag, air mattress, large and crammed full pack, a large zipper handbag, a Primus stove, a gallon canteen and a pair of climbing boots."

It was the thoroughly British Motor magazine which summed up the appeal of the Cooper so succinctly, "So much performance combined with a lot of practical merit and quite a high standard of refinement will obviously make people decide that a sum of about £600 is better spent on this model than on something bigger but no better."

Modifications to the Cooper over the next two years were broadly in line with the standard car. Within six months the clumsy Se7en name was dropped. In 1963 the front brake discs were up rated whilst at the back aluminium suspension trumpets replaced the steel ones. 1964 was a watershed year when two modifications would change the character of the car quite radically. Firstly BMC standardised the 998cc engine in January. Already used on the Elf and Hornet models, it made sense to introduce it to the Cooper, but in a modified form. Compared to the Hornet/Elf unit the Cooper had very different cylinder head, pistons and camshaft. It shared 1.25 SU carburettors and three branch exhaust system with the 997, but the camshaft and valves were different again. It had the same 0.312 lift action, but the duration was as the standard Mini (230 degree) as against the 997s 252 degrees. The inlet valves were larger at 1.219 in whereas the 997 was 1.156. The pistons had raised crowns and compression ratios of 9:1, or 7.8:1 although very few of the low compression models were sold on the UK market. Unlike the 997cc the new engine adopted floating small ends which made the unit much stronger, increasing the bore and reducing the stroke resulted in a much smoother engine, and although the maximum power at 55 bhp was unchanged, it was achieved at 5,800rpm instead of 6,000rpm. The torque was also dramatically improved at 57lb/ft at 3,000rpm rather than 3,600rpm at 44lb/ft. So it became a far more flexible and ultimately tougher engine. Then in September 1964 came Hydrolastic suspension, which made for a bouncier ride at speed. Many enthusiasts argued that it spoilt the Cooper. Certainly when Motor tested the newly suspended model they took photographic evidence to prove the change in behaviour. "On a closed throttle the Hydrolastic suspension causes appreciable nose dive: when accelerating the car squats down at the back. Jerky driving, which emphasises these characteristics, can make the ride uncomfortable."

The other 998 Achilles heel were the brakes, which just were not up to the job of repeatedly stopping a speeding Cooper. They were an improvement over the early models, but the 'S' now showed it up. Part of the problem was that the 'S' had wider, ventilated, 4.5in rims to accommodate bigger discs and the standard Cooper didn't. During its life the Mark 1 998 Cooper was subtlety updated in line with the standard model. Firstly in February 1964 the windscreen wiper arc was reduced to stop it hitting the screen rubber. By March, Dunlop SP41 radials were standardised which significantly improved handling. In July the rear brakes had lower anti lock pressure settings. With the advent of Hydrolastic suspension there were new gear change forks which had a larger contact area, whilst the clutch was now of the diaphragm type. In October there were improved drive shaft couplings and a month later the driver's seat now had a three-position setting. Things got a little quieter in 1965 when a 16 grilles per inch radiator was installed followed in May by a scroll type oil seal on the primary gears.

The 997cc Cooper was very successful. It kick started the Cooper's rallying career and scored the model's first international victory. Sales at 25,000 were impressive, especially as the original run was meant to be just 1000, with a weekly build of no more than 25 units. The 998cc version, despite getting bouncy castle Hydrolastic suspension built on the solid foundations of the earlier car and cemented the hot little brick in buyer's affections. Most important of all were the specific Cooper developments like disc brakes and remote gear change which would both eventually find their way onto the standard production Mini.

Mini Cooper Mark 2, still badged Austin and Morris, but now a common grille and plain interior.

The new Cooper was pure Mark 2 Mini with the revised grille, now standardised with a thick 7-slat design, bigger light clusters and rear window. The chrome trim around the door window frames was retained, but the bumper corner bars were deleted to leave the overriders behind. A major casualty of the change was the distinctively two-tone interior with black Super De Luxe trim. On the outside the same colour options were still available, increasingly though monotone schemes were becoming common. The boot lid was now double skinned rather than having a hard board cover. The boot board now sat on spot welded rather than riveted brackets. Mechanically Hydrolastic was still the method of suspension and a plastic radiator fan was fitted in place of the old steel one. An all-synchromesh gearbox in 1968 was the biggest change, otherwise the Mark 2 car turned out to be a very short-lived model. In view of the fact that the 'S' continued in production for three more years and in terms of comparable performance its replacement was the snub nosed 1275GT. I know we've already done the Clubman and the 1275GT a bit, but let's take another look at the GT.

My Mini Cooper it's part in my Breakdown

The reasoning behind the 1275GT was simple, it was a direct Cooper replacement. Donald Stokes did not like the way that the Cooper apparently increased insurance premiums for all Minis. Even John Cooper suggested that if that was the case, don't put a GT badge on it, use something more subtle, like 'E' for executive as a more credible and honest substitute. Certainly one thing 1275 clearly wasn't, was a GT. When it was launched all the insurance companies said was this is a Cooper in disguise so the insurance rating stayed the same.

The 'hot' Clubman was largely identical to the cooking version. The fundamental flaw was the power plant, which at 1275cc promised Cooper S performance but could hardly deliver for a number of reasons. First of all that unit was not a direct transfer from a Cooper, but an Austin/Morris 1300. What also distanced that engine from any other Cooper credentials were the single carburettor, and the fact that both head and block were different. That added up to 59 bhp as opposed to the 76 bhp, which a real S produced. To address some of those problems, BL fitted a lower final drive ratio of 3.65:1, which managed to give the car a top speed of 87 mph. However, the poor fuel consumption meant a return to 3.44:1 the following year. What the 1275GT did have in common with the Cooper was front disc brakes. Otherwise they were almost unrelated apart from the fact that all the

My Mini Cooper it's part in my Breakdown

Clubmans, including the 1275GT retained Hydrolastic suspension (as did the Cooper S until the model was discontinued in 1971).

However, there was one piece of equipment which the Cooper sadly missed out on and that was a rev counter which the 1275GT had nestling in its instrument binnacle. On the outside it was pure Clubman in shape, only a few details picked the 1275 GT out as being different. Firstly there was a black grille with a red GT badge on it. Another clue were the sill stripes bearing the legend 'Mini 1275 GT' and a stainless steel badge on the boot. At each corner were Rostyle steel wheels as used on BL's Spridget range of sports cars and shod with radial ply tyres. Inside, apart from the three dial binnacle was some sporty seat trim and a leather stitched surround on the steering wheel with 1275 GT on the centre boss.

Motor tested both the Clubman and 1275GT in 1969 and used the headline, 'At last - a comfortable Mini'. Practical considerations aside what everyone wanted to know about was the performance of the new sporting addition to the Mini stable. Motor found that the GT "Has a fairly unstressed engine giving about the same output as the 998cc Cooper; so the performance is on a par with it through the gears. However, its extra torque makes it exceptionally lively in top gear, 40-60mph taking less than half the time of the present 1 litre cars, and considerably less than the old Cooper too. It compares well against its competitors, with a 0 to 60 mph time of 14.2." In fact, pitting the Clubman against similar cars was to become a regular pastime for the motoring press over the year to find out how flawed the 1275GT really was. Autocar produced a highly detailed account of how the 1275GT measured up to the NSU 1200TT in December 1969. On performance: "The way the Mini runs out of breath is best demonstrated by its positive refusal to reach much over 90mph even when driven flat out down a long, steep hill. This indicates how fast power falls off once you are over the peak, and why there is absolutely no point in going over 6000rpm in road driving. The NSU, on the other hand, will cheerfully take you over 100mph if the conditions are right. There is no doubt that on a truly open road the NSU is the faster of the two cars." Ride and

175

handling: "We all felt that the NSU gave a better ride than the Mini...As far as straight line stability is concerned, the Mini wins hands down." To sum up, "For me, the NSU wins almost every round. Yet a lot of people now thinking in terms of a 1275GT as a purchase haven't heard of the NSU, let alone given it any thought as an alternative." Autocar revised its opinion when the low gearing was revised: "Performance brisk and better in every respect including economy. Rather noisy. Bouncy ride. Superb road holding and handling. Good ventilation and good fun...It is a better car than the original now performing well up around the top of its class and, being that still engagingly cheeky character of a car is any Mini, is highly enjoyable."

Arguably the most relevant comparison test conducted during the '70s was by Motor in 1974 when they took a 1275GT over to France and ran it against the Innocenti Mini Cooper 1300. 'Midlands Mini, or Inni Mini?' After performance testing and an 850-mile trip to the Dordogne and back the magazine concluded "The Innocenti is a nicely equipped car, more powerful than the 1275GT and slightly better in ride and handling. But we feel that it does not owe much of its success abroad to superior assembly or refinement, since it retains most of the Mini's basic faults such as excessive noisiness and a basically poor ride...Certainly we were made very aware of these faults during our Continental test - we had aching backs and buzzing heads to testify to them at the end of one particularly long day's motoring - but at the same time we acquired a renewed respect for the essential excellence of the design. Long may the Mini continue."

Last of the 1275GT line as Denovo run flat wheels and tyres are standardised.

Just like its more ordinary Clubman brother, the 1275 GT changed little over the years and kept abreast of standard Mini updates. After the final drive ratio was revised in '71, the fitting of a temperature controlled air intake system coincided with the power output dropping dramatically to 54 bhp. However, the 1275 GT did have the distinction that year of being the first Mini to have 12" (30.4cm) wheels along with larger disc brakes, plus a 7.5-gallon fuel tank. Denovo run flat tyres were also made an option at this time. The general Clubman facelift in '76 resulted in the 1275GT being stripped of its GT grille badge and getting fashionably stripy seats, a vanity mirror, a second door mirror and door pockets.

In view of the many criticisms levelled at the Cooper replacement, BL Special Tuning made an attempt to liven up the 1275GT when in December 1971 they dropped off a tweaked model at the offices of Motor. "The standard 59bhp 1275GT only does 87.5 but, worst of all, takes 14.2 seconds to struggle up to 60, and it has been embarrassing them long enough." The article was headed '1275GTS can it beat the old Cooper?' The car they tested was fitted with a Sport Performance Kit C-AJJ 4082 which comprised a polished head, carburettor, a mate for the existing 1.5in carburettor and a manifold to take them both, two air filters, a distributor plus a set of instructions. All the 1275GT owner needed was about four hours, some mechanical aptitude and £125. So was it quicker than the old Cooper S? "Yes and no. Yes, it's quicker on standing starts. No, it's less tractable and slower on top speed. But there's not much in it..." The figures were impressive as the 1275GTS hit 60mph in 10 seconds, 0.9 quicker than the old S. The standing quarter came up in 17.4 seconds whereas the S covered the same distance in 18.2 seconds. Overall though the 1275GTS was not a well-sorted package, fuel consumption was an alarming 22.3mpg during Motor's test and the transmission produced a 'vibro-massage' effect at motorway cruising speeds. Power delivery was hardly smooth so it was no surprise that they gave the 1275GTS only a qualified endorsement. "Special Tuning have added an 'S' to the badges on the boot, and there is no doubt that the car is competitive with a genuine 1275 Cooper S. Even so, it didn't seem quite like the real thing to us. It was just a quick version of the 1275GT - great fun indeed but it did not satisfy our nostalgia."

What Car in 1977 were right when they said "The sports car of yesterday has now virtually made way for the sports saloon of today. The Mini started it in the early '60s...BMC produced their Mini Cooper." But the market had moved on and the supermini era ushered in performance variants of popular hatchbacks. There was no Golf GTI, probably because it was only available to special order in left hand drive, but there was the Peugeot 104ZS and Renault 5TS. What Car? concluded that the "Mini 1275GT is the oldest design, and it shows. Its ride is poor, accommodation marginally better than it was, but standard of finish and equipment will suit most people. Performance hardly merits the GT label. Yet the Mini has a distinct price and running advantage, and that could be important." Although they found the Renault to be 'impressive and sporty', whilst "The Peugeot 104ZS is what the Mini should be. Versatile, fast, comfortable, well equipped and a joy to drive...The verdict must go to the Peugeot, but we wonder how it will fare when the sporty Fiestas appear. They will be good new for Ford dealers, bad for Leyland." Those were prophetic words as Leyland entered the '80s without a credible hot hatchback.

My Mini Cooper it's part in my Breakdown

ADO 70, Micholetti's targa topped proposal for a rebodied 1275GT, which could have replaced the arthritic Spridgets.

In 1970 a standard 1275GT was driven to Italy and coachbuilders Micholetti. There, over two months they transformed it into a stylish and targa topped two-seat sports car with the project number ADO 70. It could have formed the basis of a replacement for the MG Midget. Those removable roof panels predated the Fiat X/19, but it was arguably a more comfortable cabriolet than sports car. However, designer Rob Owen found out that the roof leaked quite badly on the return journey soaking the trim and carpets. What counted against it was the front wheel drive layout, which was considered unsporting, had they learned nothing from the Mini and Cooper? Then there was the American problem. Rumours had been circulating for some time that the regulators were poised to outlaw open cars on safety grounds. Not only that the tough emissions legislation would be costly and difficult for the 1275 engine to meet those requirements. So R.I.P. interesting concept whilst the tired old Midget was given a 'new' lease of life with the Triumph Spitfire's 1500cc engine. Oh dear.

The last big event in the life of the 1275GT was the standardisation of Denovo wheels and tyres in 1977 presumably because they had a lot in stock. Few drivers liked them, providing poor road holding and questionable run flat ability. Creeping corporate black paint in late '79 was splashed on the door mirrors and roof gutter, the final

179

funeral finishing touch before the 1275GT passed away in August 1980. There was no room for the Clubman once the Metro arrived, a car, which was designed to be boxy, rather than having boxiness thrust upon it.

Yet the Clubman in its day was a big success. With more than 110,000 finding homes over its lifetime the 1275GT comfortably outperformed the combined sales of the Mark 1 and Mark 2 Coopers. This proved that the buying public would have welcomed a more radical update to the basic model. What if the Clubman had been a bigger Haynes humpbacked hatchback? Who knows? If the Clubman is to be remembered for anything it will surely be the fact that it is the only Mini to have visibly aged.

December 1984. Mileage: 98,862 Amount Spent: £10 on the MOT plus some petrol. Minis in my Life: 1964 Austin Mini Cooper MOT: Yes. Expires December 1985

With the Cooper up and running, it was time to take it out of my parents' garage, so that they could put their car in it. I was about to embark on the longest single journey it would ever undertake with me at the wheel. I was going to drive from London to Norfolk. About 90 miles.

It was an interesting journey for a couple of reasons. Firstly it was bitterly cold, cold enough for ice and indeed snow. Luckily I was in a car that had won the toughest rallies in winter, so I had every confidence that the Cooper could cling onto the road. However, what made it most difficult was the reluctance of the gearbox to stay in gear. So once I got into fourth on I had to hold it in place. The vibration up my left arm was causing a numbness that verged on an industrial injury by the time I reached the county of Nelson's birth.

Epic journey complete, but little did the Cooper realise it would be in for an extended hibernation. It's not a sentient being of course, but if the Cooper were…well it would have probably sought out a more caring and sartorially hip owner.

13. **The Cooper but with added S which could only be a good thing for anyone who bought into new breed of sports car that didn't require the owner to have a handlebar 'tache and flat cap.**

Like the best performance cars, the Cooper's development became inextricably linked to competition, hence the 'S'. BMC and indeed even Issigonis had been mightily impressed by the Cooper's performance on the road and in competition. Issigonis not only had the time to spare, but also wanted to be involved with the Cooper this time around. A major influence behind the new car was also BMC competitions manager Stuart Turner who wanted a something that was capable of actually winning rallies.

Development work on the 'S' was actually farmed out to consultants like Daniel Richmond of Downtown Engineering. In fact, Richmond's tweaked 997 Cooper was studied closely at Longbridge before the final decision was made in the winter of 1962 to build an 'S' model in a quantity of 1000 units to qualify for Group 2 competition. Despite the involvement of outsiders, control of the project was down to Issigonis. It was decided to concentrate on an 1100cc in the interests of competition giving BMC the option of stroking the unit up or down

My Mini Cooper it's part in my Breakdown

depending on the class they were considering. The resulting over square 1071cc engine kept to this brief and the unit itself was very different from a cooking A series.

Opening the bonnet it was easy to spot the new head, which had an extra bolt and twin 1.25in SU carburettors. The block had also changed because the tappet side covers, familiar sights on an 848cc were missing because the outer cylinder bores were moved further apart whilst the inner two got closer. The engine internals were heavily revised. In particular the crankshaft was made from special EN40B steel and nitrided to make it harder. The valve guides also received a similar treatment, constructed from Nimonic 80 whilst the valves themselves had stellite faces welded on to make them harder wearing.

Although capable of revving right up to 7200rpm, the power of 70bhp was delivered at 6200rpm. To handle this power the standard Cooper gearbox was fitted, with optional lower final drive ratio and a close ratio gearbox. Stopping it all were thicker (1/8th in/0.5 cm) and larger diameter discs (7.5in, 19cm) with servo assistance, plus a tweaked rear brake pressure-limiting valve. Ventilated steel wheels helped keep the brakes cool and these were now 4.5in (11.4cm) wide, rather than 3.5in (8.8cm) on the standard Cooper, with just the standard hubcaps. Higher ratio steering, lock to lock at 2.3 turns also made the 'S' an even more wieldy performance car.

'S' specification was identical to the Cooper, save for those all-important distinguishing badges on the bonnet and boot lid. Inside, the upholstery was equally Super De Luxe although the speedometer was calibrated up to 120 mph.

Magazine road testers all responded well to the improved performance of the S, the superior braking and Dunlop SP Sport tyres. One penalty was increased fuel consumption, although the optional right hand tank would double the capacity to 11 gallons (50 litres). Firstly Autocar squeezed a 13.5 second 0-60mph time, a 91 mph top speed and a 19.2 second time for the standing quarter mile. Two weeks later Motor managed the 0 to 60mph in 12.9seconds a 94.5mph top speed and the standing quarter in 18.9 seconds. They also raved about the brakes.

My Mini Cooper it's part in my Breakdown

"The braking powers of the S are formidable and in complete harmony with its performance. The disc-front, drum-rear, combination, allied to Hydrovac servo assistance gives extremely effective braking with only gentle pedal pressure, while repeated use brought no evidence of brake fade." They summed it up very nicely when they concluded, "In all the Mini-Cooper S is a car of delightful Jekyll and Hyde character, with astonishing performance concealed within its unpretentious Mini skin."

By the time that Bill Boddy got his hands on the 1071 S for Motor Sport he had pushed the 0 to 60mph time down to 11.9 seconds and 18.7 for the standing quarter although top speed was only 92mph. He found the S almost docile, an "Excellent balance between good acceleration and civilised step-off, between ultra powerful brakes and sensitive, wet-road retardation." However, "The almost luxurious Mini-Cooper interior and a flecked upholstery and trim more suitable to a lady's boudoir than the inside of a rally car!"

The Americans were suitably impressed with their $2,500 version of the 1071 S in Auto. "A belt in the back and a few seconds later I glanced at the tach (A 10,000rpm full sweep tach is standard equipment. Ed) and then looked at the speedometer. It was swinging rapidly towards 90mph and we were still in third!" They managed to get pulled over by the Highway Patrol who could barely believe that something so small could go so fast. They had a debate about speedometer accuracy and the police followed for a few miles and confirmed that give or take a few mphs the Mini really was exceeding the speed limit by a massive margin. The police were equally impressed and never even issued a speeding ticket." Ultimately though, "It is in the areas of ride, handling and manoeuvrability that the Austin-Cooper S is truly outstanding." Typically they found the specification on the basic side: "While we could make some snide remarks about the mirror, wipers and interior light, actually few creature comforts have been sacrificed for size and performance." Their sum up was a ringing endorsement. "Not many cars come down the pike which are all sweetness and light. The Austin-Cooper S is one of them.

My Mini Cooper it's part in my Breakdown

Sure...it's an ugly little pumpkin. It has some minor faults, which should be corrected. But in spite of all this we can't imagine a sports car we would rather have. Nor can we remember a car we enjoyed more in the testing."

Car magazine enthusiastically put a Downtown tuned Radford Cooper S through its paces.

The production run for the first 'S' had been set at 1000, but of course that number was exceeded four fold when it was discontinued in March 1964. But then, as had been planned, the long and short stroke versions of this engine were launched within months of each other.

First to arrive was the 1275cc unit. This produced a useful 76bhp, which was not only torquey but also flexible and reliable. This unit was followed by the short stroke and short-lived 970S model. The nine-month production run was purely special order and homologation specific as just under 1000 were built to qualify for the 1000cc class and International Group 2 Touring Car Championship. However it's influence extended into the late '60s when it was still used by the factory to snatch a class win in certain events and interestingly Tony Fall won the 1966 Polish Rally in a 970 S. Its forte though was saloon car racing where highly tuned variants dominated the sport. This was not a cheap engine to build although its effects were widely appreciated. Despite producing just 65bhp at 6,500rpm, it was almost as quick as the 1275 S. The 970 was a smooth, high revving unit, but obviously not as flexible as the larger S which produced a useful 79lb/ft at 3000rpm against the 970s 55lb/ft at 3,500rpm. Like the rest of the range it was uprated to run on Hydrolastic suspension after just three months production. Seven months later the 970S had done its job and was discontinued.

Car magazine are still putting the Downtown tuned Radford Cooper S through its paces.

The Cooper S became synonymous with the 1275cc unit. In fact, this engine would go on to outlive all the other A series engines and keep the Mini running to the end of its life. Getting it built in the first place was not easy as George Harriman had trouble believing that that the original 850cc engine could be stretched to that capacity. In the end he trusted John Cooper's judgment and told the development team to get on with it. The result was probably the most remarkable Cooper of all. If the original 997 had been a revelation this new S reached the magic ton, 100mph, and almost halved the Cooper's 0 to

60mph time and was clearly from another performance planet.

The first versions of the 1275 S, which reached the press test fleets, had dry suspension. It was John Bolster for Autosport who managed some astonishingly quick performance figures, getting the 0 to 60mph time down to 9 seconds, the quarter mile in 17.6 seconds and a top speed of 100mph. "Up to 60 or 70 mph the acceleration is tremendous...it cannot be too strongly emphasised that this model bears no resemblance to the typical modified Mini, many of which are rough and noisy to an extent which becomes wearisome for everyday motoring."

Autocar were not successful in achieving such impressive performance times and unlike Bolster found the car a little rough on occasions. "Top-end roughness could be felt as quite a violent vibration through the gear lever...There is another vibration, corresponding with the idling speed just below 1,000rpm, which causes the steering column to shake, and the wiper blades to flutter on the windscreen." However the magazine concluded, "In almost any degree of traffic, country roads, trunk routes, or city streets, the 1275S is one of the quickest ways of getting from A to B in safety. Far from a quart squeezed into the proverbial pint pot, this car has handling and braking well within its high standards of performance."

Motor also had a few reservations when the same test car started to sup oil at 75 miles per pint and it proved to be a touch slower than tuning company specials, although they still thought it a remarkable car. "Even if some of the novelty has worn off, our enthusiasm for Mini motoring reached new peaks after only 1500 miles in this car. With a maximum speed of 96.8mph, vivid acceleration and still further improved handling, it is enormous fun to drive and just about the most practical toy that £750 will buy. It has most of the failings of other Minis - uncomfortable seats, an awkward driving position, bumpy ride - plus some of its own like very heavy oil consumption, but the sheer delight of driving was adequate compensation for us."

Mk II Cooper S seen here in constabulary trim. Never mind the decals, two-tone horns and blue light, the larger rear window and light clusters were the main changes for 1967.

Like the 1071 and 970 models the specification was identical for the 1275, although a laminated windscreen was standard. Likewise, model developments were largely in line with the ordinary Minis. So of course Hydrolastic suspension was added in 1964, but not to all round approval. Henry Manney took a Hydrolastic S for a spin on the Goodwood race circuit for Road & Track in 1965. "The increased suspension movement necessary for carrying Auntie Dollie and her parcels doesn't seem to agree with it at speed, There was more lean and the customary Mini on rails feeling was slightly lessened, even if you could stuff it through tight corners on full understeer as before."

By contrast devout Mini-ist John Bolster thoroughly approved of the new system. "On the road, the Hydrolastic Mini feels almost soggy at parking speeds, but the suspension seems to become progressively harder as the velocity increases. The improvement in riding comfort is very great...For use on the road, though I am completely sold on it, from every point of view."

**Mark II Austin Cooper S without all the Police
fixtures and fittings.**

Motor were sceptical about Hydrolastic, which
"Has improved the ride -mainly by converting pitch into
bounce - but it also gives the impression that there is a
good deal more roll than occurred in earlier Minis." Some
of these criticisms were addressed with an improved
system from 1966. These were higher rate units with a
steel/rubber lower wishbone bush, strengthened
suspension mountings and a flange to fix solid universal
joints onto the driveshaft. Other significant changes were
an oil cooler and twin fuel tanks in 1966. Lots of road
testers had commented on the fact that the S seemed to
burn a lot of oil and would benefit from the addition of a
cooler to reduce consumption. Fuel consumption was the
other worry as a hard driven S might struggle to 150
miles on a tiny 5.5-gallon (25 litre) tank. However, a
second right hand tank had been an option for some time,
doubling that capacity was sensible, and balanced the cars
dramatic rear profile.   Significant options included
reclining seats in 1965 and a heated rear window a year
later.

The Cooper S entered its second phase in line with
other more mundane models and ended up looking just as
standard because a contrasting roof colour became less

189

common. Inside, Super De Luxe trim took the place of the more flamboyant two tone variety. A new Mk II 1275 badge and either a new oval Morris (white background), or Austin (black background) S badge at the front helped distinguish the S, whilst 4.5in (11.4cm) rims of course also set the car apart. An all-synchromesh gearbox in 1968 was the only significant update.

Mark III Mini Cooper, which looks identical to the cooking Mini 850. Only the wheels and a close look at the badges are the giveaways.

Announced in November 1969 the Mk III 'S' was the sole surviving Cooper representative to take the great name into the '70s. First of all though the production of separate Austin and Morris variants continued until March 1970. From then on the generic Mini marque took over as the Cooper S entered its final Mark III phase. If enthusiasts thought that the Mark II was indistinguishable from a cooking 1000 model, the latest model, with no duo tone paint option became completely anonymous. The grille was the same, as was the corporate 'Mini' bonnet badge, whilst the door trim and seats were shared with the Clubman, blink and you could miss the oblong badge on the boot which still bore the legend Mini Cooper S. What the Cooper did retain from the old model was the Hydrolastic suspension. Although the rest of the range (except the Clubman) had switched back to the dry rubber cone system, the surplus supply of Hydrolastic sub frames were foisted back onto the Cooper.

This is where the Cooper connection ends for the time being. Donald Stokes had taken over the reins at BMC, turning into an even bigger conglomerate called British Leyland. Astonishingly there was never any official agreement between Cooper and BMC about developing the Coopers. There was a straight £2 royalty on each unit sold. When Stokes came along that nominal sum was regarded as extravagant and Cooper's involvement unnecessary in the new BL scheme of things. Surprising really, the Cooper and its unprecedented sequence of sporting success had paid off handsomely for BMC in terms of sales, international publicity and prestige.

The Cooper could not really be replaced and BL did not really try. The 1275GT and 1300GT were marketing exercises rather than serious attempts to develop the small sporting car. The same could be said of the future Cooper. At least the Cooper concept was not quite dead, only resting and waiting for a far eastern revival. Before we get there though, what about all those Mini tuners in the 1960s determined to make the Cooper S go even faster?

A class apart from the rest was Downton Engineering. Proprietor and tuning genius, Daniel Richmond had official endorsement from BMC and was in close contact with all those involved with the Mini: Issigonis, Moulton, Cooper, competition boss Turner and company boss Harriman. Based in Downton, Wiltshire Richmond began tinkering with the Mini back in 1959 and the results were always incredible. As well as official projects for BMC, which included work on the Cooper and the cylinder head on Group 2 1275s, which was never bettered, Richmond had a roster of eager clients. After Radford had finished adorning Coopers, Richmond would put the performance back plus a little more. Steve McQueen, racing driver Dan Gurney and Enzo Ferrari all owned Minis, which passed through his spotless workshops. Richmond claimed that he achieved his remarkable results by attention to detail. The company proved to be a finishing school for many A series exponents including racer Gordon Spice, Jan Odor who went on to found Janspeed and Richard Longman.

An equally evocative name from the '60s was Broadspeed, best known for running a team of highly competitive Coopers would also prepare cars for private customers. Car & Car Conversions took a 1275 for a spin in January 1966 "The chief weaknesses of the Cooper S are noise, vibration and, driven, an excessive oil consumption. The car we've been testing is quieter, suffers from practically no vibration, despite its ability to survive a 2,000 rpm in crease in engine speed...This car did 113mph in one direction, and will get to sixty, two up, in under nine seconds." That conversion cost £100 and comprised a modified cylinder head with larger inlet valves, ports and tracts; polished ports, recontured combustion chambers a compression ratio of 10.5 to 1, modified inlet manifold, 1.5 SU H4 carburettors, a road/race camshaft and modified exhaust manifold.

Among the many hundreds of companies, which made Minis go faster, was Yimkin Engineering based in central London who tweaked the basic Minor and Seven. They simply used a modified cylinder head and special needle for the SU carb. With a raised compression ratio 8.8 to 1 the performance improvements were marginal and added just 5mph to the top speed and knocked jut 5 seconds off the 0 to 60mph time. The car was made famous for being motor racing legend, Fangio's introduction to Mini motoring.

Arden Racing from Solihull was quick off the mark with an uprated 850cc. A modified cylinder head, revised inlet and exhaust manifold, an additional 1.25 SU carburettor and new exhaust silencer were part of the package with an optional electronic rev counter. Top speed went up to 85 mph and 60mph was a 20 second job.

When it came to tuning equipment Speedwell produced a large range of A series compatible parts. They also built some radical road cars, the most notable being the Courier, a sort of '60s BMW Touring because it was based on the Mini estate. The 850cc engined was enlarged to 1152cc, with a special crankshaft, flowed cylinder, performance camshaft and H4 carburettors it all added up to 91bhp at 6600rpm. Lowered suspension and Girling servo assistance with anti fade brake lining meant that the 100mph estate could handle and stop safely.

And that is just the very tip of a huge tuning iceberg which also included such famous names as Oselli and Janspeed and would never, ever include **Rüpp***Speed*®

Date: November 1986 Mileage: 98,862 Amount spent: MOT plus £218.05
Minis in my Life: 1964 Austin Mini Cooper MOT: Yes. Expires November 1987.

Mini in Limbo. One whole year after that epic journey north the Cooper had not even covered a mile before it was MOT'd. First of all though I contacted a local mechanic called Alan Bridle that my Dad knew to sort out the gearbox. That involved taking out the engine, separating the gearbox, replacing it with an exchange item and then changing the gaskets, filter and refreshing the oil. He was a lovely chap and got on the with job from his small cottage.

Twenty years later, when Alan had passed away, his house was occupied by a valeter. He cleaned up a Volvo V70 for me (and cleared away a long dead prawn sandwich squashed flat under the rear seats) and I told him about a previous occupant of the house who was a mechanic. 'Oh that explains it. My Mrs is really into gardening and every time she digs the garden up, she gets a shovel full of spark plugs.'

The MOT advisories mentioned that the headlamps were out of line, and that I should keep a check on the tyres. Actually the headlamps would remain out of line and I didn't check the tyres for the next half dozen years.

There is a reason for this when I had a slight family estrangement but I won't go into any grim details. Suffice to say that the Mini was wrapped in plastic and pushed into a barn, which led directly to the madness, which followed in the early '90s. But that's another chapter.

Hibernation.

14. Mini Goes Motorsport when all of a sudden the smallest car in the race, beat the biggest, here's how the whole world fell in love with the racing underdog that more often than not got the chequered flag first, except when the French cheated in the Monte Carlo...

'...I thought there was something wrong with his car when I was able to overtake him; it was only then I realised how fast the Mini was on slippery surfaces. And that was my first drive in a Mini'. This was Paddy Hopkirk's reaction on overtaking an Austin Healey 3000 when he was competing in the 1963 Monte Carlo Rally.

A major part of the Mini legend is its racing history. Not only did the little car win races convincingly, there is an amusing anecdote for just about every competition it entered. However, the Minis official factory backed involvement in motorsport was relatively brief, but the '60s were never brighter than when a Mini was mixing it with all comers. On both road and track it was unbeatable, humiliating much larger and more expensive cars in the process and kick starting thousands of motorsport careers.

The Mini was always cheap to buy, fun to race and easy to develop. In standard tune it proved the front wheel drive point and led directly to the competition honed Cooper. Best of all, the Mini has never gone away, turn up at any weekend race meeting, from circuit meeting to classic rally and you are bound to find a Mini lurking in the line up and probably finishing in the top five. There are better books than this to read about the exploits of the Mini and Cooper, but here is a potted history of the official works involvement.

Amazingly it was the old A30 and A35, which led the way in motorsport terms and proved what a small, agile, A series powered BMC car could do. In 1956 the father and son team of Ted and Raymond Brookes won the Tulip Rally outright in a standard A30.

However, BMC were characteristically slow to see the competition potential of their new Mini car. Despite the almost Formula 1 nature of its design, the engine, suspension and gearbox package being as one, official interest was minimal. Despite encouraging road test feedback, the chuckable, lovable nature of the Mini was being overlooked and when parked in the Abingdon competitions department it was largely ignored. Apparently the first person to buy a Mini specifically for competition was famed circuit racer John Handley. The first day that the car went on sale he persuaded his local dealer to part with their demonstrator and promptly drove off in the direction of the Worcestershire Rally. However, works drivers Pat Moss and Stuart Turner were credited with a very early win in a minor 1959 event called the Mini Miglia and organised by the Knowldale Automobile Club, although Moss was reported as saying that the Mini was too slow, whilst Turner thought the car particularly uncomfortable.

Nevertheless a team was entered for that year's RAC Rally. Three Minis were entered and they all dropped out with the same trouble: faulty oil seals allowed the clutch to slip despite the best efforts of service crews squirting in powder from fire extinguishers and even road grit. Minis tackled their first international event in the 1960 Monte Carlo. It was a reasonably successful expedition, as a works team comprising TMO 559, 560 and 561 competed alongside three private entries for glory. These accident prone cars had an eventful time, 559 collided with a private entrant, 560 was almost written off and limped home, while 561, hit a rock. Nevertheless 73rd, 55nd, 33rd and 23rd position were respectable results.

The Mini recorded its first International win in the 1960 Geneva Rally whilst other 850cc models went on to contest all the major events, which included a historic first in class for TMO 561 at the Alpine Rally. This car scored another class victory in the 1961 Tulip Rally, but this was to be the last year of competition for the plucky 850cc, eclipsed by the arrival of the Cooper. However, the Mini had proved the point that despite negligible ground clearance, tiny wheels and occasionally obstreperous components this was a rally weapon to be taken seriously.

Stuart Turner became the new competitions manager for BMC and not only inherited a very well run team, but was able to give the Mini which he had initially found so uncomfortable, its big Cooper badged break. On the team were two very talented Scandinavians, Timo Makinen and Rauno Aaltonen, plus the cars were now painted in the soon to be familiar red with a white roof, so all the elements for rallying success were in place.

Their first event was the 1962 Monte Carlo, which almost ended in tragedy when Aaltonen lying second crashed into a wall, caught fire and co-driver Geoff Mabbs rescued his unconscious team mate. It was better news for the ladies, Pat Moss and Ann Wisdom who finished 26th overall, 7th in class and scooped the Coupe de Dames. This pairing performed even better in that year's Tulip Rally, winning it outright, the Mini's first International win. Then in 1963 a very important driver was recruited to the Mini Cooper team, Paddy Hopkirk.

The omens were good at the start of the season as the Cooper achieved 3rd and 6th places in the Monte Carlo. This success was followed by a second and class win in the Tulip. New signing Val Domelo who replaced Pat Moss finished 4th in class. She went on in the following Trifels Rally to score a significant class win. The stunning arrival of the 1071 Cooper S was marked by a first overall win for the mixed sex pairing of Aaltonen and Anne Ambrose. Paddy Hopkirk, partnered by Henry Liddon followed this up with a 3rd overall, but a class win in the Tour de France and 4th overall in the seasons last event, the RAC.

Not surprisingly for the 1964 season, with a few exceptions the S was now adopted as the main BMC car. They got off to a good start too as Hopkirk scored the Minis most important win to date at the Monte Carlo with other team cars finishing 4th and 7th. These winning ways continued in the Tulip with another overall victory. However, the rest of the year did not go so well. The new 1275 version proved unreliable in the Acropolis Rally, although it managed a class win in the Alpine. To confuse the S issue the short lived 970cc participated in a few events and acquitted itself very well winning the Ladies Cup and a Class victory in the Alpine and scoring another class win in the Tour de France.

**Paddy Hopkirk and Henry Liddon on the way to a
historic victory in the 1964 Monte Carlo Rally.**

1965 was a busy season and a much better one
for the Coopers. They got off to a terrific start as Timo
Makinen and Paul Easter overcame appalling weather
conditions to take victory. Having started their run in
Stockholm they were among only 35 of the original 237
starters who qualified for the elimination tests. Despite
sub zero temperatures, huge snowdrifts and treacherous
ice, Makinen and Easter took the now famous AJB 44B to
victory. They were ably supported by Hopkirk and Liddon
at 26th overall, but first in class, followed closely in 27th
by the Morley twins. Frozen transmissions put paid to the
teams ambitions in the Swedish Rally, as all four cars
retired with seized differentials. Hopkirk was back on
form though for the Circuit of Ireland which was won
outright, followed by a class win in the Tulip. The Altonen
and Ambrose partnership won the Geneva Rally, followed
by the Czech and the nearby Polish event. This left
Altonen in clear sight of the European Rally
Championship with just two events remaining. The so
called Three Cities Rally, or to give it the clumsier official
name, Munich - Vienna - Budapest Rally, was also a happy
hunting ground for Aaltonen which just left the RAC. A

huge works entry of eight Coopers, not to mention big Healeys tackling the last event of the season. In fact a Healey 3000 piloted by Timo Makinen finished runner-up to Aaltonen who was crowned European Champion, the first time that a British car had won the title.

As psychedelic years go, the BMC competitions department would never have a stranger trip than 1966. Most bizarre and notorious of all was the Monte Carlo Rally. The circumstances surrounding this event are well documented but bear a certain amount of repetition and maybe understanding. First of all it had been well telegraphed that the French would be reluctant for the British cars in general and Coopers in particular to make much of an impression on the Rally. Apparently a home win for Citroen would make a much more popular result. The British contingent had no reason to doubt the officials intentions as rumours circulated that BMC had failed to homologate the Cooper S. Actually they had, exceeding the 5,000 Minimum by 47. However, there were suggestions that the rally version of the Cooper had little in common with a stock showroom model. More worrying were the exceedingly late regulation changes by the ruling body. However, all the British teams believed that they had complied.

Never mind the great drivers, brilliant little cars and excellent mechanical back up, a major factor in the Mini's rally success was innovative preparation. Tony Ambrose when he joined the team in the early '60s pioneered the use of detailed pace notes, which made the co-driver's role crucial. Also Stuart Turner was the first rally manager to employ recce vehicles, which ran ahead of the rally to report back on conditions. The benefits were obvious and the results followed, so it was no surprise to find that the finishing order on the 1966 Monte was Makinen, Aaltonen and Hopkirk, or Mini-Cooper, Mini-Cooper and Mini-Cooper. But of course, the French did not see it this way. The post event inspection turned into an autopsy as the officials pulled the cars apart for technical infringements. They found plenty of irregularities between the cars specification and homologation papers, but the BMC mechanics consistently proved that the officials were wrong. Track an extra 3.5mm wide? No the suspension had simply settled after the exertions of the Rally. Stroke too long? This was 1275cc not an 850cc unit. To cap it all, highly inaccurate bathroom scales were used to measure almost every component.

Almost in desperation the official turned their attentions to the car's lighting system, which they claimed, failed to comply with French traffic laws even though they were allowed under Appendix J of the Rally regulations. Apparently the fog lamps could be used as dipped beams because the headlights contained single filament halogen bulbs. Not only were the Minis disqualified, so was the 4th placed Lotus Cortina driven by Roger Clark which put a Citroen DS21 in first place. Appeals failed, even though there was photographic evidence that Citroen had changed their lighting system late in the event. Never mind, things could only get better, only they didn't.

In Sweden, Makinen suffered a broken driveshaft, and Aaltonen hit a rock and subsequently overheated, so both cars retired. On the San Remo, Hopkirk finished 6th in class whilst Tony Fall was disqualified for having non-standard paper air filters. Then things started to pick up. Fall and Henry Liddon won the Circuit of Ireland. Hopkirk and Crellin the Austrian Alpine Rally. Hopkirk then took a class win in the Acropolis. Tony Fall won the Scottish Rally and followed that up with a second overall in the Geneva event. Three more major victories followed for Aaltonen on the Czech Rally, Fall on the Polish and Makinen on the Three Cities.

The usual large entry for the end of season RAC included world Formula One Champion Graham Hill piloting one of eight cars. Finishing 2nd, 4th and 5th overall meant a 1-2-3 in their class. Despite this BMC did not see the positive side and they started to restrict funds. It was hardly surprising that faced with such difficult circumstances Stuart Turner left, handing over the operation to Peter Browning, although both men were scheduled to mount the assault on the 1967 Monte Carlo Rally.

Inside the compact and not especially tidy competition department which was located in the MG factory.

Revenge for the 1966 nonsense proved to be sweet, although conditions were again difficult and the rules were revamped. Only a limited selection of tyre options were available for special stages which required the Coopers to have a substantial roof rack each. This did not stop the team posting another historic win. Aaltonen and Liddon beat of a strong challenge from a Porsche 911, whilst the rest of the team finished 6th with the Hopkirk/Crellin pairing, 10th in the hands of Tony Fall, 15th for the relatively new pairing of Lapinen and Wood, with Makinen and Easter at 41st position.

The rest of year was just as encouraging with six outright wins, nine class victories and plenty of high placings. There were some fresh challenges for the Mini Cooper too as BMC took their first shot at the notorious East African Safari. Aaltonen drew up a specification sheet for his car, which included fully adjustable Hydrolastic suspension, pumped-up by a rear-mounted device for increasing ground clearance. In addition there was a high exhaust, and air intake to stop the engine taking any mud on board. Everything was beefed, the visible sign being a massive sump guard and large handles mounted on the front wings and back of the roof to allow the car to be manhandled out of any trouble. Top mounted windscreen wiper, which could also be operated manually. In the circumstances this car needed all the help it could get as monsoons turned the event into the stickiest ever. Not surprisingly the car came to grief in a mud filled hole as the engine gummed up with the brown stuff. Never mind, because Hopkirk realised a long held ambition to win the Acropolis. On home soil in the Thousand Lakes, Finn, Timo Makinen won despite having his view of the rally obscured by a bouncing bonnet, released to aid cooling.

Timo Makinen and Paul Easter with all the trophies from the 1965 Monte Carlo victory.

1967 was the year when the RAC event was cancelled due to an outbreak of foot and mouth disease so the last two events were the Alpine followed by the Tour of

My Mini Cooper it's part in my Breakdown

Corsica. Although four cars started the event, three retired leaving the popular pairing of Hopkirk and Crellin to battle through very foggy conditions at the end of the event to claim victory. However, in the Corsica there were no pleasant surprises, only a series of upsets related to faulty fan belt material. Slipping badly, they failed to properly cool the engine and caused two premature retirements. That was the end to an eventful '67 season.

It was clear that BLMC were still behaving like amateurs in an increasingly professional sport, as they quaintly drove to and from events whilst all about them took trailers. But that was only part of the problem, the Mini-Cooper had a good run. Better than most. Six years at the top was impressive, but lots of other cars were not only catching up, but overtaking. To take on big budget teams like Porsche and Renault, BLMC would have to spend some serious money, money that they did not have. So the omens for 1968 did not look good and got a little worse at the Monte Carlo.

To make up for the 1275s bhp shortfall, twin choke Weber carburettors boosted the output by a token 7bhp, but the update caused consternation amongst the French officials. Were these modified carburettors? The regulations certainly forbade it. In the end a compromise was reached whereby if a fellow competitor objected, then the Minis were out. In the event itself the Minis may not have been in contention for the top place, but they finished strongly, Aaltonen, Fall and Hopkirk registering 3rd, 4th and 5th and top three in their class.

Potentially there were eleven championship events in 1968, but the team only challenged eight of them. Although it was becoming clear that the Mini-Cooper was being regularly outclassed by more powerful opposition, t the results were still impressive. After a wipeout in the Flowers Rally, Belgian driver Vernaeve drove to 3rd and a class win. Aaltonen followed up the previous year's Acropolis win with a 5th and class victory. The last two events for the team were the Scottish Rally, which yielded a class win. Four months later Hopkirk took one Cooper S to the TAP Rally and came away with a very creditable second place after leading for most the rally.

My Mini Cooper it's part in my Breakdown

Hopkirk was retained for one more season and works Coopers participated in just two international events in 1969. He always excelled in the Circuit of Ireland and despite experimenting with 12" (30.4cm) wheels, a misfire and some suspension problems, came in third. This was followed by the Tour de France where fuel injection was used and Hopkirk was joined in his assault on the road rally by John Handley in another Group 2 car and Brian Culcheth in Group 1. Hopkirk finished 14th overall, but won his class, whilst Handley went out when lying 6th, whilst Brian Culcheth managed a strong class second beaten by a Julian Vernaeve's privately entered Cooper S.

Leyland's official participation was virtually over, many of the works cars were dispatched to bounce around televised autocross events in the late '60s. For 1970 two very minor rallys were contested in Australia. Brian Culcheth did the honours retiring in the Southern Cross and finishing fourth in the Rally of the Hills. And that was it for the Cooper...

Paddy Hopkirk is back! He lines up with the original Monte winning Coopers, plus four '90s Coopers to tackle the 1994 event. Hopkirk and Ron Crellin finished 52nd overall and 4th in class.

...until 1994. Project Mini Monte Carlo was an attempt to get the car back into the Rally it had dominated in the '60s, with the same driver/navigator combination of

204

My Mini Cooper it's part in my Breakdown

Paddy Hopkirk and Ron Crellin. The idea was to find out just how competitive the Mini was in a modern World Championship rally. Preparing a car for Group A regulations was hardly straightforward especially as the engine had to be a substantially standard unit. However, Brigden Coulter Motorsport managed to get an engine to produce 97 bhp at the wheels. Despite some electrical problems and the cars inability to finish they were still classified in the results. Philippe Camandona finished 47th overall a 3rd in Class. Hopkirk and Crellin finished 52nd overall and 4th in Class. Already a popular and successful sight on numerous classic rallys, the Mini also returned to the RAC event in 1994 driven by Russell Brooks.

History was made in 1995 when Daniel Harper and Les Reger steered the Mini to its first international win since Paddy Hopkirk won the Acropolis Rally back in 1967. The event was the Vauxhall Rally of Wales and the Class was A5, beating off numerous Peugeot 306s and Vauxhall Novas to take the title. But that was not the end of the Mini's Rally revival, specialists Mini Sport entered two cars to challenge for the Mobil One/Top Gear RAC British Rally Championship with Daniel Harper and Les Reger in Group A and Dave Johnson and John Flynn in Group N. After gruelling rounds in Wales, Scotland, Ireland and the Isle of Man they came out winners of Group A and runners up in Group N. In rallying, the Mini in never went away. And how did it do on the track?

The Mini's potential for circuit racing in the '60s would seem to be as limited as their dimensions, especially in view of the hugely powerful cars they were up against, which included huge Jaguar saloons and American Ford Galaxies. Size did not matter as ability counted for so much more. On the track Minis proved to be astoundingly quick. Cheap to buy and prepare Minis provided the perfect progression from karts for a large number of Formula 1 stars who got their start in the little cars including James Hunt and Nicki Lauda. Incredibly the Mini stayed competitive at a national level well into the 1980s. Even today the Mini is still hugely popular as a racer, not only because it costs so little take racing for a season, but also there are lots of opportunities for close competition with the popularity of one make series like the Mini Miglia. Of course, there is no way that the whole story could be detailed in just a few pages, but here's some of the highlights from an illustrious and very long career on the track.

The Cooper Car Company raced Minis which bore their own name and distinctive British Racing Green and white bonnet striped livery from 1962 with a certain amount of backing from BMC. It paid off because John Love won the British Saloon Car Championship that year. In 1963 Sir John Whitmore was the runner up to the huge Ford Galaxie driven by Jack Sears. Ralph Broad entered a modified Cooper which was driven by John Fitzpatrick, John Handley and Jeff May which proved to be highly competitive. So competitive that Fitzpatrick was procured to join Cooper and he finished runner up in the 1964 British Championship and class winner for 1300cc cars.

In Europe a Downtown Engineering tuned Cooper with Rob Slotemaker at the wheel won the 1300 cc class of the European saloon Car Championship. Ken Tyrell ran a two car team for Cooper with Warwick Banks and Julian Vernaeve. Banks won the European title in 1964. On home ground in 1965 the Banks roller coaster rolled on. Driving for Cooper he scored 8 out of ten victories, taking the class award in the up to 1000cc category, but deprived of a Championship win because of a technical protest.

Ralph Broad operated on a shoestring budget but benefited from works updates to specification, in particular tougher gearboxes. His success in Europe resulted in BMC offering him the contract to race on the continent in preference to Tyrell for 1965. John Fitzpatrick rejoined the team alongside John Handley and spare driver John Terry. It was not a successful season. Budgetary restraints were the problem, which meant missing some races. Back home though Broadspeed Coopers often beat Cooper Coopers. BMC therefore cancelled the European agreement. In 1968 BMC extended its support to British Vita who contested European races in the one litre class with driver's Handley and Alec Poole. Handley won the championship.

It was all change on the home team front in 1966 when Broadspeed turned to Ford, racing Anglias and later

My Mini Cooper it's part in my Breakdown

on, Escorts. Driver Fitzpatrick went with him whilst over at Cooper Warwick Banks went off to concentrate on single seaters to be replaced by John Handley. Engine preparation was now a matter for Downton Engineering rather than BMC. Homologated fuel injection meant they were fast and reliable, but John Rhodes just missed the title which was taken by ex Mini man Fitzpatrick. In 1968 the Cooper team retained Rhodes who was joined by Steve Neal, but it was a repeat of the previous season as Rhodes finished runner-up again, but bagged the 1300cc Class.

The creation of the Leyland Group was not good news for Minis and motorsport. Already the rally operation was being scaled down due to the expense of contesting these events and the emphasis was being switched to rallycross and circuits. Already Cooper were dropped although they stayed with Downton to form the Cooper-Downton-Britax team with Steve Neal and Gordon Spice doing the driving duties. The outstanding problems that affected the works Rally programmes were exactly the same when it came to breathing life into the racing side with the increasingly professional approach of other factory backed teams and the fact that the Mini was now a decade old. That did not stop the Equipe Arden organisation with Spice driving, from picking up the 1000cc class award in 1968. For 1969 the works drivers were Rhodes and Handley who benefited from the newest development: 12" wheels.

The Leyland logo was not to be a lucky charm. Both cars were written off in accidents at the first Brands Hatch meeting. At the following Silverstone meeting things got a little better with 10th and 11th placings, which meant 4th and 5th in class. A 3rd and 4th at Crystal Palace saw even more improvements. Them it was on to the continent and a 5th and 6th at Hockenheim, but both cars at the Nürburgring 6 hours retired with broken rear trailing arm pivots. On to the Spa 24 hours modified Coopers failed to stay the distance. Back in Blighty the Oulton Park Gold Cup saw Rhodes car, with a Weslake tuned 1299cc engine, trailing twelfth.

A final continental fling for the Coopers at Salzburg saw Rhodes and Handley score an impressive 1-2. Unfortunately that did not stop the factory abandoning the Cooper for competition purposes. Although the season finished well, throughout they had found the going tough against entries from Cooper and the Broadspeed Fords. It did not help that concentrating on outright wins with 1300cc category Coopers left the 1000cc open to others, namely Alec Poole and an Equipe Arden prepared Cooper which won the class title and the RAC Championship outright in 1969. Add to all that the fact that Abingdon were new to circuit racing and the restrictions on development due to the engine/gearbox set-up it is remarkable that the team achieved so much. But Leyland were in no mood to be patient.

In 1969 Richard Longman won the first ever motor race 'in colour' on British TV which was an omen of sorts as he fought off the attentions of a huge Ford Falcon in a Downtown 1300 Cooper. In fact that was just one of 27 races in which he was successful that season and he loyally stuck with the Mini for another decade finding fame as an expert tuner of A series engines. When production saloon car racing was re-established in 1972 the winner of the 1300cc class was Jonathan Buncombe with a Longman engined Cooper S.

Once the Cooper's homologation period expired Longman turned his attentions to the 1275GT and in 1977 revived the Minis competition credentials in national terms. British Leyland should be given credit for helping qualify a number of parts including twin SU carburettors, sportier camshaft, close ratio gearbox, 12" wheels and better Dunlop tyres. Up against a Chrysler Avenger driven by Bernard Unett who had dominated the 1300cc class for the previous three seasons, Longman got the better of him on a couple of occasions. However he finished second, with Alan Curnow in an identical 1275 GT third.

1978 was the year that Longman put the Mini back on top with an overall win in the RAC British saloon car championship. Sponsored by Patrick Motors Longman also went on to fly the flag yet again in 1979 by winning the group 1 British Saloon Car Championship with Curnow as the runner-up. The car's success ended in the Saloon Car Championship when a change in the regulations meant a higher Minimum weight limit.

My Mini Cooper it's part in my Breakdown

Undoubtedly a key to the Clubman's success was BL's one make 1275GT racing series, although of course they switched to the Metro Challenge with the announcement of the new car. Despite that the Mini has raced on and you can cheer a grid full of Minis on at most meetings during the season at a Mini Miglia, Mini Se7en, Ministox and sundry other Mini Challenges.

September 1991. Mileage: 98,862 Amount spent: £0 on the Austin Mini Cooper but, Cost of Austin Mini 850cc and a Morris Mini Cooper £750.
Minis in my Life: 1964 Austin Mini Cooper, 1967 Austin Mini De Luxe, 1967 Morris Mini Cooper MOT: Austin Cooper No. Morris Cooper Yes.

A tale of two Minis. I really missed having a Cooper around, what with it being in Norfolk and me in London. So I went to Suffolk and bought a couple more Minis, it was an absurd thing to do. I justified the purchase of two

My Mini Cooper it's part in my Breakdown

1967 Minis a 998cc Morris Cooper and an Austin De Luxe on the grounds that I needed a spare. Well I think it may have been an attempt to recapture my youth and also check and see whether it was still possible to go out and buy a Mini Cooper for a few hundred quid.

Deep in Ted Sparrow's workshop was a Mini Cooper suitable for treatment. It looked exactly like a 24-year old Mini should: bloody awful. The floor was held together with plates and the upper body with even more plates and bodger's filler. The nightmare continued on the roof, which had a new skin riveted on top of the old one.

Originally Sparrow thought that he had struck gold with an ex-police constabulary car which would have been worth a fortune at the time. That's because underneath the layers of thick black paint the original colour was white and what remained of the interior was just about red. However, the more mundane explanation is that it had turned turtle at least once or twice in its eventful life and someone had just tacked a second hand roof panel on top. Not only that, the rear Hydrolastic set up had finally expired. It then listed into Ted Sparrow's Mini Centre with the rear wheel arches cutting huge grooves in the tyres.

Under the bonnet the good news as I found a genuine chassis number and the engine details which indicated it was a high compression version of the 998cc unit. So it was a case of nice running gear, shame about the body.

The original plan had been to simply transplant all the OK mechanical bits from the barely alive Cooper into the reasonably sound Austin. Actually the standard De Luxe Mini was a one owner example. However, it wasn't as simple as that. Things needed doing to the shell which included a new wing and A panel and some other bits of bobs which then led to a complete respray. The interior of the Cooper was shot and had in fact been painted black with, er matt black undercoat paint and could not be cleaned so the plain Austin trim had to do.

Cannibalising two Minis to make one isn't everyone's idea of car restoration, but hey, the alternative, as I will find out in another 20 years is actually more expensive and complicated than I could ever have imagined. So making use of two contemporary cars that would have shuffled down the production line at similar times seems like a sensible thing to do. Especially as there isn't that much structurally different between a standard and Cooper save for a few brackets, fixtures and fittings. As for the originality bores, well I was happy to give them a fight back in 1992. It never came to blows, but I did make the middle shelf of the newsagents.

That used to be a Mini Cooper.

15. The Mini was truly cosmopolitan, it spoke every language and translated seamlessly into any environment, trouble is BMC and BL weren't nearly as clever as VW so the Mini was no Beetle when it came worldwide sales, however, it got sold and knocked together in a quite a few corners of the world.

Here's a Mini Minor working for the Sheriff's department in Nevada USA. Is that John Wayne?

'World cars'. That's been the buzz motor industry phrase for a long time now. Apparently every manufacturer ought to have one, that is, a model which has global appeal, can be assembled cost effectively by the locals and even be adopted by them as one of their own. But the truth is that the Mini has always been big abroad. Ever since it was launched the Mini has been completely cosmopolitan having been widely exported since 1959 without interruption. Not only has it appealed to markets in all corners of the world, it has been built there too.

Indeed, at times it has been the worldwide demand, which has kept the Mini in production during the dark days of the mid '80s. Luckily the Japanese, French, Germans and Italians loved the Mini enough to help Rover make the decision to keep the little car in production.

Essentially Minis remained remarkably similar to British specification cars with some minor revisions to conform to local regulations. For instance Canadian and American Minis had 'bull bars', whilst in Chile and Venezuela, they were made of plastic. There were name changes too as in Denmark a Mini became the Morris Mascot whilst the Kombi moniker was applied to German estates. Inevitably they had their own special editions too: fancy an After Eight? The French did. Over in Italy Innocenti not only built their own versions of the standard Mini, Cooper and estate they took the concept one stage further and came up with a brand new Bertone styled supermini. In fact, the Cooper was not just a British phenomenon, being built in several other factories across Europe long after production ceased in the UK. The Moke has also travelled particularly well having been built in Australia, Portugal and more recently Italy.

Here's a Canadian spec Mini leaving Longbridge with a raised bumper which doesn't look pretty, but regulations demanded it.

Export Minis were always close relatives of home market models. Obvious changes have been kilometre calibrated speedometers and left hand drive set-ups. For many years models exported to Europe have been badged as Mini Specials, changed to Sprite in the '90s. Occasionally these markets also benefited from a unique model, which was never officially launched in the UK like the 1300 Special, a saloon with a 1275cc engine, which looked like a Cooper Mark 3 but had GT power.

In the beginning BMC offered two levels of export trim, De Luxe and Super De Luxe and badged as an Austin, or Morris 850 and Super 850. A Basic and Export Saloon were added to the range in 1961 and replaced the De Luxe in 1963. The three trim levels remained for the Mark 2 in 1967. As the Austin and Morris names were dropped two years later the 850 Special De Luxe, 1000 De Luxe and 1000 De Luxe were added to the line up. Of course Clubman and 1275 GT models were also destined for the major export markets

Innocenti's version of the Cooper, which continued after the UK version, was dropped by BL. This is the Mark III Export model finished to German specification. How truly international.

My Mini Cooper it's part in my Breakdown

Although Complete Knocked Down (CKD) Kits were sent to assembly plants worldwide, some of the most fascinating, distinctive and original concepts were built at dedicated Mini production plants around the world.

Arguably the best-known Mini manufacturer outside of the UK was Innocenti. Their models were not just rebadged and rehashed Minis, but often thoroughly reworked and remodelled with their own distinctive character.

Founded by Ferdinand Innocenti in 1933 the company was better know for manufacture of the mod's favourite motor scooter in the shape of the Lambretta. However, Innocenti was ambitious when in 1960 it began production of licence built Austin A40s, which initiated a long association with the British company, which included the Austin/Morris 1100. They also reproduced the Austin Healey Sprite and beautifully rebodied it with coupe' styling by Osi and a convertible by Ghia.

Production of Innocenti's version of the Mini began in October 1965. Mechanical and certain body parts were imported and it was badged as the Innocenti Mini-Minor 850. The specification was British based with Hydrolastic suspension and virtually a De Luxe level of trim with opening rear quarter windows, lever door handles, vinyl trim, rubber mats and three instrument binnacle. Compared to the Longbridge model there were side indicators mounted on the front wings, reversing lights and a distinctive nine bar grille. A year later the company quickly followed this up with their own version of the Cooper. It had 998cc power just like the original, but was badged as a Mini Cooper. Then at that year's Turin Motor Show the company added the 'Mini t' to its range, which in English translated into estate car. Like the UK market counterpart, customers could choose between mock Tudor timber decoration, or a plain all-steel model.

The Mini Minor went Mark 2 in 1968 just like the UK version although the 848cc engine had a mild state of additional tune with a 9:1 compression ratio and HS4 carburettor, which produced 48 bhp, and a top speed of almost 85 mph. The Mini Cooper Mark 2 came with new wheels and interior trim with a 9.5:1 compression ratio and 60 bhp and a 93 mph top speed whilst the British 998cc model ran out of puff at 90 mph.

Not surprisingly, the range went Mark 3 in 1970 with all the bodywork and trim changes first seen on the British cars in 1969. The big differences were the retention of Hydrolastic suspension and unique wind-up windows with quarter lights. Inside, it was full width fascia time, featuring five dials, with the speedometer and rev counters mounted in the middle and three minors dials in front of the driver. Italy finally got a Mini with an automatic gearbox, which was called the Mini-matic.

Innocenti Mini 120. Underneath the unique, hatchbacked body are standard A series mechanicals. The perfect marriage between Birmingham and Milan, which never officially came to the UK.

With the passing of Ferdinand Innocenti in 1972, BL stepped in and the new company was called Leyland Innocenti SpA. Not only did they get a new boss, Geoffrey Robinson, the whole range was renamed. The quaint Minor Minor, became the much more mundane Mini 1000 and an upmarket 1001 which had a timber finish on the instrument binnacle and a 51 bhp engine. The Mini-Matic retained its name, whilst the estate got an upper case t to become the 1000T. A new Mini Cooper 1300 came with UK Cooper S power and was an important revival of a charismatic name for the simple reason that the company never signed the same agreement as BMC. Apart from the badging the tyres were wider and came with wider arches which would eventually appear on UK cars. The last Cooper the company built was an Export model in 1973, with a rod gear change, dual circuit brakes, Rostyle wheels and ribbed vinyl trim.

Here's the back end of a Mini 90, which had a tailgate.

The most exciting Innocenti development during this period was the Mini 90 and 120. This was the first official hatchback based Mini which preceded the Metro by six years. Styled by Bertone it was a contemporary square cut design and was arguably one of the first Euro superminis. Underneath it all of course was the standard A series Mini running gear yet it was only marginally larger than the old car being just 2.6 in (6.6cm) longer and 3.5in (8.89cm) wider. The Mini 90 had the 998cc engine producing 49bhp, which translated into an 87mph top speed and was distinguished by its black bumpers. The 120 had a detuned 65 bhp 1275cc unit with twin carburettors, which would reach 96 mph and was topped off with chrome bumpers. The only mechanical changes were a resisted radiator now mounted at the front and a revised exhaust. Inside, the rear seat folded forward and despite a high loading lip, offered a usefully large luggage area. The most distinctive part of the interior was the dashboard which echoed the original Mini's central pod, though only a stylised Mini logo occupied this space whilst in front of the driver though were rectangular cut outs.

Of course the big debate back in 1975 when cars were tested in the UK was, 'Will it ever come to Blighty?' Leyland seriously considered the possibility, especially as most of the mechanical components and some of the body pressings originated in Britain. Plans were drawn up for a limited run of 5,000, but BL pulled out. Production costs on this car proved to be very high and anyway the prototype ADO88 was well under way at that time and would eventually metamorphose into the Metro. In fact, it may be a good thing that the Innocenti never came here officially. That's because all the models, which were imported unofficially, seemed to fall apart and then rust to bits in a very short time. Something to do with low grade Eastern Block steel and Italian build quality. As if Leyland's troubles weren't bad enough, adding an Italian built car to the range could have finished them off much sooner.

In fact BL's financial woes were not unconnected with Innocenti's bankruptcy in 1975. Fiat were interested in buying the company, but De Tomaso beat them to it. The standard Mini was discontinued although Cooper production staggered into '76 thanks to factory left overs. De Tomaso had plans, and this included the Mini De Tomaso based on a 120, but with a 74bhp engine. It was a very welcome mid '70s Cooper S and headed a three car range that comprised the 90, 120 and De Tomaso. In 1982 the A series power plant was replaced by a three cylinder Daihatsu unit to make the Mini 3. That car became the Innocenti Small and in 1990 Fiat finally got their hands on the company. In 1993 the car was discontinued.

The Australian part of the Mini story all started as just another big export market, then changed into a CKD operation and ultimately a full production facility with a large local content. The Minis originally assembled in 1961 were 848cc cars and badged as Morris 850s. Not far behind were Mini Coopers a year later. The 1275 S followed in '65. Incredibly, Australia was the first market to produce a Mini wind up windows in 1965. Their system bore no relation to the Elf/Hornet one-piece arrangement and featured a hinging quarter light. This conveniently luxurious touch was even extended to the van, which was launched that year. Otherwise Australian Minis kept abreast of UK developments by introducing Hydrolastic suspension in 1965, 998cc power in 1967 an automatic Mini-Matic and the Mark 2 in 1968, although the Cooper S Mark 2 was not launched for another year.

To celebrate the fact that the Mini was now almost Australian, about 80% local content, they launched in 1969 the Morris Mini K, which stood for Kangaroo and was reinforced by a marsupial logo. Power was supplied by the 1098cc unit producing 51bhp. For 1971 the corporate nose became the Clubman, hence the name change to Mini Clubman 1100, whilst the Cooper was transformed into the 1275cc Clubman GT. One anomaly though was the external door hinges whilst Hydrolastic suspension survived until 1973. Australia scored another Mini first though with recessed door handles. The Morris name was dropped in 1972, and so was some of the Kangaroo's local content in the shape of the 1098cc engine, whilst the UK built 998cc was re-imported. The company took the special edition route in the late '70s with some quite highly specified models, which included alloy wheels, metallic paint and radio cassette. By the launch of the 1275LS which even had 12in (30.4cm) wheels it was all over for the Mini in Australia.

Leyland had managed to mismanage just about every aspect of their overseas operation. Developing the P76 saloon specifically for the Australian market had sapped the resolve and the finances of Leyland. As the Mini faced increasing Japanese competition it was discontinued. However, there was still one more Mini based model left in production.

My Mini Cooper it's part in my Breakdown

Flatbed Moke, the Utility from 1972, unique to the Antipodes. The 'off road' Mini flourished in a more favourable climate and was Australia's cheapest car.

Australia started producing the Moke under licence in 1966 with a 998cc engine. In 1968 optional 13in wheels meant much better ground clearance than before and the Australians embarked on a development programme. The heavily revised Mark 2 Moke, later named simply BMC Moke, had standard 13-inch (33cm) wheels. Power was supplied by a locally built 1098cc unit, which had better cooling, and a revised oil filter. Cooper S universal joints, larger brake cylinder and lower final drive combined with wider tracks to improve the outback performance.

Then the Australians seriously upgraded the Moke with the limited edition Californian, a name that would endure for many years afterward. Firstly they imported the 1275cc engine producing a useful 65bhp and installed it into a slightly more garish machine. There was more than Spruce Green paintwork on offer whilst the roof was a paisley patterned vinyl affair and the spare wheel had a cover. Two speed wipers, hazards and a reversing light made this the most high spec Moke yet. The fuel tank was also moved from the vulnerable side position to the rear. Obviously the ultimate Moke, but it did not last because the 1275cc engine could not meet local emission requirements and was deleted in 1972.

My Mini Cooper it's part in my Breakdown

Back came the 1098cc engine and a so-called Moke Utility, essentially a two-seater pick up model. Then Leyland decided to switch to the 998cc engine and fitted emissions equipment in 1976. The Moke was back on track when the Californian was reintroduced in 1977 with white spoke wheels, bull bars and sports steering wheel with a Californian bonnet decal. Clearly off road chic had arrived a couple of decades early in the '70s.

Moke development did not end with the Californian, in 1979 the bodywork was galvanised for the first time that put an end to any corrosion worries. Mechanically it was overhauled for better performance. High back, tilting seats made it even more comfortable and new stalk controls easier to operate. Californians had a full roll cage, the hood was improved with side screens and there were now deflector screens on the windscreen. Not only that, there was an optional 1275cc engine. Even so, the Moke was a tired old model and coming to the end of its useful life in the Antipodes. Production was discontinued in 1981, but the Moke story did not end there, it restarted slightly closer to its original home.

Even before the Moke was cold in Australia, CKD kits had been finding their way to Setubal in Portugal. It was no accident that Mokes were ending up there because at the Industrial Montagem factory owned by Leyland, building up the vehicles allowed the company to sell Metros. A smart way around import restrictions meant building vehicles locally and there was nothing easier to bolt together than a Moke. So no big start up costs, or skilled labour and lots of profitable Metro sales. The Moke they built was essentially an Australian spec. Californian. That meant 998cc, 40 bhp engine from Britain, 13in (33cm) white spoked wheels, roll cage, high back seats and zipped side screens. Several of these models even made it officially back to the UK although Dutton Cars imported no more than a handful.

Problems at the factory resulted in bankruptcy. So a new company, which was majority owned by Austin Rover, with new management, a move to a new plant and a model revamp all had to work. And it did. The Moke never looked back after standard Mini running gear was fitted including 12in wheels disc brakes, 998cc City engine, gearbox and differential. Demand in Europe and far eastern markets soared and possibly for the first time in its life, the Moke was profitable. Once again the Moke came back to Britain marketed very successfully this time by Duncan Hamilton. Austin Rover though did not need the bother of running such a small operation especially as Portuguese membership of the EEC and freer trade meant sneaking Metros into the country was no longer necessary.

Production ceased in 1989 and the whole enterprise, including the Moke name, put up for sale. The Italian concern Cagiva, best known for building motorcycles bought the rights and restarted production of the 'Moke' as it now had to be called, in 1991. Inevitably it was decided to build the Mokes in the company's Italian factories. Portuguese production ceased in 1993. Supplies of mechanical parts from Longbridge were proving to be a problem and reengineering it to accept other donor items proved to be very costly. The Moke ran out of puff in Portugal and stalled completely in Italy thirty years after it was written off in the UK.

One of the Belgian built Mini Specials.

The majority of Minis for sale in Europe were built at BL's plant in Seneffe, Belgium. The best known was the Mini Special, a standard saloon and 1098cc Clubman engine concoctions and the Cooper 1300 Export. Some even made it back to Britain in right hand drive form as personal imports. The plant was closed in April 1981.

BMC had a Madrid based subsidiary called AUTHI, actually Automobiles de Turismo Hispano Ingleses SA, were production of several models took place, principally based on the Morris 1100 and MG 1300 including some South African variants that were only sold in Europe. The Mini came to Authi's Pamplona factory in 1968. Starting with the 1275C they added the 1000E and 1000S models to the range. A buy out in 1969 meant a new name Leyland Authi, and a line up of Mini models to include the 850 and 1275 GT. Mini Cooper 1300s were also built by Authi, being very similar to the Innocenti. Production ceased in 1976 when General Motors bought the factories. Ironically, a '90s supermini is now built there: the Corsa.

South Africa has one of the largest concentrations of car factories outside Europe it is no surprise to discover yet another Leyland subsidiary operating on this continent. Odd automotive concoctions were, and still are a speciality in this unique marketplace and there was nothing odder than the sight of a standard Mark 3 front end with a tail form an Elf/Hornet.

Otherwise the standard engine was a 1098cc unit in the standard, or Clubman body. They also had their own version of the 1275GT called the GTS. Production finished in 1980 with the 1275E on titchy 10" (25.4cm) steel wheels and rather frightening drum brakes.

Plastic Mini, big in Chile, banned in Britain. Yes it's the Chilemini.

My Mini Cooper it's part in my Breakdown

Import quotas and limited industrial resources have always meant that getting cars into South America was always difficult. Overcoming these problems first in Chile meant involved plastic Mini bodies. Easily assembled by a local workforce it looked similar to the original, but did not need the welding seams. It was even mooted that production could start in the UK, but the unions objected. Rover managed to pull off the same glass fibre trick again in Venezuela with the Minicord.

October 1992. Mileage: 98,862 Amount spent: £0 on the Austin Mini Cooper but, cost of making two Minis into one Cooper, £3050.
Minis in my Life: 1964 Austin Mini Cooper, 1967 Morris Mini Cooper
MOT: Austin no. Morris Yes.

My brand new Cooper was part of a prominent Car magazine article in July 1992. It was so prominent, me and the Cooper even made the front the cover along

My Mini Cooper it's part in my Breakdown

with Editor Gavin Green's Citroen Light 15, Art Director Martin Chappell's Fiat 500, Deputy Editor Richard Bremner's Alfa Giulietta, Features Editor Paul Horrell's Fiat 124 and Assistant Road Test Editor Colin Goodwin's Datsun 240Z. However Colin was underneath an old E-Type on the cover that he drove, or rather endured for a week. Pretty to look at, but a pain to live with and held together with loads of filler. But I digress. The article was called Static Classics. It was all about the madness of running a silly old car. We even costed ownership out on a per mile basis and I thought that £8.28 after 500 miles was pretty embarrassing. Luckily Martin Chappel had calculated his 4 miles with the Fiat at £432.50 and Richard Bremner who had never driven, but only pushed his Alfa conservatively put the figure at £149 a yard. Perhaps I wasn't so bad after all.

The end though wasn't good. My Cooper was in a garage being MOT'd when I got a cash offer. I was in the middle of organising a house purchase and needed every extra quid I could find. So in a moment of weakness I said yes but the trade buyer was a piece of work. He was in the bank getting the draft made out to me and kept slicing the price. I should have told him to stuff it instead I said yes to £1300. Yes £1300, what an idiot. With that it was on its way to Japan for goodness knows how much. It still needed plenty doing to it to satisfy those who wanted utter originality, but it was a solid little Mini shaped box. To this day I think of it and shudder at the sheer stupidity of letting such a sound Mini go for so little.

**A Mini Cooper. Not for the purists, but they were both
1967 Minis and one was complete rubbish, so instead
of throwing it away we made a brilliant one.**

16. **It's the 1980s and the Mini is winding down for retirement, which actually was a bit premature. Sadly Issigonis leaves the Kremlin for good.**

As the Mini entered yet another decade it had a new rival to contend with. This new small car came from the same organisation, so they had plenty in common, not least the ancient A series engine. For a while they even shared a name, officially referred to as just Metro, yet for the first couple of years the car was generically a 'Mini Metro' to the great British public. With the Metro's hatchback, Eurobox styling, purpose built, robotised factory and huge marketing push the Mini's days had to be numbered.

However, although market research revealed to British Leyland that the Mini should stay in production, the intention was still to replace it by the early '80s. Michael Edwardes had envisaged a product led recovery which meant direct replacements for the Mini, Allegro and Marina, but this could hardly happen overnight. When they finally arrived, with the exception of the Metro, both the Maestro and Montego were not worth the wait. In fact, there had always been a curious reliance by BL and BMC on the loyalty of private UK customers. Time and again these regimes failed to make any conquest sales by snatching customers away from the likes of Vauxhall and Ford with a better product. All that seemed to happen was that the new model ended up selling in the same quantities as its predecessor.

Metro, the Mini's replacement. Except it wasn't.

The root of the problem with the new Metro an otherwise competent addition to supermini league, were the wildly over optimistic predictions for sales. Edwardes may have initiated the styling rethink, but sales forecasts remained the same. The BL board simply did not consider the impact of competing with the new superminis in the marketplace, like the Fiesta and Polo, which would inevitably end up pinching sales from the Metro. The original sales estimates dated from the late '60s, related to the prototype 9X and predicted a minimum of 350,000 units. However, the Metro never sold even half that figure. Yet the Mini was being produced at a rate of 200,000 between 1975 and 1978. However, those volumes were reduced dramatically to make way for its replacement and by 1982 worldwide sales of Minis ran at 52,000, whilst the Metro chalked up 174,000 units at its peak. This meant that BL made no increase in small car sales and had in fact started to lose out as volumes of both cars started to plummet as the '80s wore on. Mad.

So the Mini entered a new decade as a neglected model, which nevertheless had a loyal following and after twenty years was proving to be profitable. Any changes were forced by emissions, or safety legislations and sales were stimulated by special editions. For the Mini enthusiast the situation was far from perfect, but at least their favourite car was surviving and by the '90s, even starting to prosper.

1980 Mini 1000 which was up against the Metro.

The imminent arrival of its close relative and rival, the Metro, triggered a number of changes in advance of that launch which would also see a large number of common parts shared around the range. First of all in October 1979 the 1000 was renamed the Super. And with the passing of the basic 850 the City name was now transferred to the 1000 model in September 1980 with a similarly poverty stricken specification. At that time the Super was rebadged 1000 HL, a designation used liberally throughout the British Leyland empire to signify a 'high line' level of specification. With the Mini, the HL signalled a whole host of changes from the purely cosmetic adoption of the Clubman interior to Metro running gear.

So out went the old centrally mounted binnacle and in came a Tupperware box like double instrument pod. In addition there was tinted glass, larger door bins and a Metro steering wheel, gear knob and window winders. Under the bonnet was the Metro's A-plus engine and gearbox. On top of the bonnet was a new Mini badge fitted to the saloons a incorporating a cross of St George mounted on the usual shield, whilst in the middle of the grille was the Austin Morris Corporate logo. Unofficially models built from this point onwards are regarded as Mark IV Minis, even though some pedants might argue that the changes in 1984 were more far reaching.

Motor magazine liked the new line up and tried one of the new 1000HLs in July 1981. "The best things about a Mini are still, in 1981, at least as good as they ever were. Its combination of diminutive dimensions, panoramic visibility, eager engine, snappy gear change and scampering manoeuvrability still make it a cheekily effective town car which is great fun to drive...and in it's latest form we see no reason it shouldn't continue to feature in the best-sellers list for years to come."

Mayfair the upmarket Mini, with plastic wheel trims, coach line, decals and passenger door mirror set it apart from the City. The fancy touches were inside with a triple instrument binnacle, three spoke steering wheel and new cloth on the seats. Now that's luxury.

For 1982 the emphasis was on economy. The City E and HLE models featured 2.95:1 final drives and high compression cylinder heads. Upmarket Minis were repositioned and renamed as the Mayfair in October with some significant trim improvements including Raschelle velour upholstery, pile carpets, tinted glass, radio, passenger door mirror, head restraints and locking petrol cap. By 1984 the Mini caught up with braking technology by finally fitting front disc brakes. It seems incredible that this was not done earlier in view of the specially made Cooper discs in 1961, which were small, but very effective for the time. This development was also joined by 12" (30.4cm) wheels. Surrounding them were wider plastic wheelarches.

Almost luxurious interior for the base City with air vents and a double instrument binnacle.

In 1985 the City E finally got decent air ventilation courtesy of corner mounted swivelling eyeball vents, which had been available since 1969. One of the most enduring interior features had been the single central instrument binnacle, but even that was replaced by the two-dial pod. A four spoke steering wheel and revised stalk made control easier. On the outside the all-important City logo was shifted to the rear three quarter panel and there were new wheel trims. The Mayfair also benefited from several changes. Inside the instrument binnacle now had a rev counter which was framed by a three spoke steering wheel, new gear knob, revised trim and on the outside full width wheel trims. Both models gained side indicators on the front wings and there was some new branding on the grille, which bore the legend Austin above the corporate logo. True to form that name only lasted until 1987 when a new Mini badge took pride of place on the bonnet.

The revised Mini City had 12" wheels, disc brakes, and economy 'E' engine.

Autocar tested the revised Mini in 1985 and compared it with five cars similarly priced but significantly larger, in the shape of the Skoda Estelle 105S, Lada Riva 1200L, Yugo 45, Fiat Panda 45CL and Citroen 2CV Charleston. "Twenty five years after its launch, the Mini is selling 23,000 cars a year comfortably ahead of any other in its class. Why? Probably because today the Mini's virtues of compactness and economy are as relevant as they ever were. The Mini is to the small car what Hoover is to the vacuum cleaner and Kodak is to cameras...The Mini is the least powerful car in this group, but with an unladen weight of 11.9cwt it is easily the lightest. Thus it has respectable performance, which is not far short of the newer Panda...with a wheel at each corner and Minimum suspension travel, the Mini is but one step removed from a go-kart and feels it. In sheer handling agility the Mini makes the other cars in this group seem positively leviathan by comparison...Above all, it's still fun."

In 1986 BL reported losses of £892 million. The British Government and Prime Minister Margaret Thatcher in particular insisted on new management and Chairman at British Leyland. That man chosen was Graham Day a tall Canadian lawyer who had been running nationalised British Shipbuilders. By 1987 Day had disposed of some corporate assets and the company recorded a £27.9 million pre tax profit. Then in 1988 British Aerospace bought the renamed Rover Group.

Meanwhile the Mini's future was being seriously debated and in 1986 the idea of dropping the car was being seriously considered. Of course, Day was inundated with protest letters when the news leaked out. The development route that the company chose initially was the special edition one. For the full horrific detail, please see the next chapter.

Issigonis retires from BL in 1972 and is pictured with his finest creations from Morris Minors, to an 1800 Landcrab, one of his favourites. He remained as a consultant to BL and Rover until his death in 1988.

Official recognition for Issigonis came first with the CBE (Commander of the British Empire) in 1964,

My Mini Cooper it's part in my Breakdown

followed by a well deserved Knighthood in 1969. However, his influence ended with the creation of BLMC. Key posts were allocated elsewhere, but he never stopped working eventually being retained as a design consultant for Austin Rover until his death in October 1988. But did they consult? Unfortunately not and Sir Alec was disappointed that none of his suggested refinements were ever adopted. Issigonis never stopped building advanced Mini based prototypes from his base in the basement of the main building at Longbridge, affectionatly referred to as 'The Kremlin'.

A favourite project of his was the gearless Mini, which had a long stroke big torque engine driving through a hydraulic torque converter. During Michael Edwardes reign Issigonis lent an example to the BL chief for commuting around London, but nothing came of it. Pity, this car was an interesting concoction of Issigonis ideas. The overhead camshaft engine had been developed for the hatchbacked 9X. The suspension was almost conventional, featuring coil springs which increased roll, but did not hamper the car's overall nimbleness. Inside this Mini was converted by Issigonis to have sliding windows and door pockets. As a driving experience it produced less noise, a vastly more compact powertrain, less complication, and less work for the driver.

Issigonis also spent time developing innovative power plants for Minis, including a steam unit, a 1500cc diesel and a 1100cc six-cylinder engine. Talking to old friend Ronald Barker, Issigonis outlined his new Mini car philosophy, "We're looking for refinement, not power, and in this respect the difference between the four and six [cylinder] is dramatic. The small car of today is screaming for refinement, less road noise as well as less mechanical noise, because it's a complete waste of time to have one without the other."

Issigonis was not just a design genius. He was singleminded, obstinate and egotistical, traits which Donald Stokes loathed, but they explained his success and eccentricities. A preference for sliding windows over wind-ups and a ban on in car radios only added to his mystique. Issigonis realised that the Mini was a one off and this quote serves as an epitaph and a warning to all manufacturers, "If one pioneers something, and it is not copied, then it's a failure...Small cars are so boring, they are ghastly, they all look the same because they are designed by committees trying to copy the Mini."

The 998cc engine's time was limited as the E type tag was dropped in 1988 and it became the simple City again. Head restraints and three spoke steering wheel made a significant difference inside and there was even an extra 1 bhp under the bonnet. Mayfair models now had radio/cassettes and minor trim changes to tempt buyers. A standard brake servo certainly made them safer in 1988 and an optional catalytic converter a year later meant that they could be fashionably green too. In spite of this, the most ancient A series power units had to die, but not before some serious marketing attention had been turned to the run out models. On the City this meant full width wheel trims a return to chrome bumpers and snazzy harlequin trim. The Mayfair also got the glam treatment with a chrome effect grille, chrome Mayfair badge on the boot, colour keyed door mirrors and number plate lamp.

September 1993 Mileage: 98,862 Amount Spent: £0. 1967 Morris Mini Cooper sold for £1300. Minis in my Life: 1964 Austin Mini Cooper.
MOT: no

My Mini Cooper it's part in my Breakdown

With the Morris Mini Cooper sold for peanuts I thought it was time to sort the original one out. So I packed it all off to The East Anglian Mini Centre in Ipswich. Ted Sparrow had done such a good job with the Morris. So it seemed logical that he should have a crack at getting the original Cooper in my life sorted out. So I dragged the Mini out the barn. Well towed actually. Had to hitch a rope to it and the other end to my Golf GTI and pull. Seized solid, I managed to free it up eventually and stick on a trailer and send it in the general direction of Suffolk.

Ted started work as promised and stripped it right down to the bare shell, which is when the trouble started. Criminals wrecked his business by breaking in and pinching all his tools. Ted not surprisingly lost the will to carry on. With no where to store cars anymore the Mini Cooper came back home, but not in one piece. There were boxes and boxes and a gearbox attached to an A Series engine, and even more boxes. The lovely spacious double garage I had was now full of Mini Cooper reduced to its constituent parts. It wasn't a pretty sight.

I was busy and this was the last thing I needed. It was all a little depressing, and then I got something in the post. It was the Heritage certificate. British Motor Industry Heritage Trust who administered all the old vehicle records from BMC. It was a relatively new service in the early 1990s and for a few quid I could find out the build date and what the original specification was. Printed on mottled paper with fancy blue edging, a gold crest at the top and archivist Anders Ditlev Clausager's signature at the bottom, it was fascinating reading. The first owner had wisely ordered a fresh air heater. Its date of birth was 17th June 1964. The colours, Almond Green with Old

My Mini Cooper it's part in my Breakdown

English White Roof with Porcelain Green and Dove Green interior, despite my attempts at respraying and retrimming, were also correct. Oh yes, and that the engine under the bonnet was 1cc smaller than anyone had originally realised.

I had always been told that what I had was a 997cc Cooper, those rare first generation models which wasn't that quick, but was the beginning of something special. In fact the V5 registration document also believed that it was a 997cc. I didn't know why it was changed, whether someone lied for insurance or resale purposes, but the truth was in bold type at the top of the certificate and read AUSTIN MINI COOPER MARK 1 (998cc).

By now I really didn't care. I had a rusty old Mini in bits and not a clue as to what I should do next. I pushed down the garage door and walked away. Sobbing.

17. **That grim special edition period when the Austin Rover/Rover Group marketing departments suddenly discovered that they could tart up the Mini and then sell it for a few extra bob to loyal but gullible customers, so here is a roll call of shame, detailing those dreadful special editions, *'Mini Cock-Ups, the lot of them'*, said Rowan Atkinson, and he was right.**

Just when the Mini looked as though it was heading for retirement in the '80s, Austin Rover suddenly discovered that they could never create enough special editions. In marketing terms it was a relatively simple repackaging exercise, which meant that it brought the car to the public's attention for a token outlay. For the price of some decals, maybe a snazzy paint scheme and a creative approach to the options list, the Mini was dangled in front of consumers who behaved as if the car had never existed. The truth was that many buyers actually needed reminding that the Mini was still on sale and this was a cheap way of doing it. Certainly a lot cheaper than actually spending serious development money to upgrade the car mechanically. It was not just in the UK that the specials struck a cord, in certain markets, like Japan and France, they could not get a enough of them. The Mini may have been a mass market 'people's car' but it was now the most niche of automotive products. As every limited edition sold out, the accounts department celebrated as profits and volumes soared.

The special edition syndrome was not a new phenomenon, BMC had begun celebrating production milestones with the millionth Minors in 1961, badged Minor 1,000,000s. The Mini first entered the special edition zone in 1976 and this trend looks set to continue for as long as the car stays in production.

One can only speculate what Issigonis made of such frivolous marketing exercises. To the Mini purist each adventure down the slippery special edition route was a disaster. Writing in 1991 about a Mini Cooper that Car magazine were giving away in a competition, Rowan Atkinson took the time to identify the enduring appeal of the Mini and launch a well-deserved attack on the roll call

238

of minimum production Minis. "Endless limited editions have attempted to maintain the appeal with only cosmetic titivation. We hereby recall, with fond memories, the Mini Sprite, Ritz, Chelsea, Designer, Advantage, Park Lane, 30, Studio 2, Sky, Flame, Rose, 25, Checkmate, Piccadilly, Jet Black, Red Hot, Flaming Stupid. An absurd Odyssey of marketing speak, being merely applications of make-up to what was perceived to be a tired old face, when in fact the Mini has elegant, classical features, that are ruined by crude face paint. Mini Cock-Ups, the lot of them."

Just in case you wondered about the name, launch date, approximate production and retail price of all those Minis, here in full are 20 years of special editions... Please note: the production figures for UK only.

Under all those 'period' extras is the first in a long line of limited edition Minis.

Limited Edition • January 1976 • 3,000 • £1,406

This is where it all started. With no particular anniversary in mind, not that any manufacturer ever needs an excuse, British Leyland introduced the cosmetically enhanced Mini Limited Edition. Based on the 1000 the paint work was green and white with a gold coach line. If that was not bad enough a distinctly '70s interior comprised an orange-striped brush nylon seats similar in style to contemporary MGB upholstery. At least the seats reclined and there were eyeball fresh air vents, yet to be standardised on the 1000. This was the style of things to come although the British public had to wait another three years for a follow up.

1100 Special • August 1979 • 5,100 • £3,300

Here is the first and one of the very few Mini limited editions with a point: the celebration of 20 years of Mini production. It was the most clearly thought out special edition with tangible differences from the standard model. Consequently it was also the most successful, as the projected run of 2,500 was upped to 5,000 units, with 5,100 eventually shifted.

Based on the 1000, with the familiar Mark III body, there the similarity ended. Under the bonnet was the Clubman's 1,098cc, 45bhp engine. This meant better than 998cc average performance with an 84mph top speed and sprightly 16.6sec to 60mph acceleration. On the outside customers could choose a Rose metallic paint with tan vinyl roof, or Silver metallic with black vinyl on top. Graded side stripes ran a few inches above the sills, leading to prominent matt black wheel arch extensions, over wide 165/70 tyres, which surrounded 5 x 10 alloys. On the front wings were side indicators. There was Clubman bumpers front and rear, locking petrol cap, tinted glass and a 'Special' badge on the boot lid.

On the inside the Special had numerous 1275GT features including sports steering wheel, centre console and a three-instrument binnacle. A radio, clock, lighter and cubby tray occupied the console and there was even more storage space with an additional tray above the passengers knee. Tartan check upholstery and cut pile carpets completed the highly successful Mini 1100 picture.

Sprite • October 1983 • 2500 • £3334

Based on the City the Sprite had bright Primula Yellow, or Cinnabar Red paint with wide side stripes separated by a 'Sprite' logo on the rear side panels. There were several carry overs from the 1100 special, including identical alloys and wheel arch extensions. Inside was a three-dial binnacle, eyeball vents and four spoke steering wheel. Inside the seats had grey herringbone material topped off with black plastic head restraints.

25 • July 1984 • 5000 • £3865

Another celebration, another Mini special, this time the car's 25th birthday. The silver anniversary meant giving a Mayfair a silver paint job and a bucket load of logos. A grey and red coach line ran around the bodywork with Mini 25 on the rear panels, boot and even the wheel centres. A silver grey paint scheme extended to the wheel arches, bumpers, grille, door mirrors and handles. The silver 25 theme extended to the interior with 25 logoed Flint velvet seat trim (the front seats even had zippered pockets in front of the squabs), edged with red piping plus grey and red carpets. A three-instrument binnacle faced the driver who grabbed hold of a leather bound steering wheel with a '25' on the boss. In car entertainment came in the shape of a radio/cassette conveniently positioned for passenger operation with two rear parcel shelf mounted speakers ready to fill the cabin with noise. The most notable innovation was the 12in (30.4cm) wheels and front discs, which had yet to find their way onto the standard production car.

241

Ritz • January 1985 • 3725 • £3798

First of the mid '80s special edition cascade, which involved tarting up a basic City. The initial theme was upmarket London locations, hence the Ritz. Obviously Austin Rover was inspired by the success of the 25. A Silver leaf metallic paint scheme, a red triple coach line ran around the body broken up with Ritz logos on the rear side panels and boot lid. Nimbus Grey paint was used to colour key the grille, wheel arches, roof gutter and driver's door mirror. There was more grey on the alloy wheels and proper chrome on the door handles, bumpers, boot handle and even the exhaust pipe. Inside the Mayfair equipped cockpit there were more Ritz logos on the seats with colourful red, blue and grey velvet striped trim. Blue extended to the fascia, seat belts, carpets and door pockets.

Chelsea • January 1986 • 1500 • £3,898

More SW postcodes, this time in the shape of the Chelsea. City E based it followed a familiar pattern. Mayfair instrumentation, alloy wheels, three Chelsea logos on the outside and inside on the seats. Although the seat trim was grey with red piping the exterior colour was Targa Red with twin red/silver coach lines.

My Mini Cooper it's part in my Breakdown

Piccadilly • May 1986 • 2500 • £3928

Austin Rover had hit their stride by now and moved into the West End with the Piccadilly. Yet another City E, this time with full width plastic wheel trims, although chrome made a welcome return to the bumpers and door handles. Cashmere Gold was the exterior colour whilst the velvet interior was dark, with beverage based, Chocolate, Coffee and Claret, brownish clash. This model set the trend for most future limited editions: few luxurious touches and plenty of cosmetic frippery. Standard push button radio, head restraints and three spoke steering wheel were not much to get excited about, yet these packages proved to be a roaring success in both home and export markets.

Park Lane • January 1987 • 4000 • £4194

The final model in the otherwise curious quartet of London based limited editions, saw Rover back in Mayfair with the Park Lane. All black paintwork this time contrasted by chrome bumpers and door handles. The logo was a little bolder this time as it occupied the lower part of the rear panel and extended onto the door. Inside it was stripy beige and black velvet, plus logos and a stereo radio/cassette.

Advantage • May 1987 • 4675 • £4286

My Mini Cooper it's part in my Breakdown

An iffy play on the rules of tennis perhaps, but this untapped seasonal theme proved popular enough for the company to return to it repeatedly over the years. If Queen's Club had not been so stuffy, this could have been the Mini Wimbledon, allowing Rover to explore all sorts of new SW postcodes. Instead it remained the Advantage, launched to coincide with Wimbledon fortnight. The promotional picture is not remotely sexist or reminiscent of a certain poster that adorned many an adolescent bedroom wall.

Of course the colour scheme had to be pure Diamond White, with colour keyed wheel trims. The logo featured a tiny tennis ball full stop and running along the flanks was a tennis net inspired pattern. Otherwise it was City E matt black bumpers, grille, wheel arches and door handle. Inside there was the usual Mayfair instrument installation with more tennis net type upholstery patterns finished in grey and green.

Jet Black & Red Hot • January 1988 • 6000 • £4382
As the names suggested, the Red Hot was painted red with contrasting black coach line and logo. The Jet Black was exactly the opposite. What they both had in common was chrome bumpers and door handles with silver and red lined wheel trims. Inside were black velour seats with red piping, black carpets and trim. On the grille was their own identifying badge. Tinted glass, push button radio and three spoke steering wheel were all part of the very simple package.

Designer • June 1988 • 2000 • £4654

The Designer Mini is the point at which Rover fully embraced '80s marketing values without a hint of irony. Well actually, there was a proposal to name it the Mini Mary Quant to associate the special edition with the swinging '60s and all that. In the end they settled on Designer, although the Mary Quant daisy logo survived on the bonnet in place of the usual Mini badge and her influence extended to a heavily branded Quant interior.

Available in either black, or white, the usual items of chrome, or matt black exterior trim were finished in grey. Inside the upholstery was black and white striped with Quant's signature on each seat. The leather-trimmed steering wheel had another Quant daisy on the boss and the driver even had a vanity mirror to gaze into.

My Mini Cooper it's part in my Breakdown

Racing • Flame • January 1989 • 2000 • £4795
Here Rover was feeling their way back towards
the retro appeal of the Cooper. The Racing was finished in
British Racing Green with a contrasting white roof whilst
the Flame was red and white. Unfortunately alloy wheels
were not on the Cooperesque menu, owners had to make
do with full width white trims, but a couple of nods in the
direction of performance were the sports steering wheel
and rev counter.

Rose • Sky • January 1989 • 1000 • £4695
The Rose and Sky was Rover's soft touch to the
hard-nosed Racing and Flame. The colour schemes for
these models were almost offensive, finished in white with
either a pastel blue (Sky), or pastel pink (Rose) roof. It got
even worse inside with pink and blue upholstery.

Thirty • June 1989 • 3000 • £5,599
Happy 30th birthday. Not only was this a pretty
decent limited edition in terms of presentation and
equipment, it also represented a watershed in modern
Mini development, providing the basis for the imminent
relaunch of the Cooper.

Based on the Mayfair the effort put into the two
pearlescent paint colours, red and black was the most
immediately striking feature and given extra sheen by a
coat of lacquer. The logo was actually more of a crest, with

elements of the old Austin marque crossed with rampant British lions and the legend 1959-1989 running beneath it. A feature of the bonnet badge the crest was also applied to the rear side panels with twin coach lines leading from them. The door mirrors and wheel arches were colour matched, but the most welcome retro element was the increase in bright work, as the grille, door handles and bumpers shone brightly again. Best of all the car sat on eight spoke Minilite-type alloys. As usual the interior had seat logos, but there was a real touch of luxury about the black leather seat bolster, red piping, red leather steering with a logo on the boss and red pile carpet. Not only that, there was a leather bound Mini book waiting for every buyer.

Racing Green • Flame Red • Check Mate • February 1990 • 2500 • £5455

These models were the clearest indications yet that a full scale Cooper revival was just around the corner. Two old names were lengthened into Racing Green and Flame Red and were joined by a new one, Check Mate. Chrome bumpers, those lovely eight spoke alloys and two-tone paint schemes, the Check Mate being black with a white roof. They all had a crossed chequered flag badge on the bonnet and inside it was black seat trim and three-instrument binnacle. A significant technical update was the adoption of the original Cooper S final drive ratio of 3.44:1. An automatic gearbox may have been an option but the most exciting add on goody was the Rover approved John Cooper performance kit which actually turned it into a Cooper.

Studio 2 • June 1990 • 2000 • £5455

Just when you thought that Rover were getting the hang of these special editions they went back to their bad old ways. Maybe they had some old graphics left over from a Metro Special of the same name last seen in '87 and '88. The logos were stuck to the front edge of the doors and the rest was limited edition business as usual. Based on a City, the grille was now chrome, but the bumpers weren't. Colour schemes were Black, blue, or grey. Inside there were doeskin seat covers with a green diagonal stripe.

1990 Mini Minor • 1990 • 1 • £?

Here's a special edition that never was. Occasionally Rover's special vehicles department come up with a concept that does not hit the marketing spot. If rejected they disappear, but this one sneaked out. Based on a Studio 2, it was intended specifically for the Japanese market as a 30th anniversary special edition. The idea was to make a modern copy of the oldest production Mini, registered 621 AOK and parked in the Heritage Motor Centre. Painted a very special creamy shade of Old English White the special vehicles department went as far as sticking dummy exterior door hinges on according to surviving studio pictures, plus mark I hub caps. Inside the original red and cream upholstery was copied, but stripped out before the car was sold. However, the red carpets, headlining and unique 'M' logo gear knob remained. This example belonged to Lynn Thompson.

Neon • February 1991 • 1500 • £5835

Yet another City with an unwise makeover. The name suggested brightness when it was in fact quite dull. The only real bright spots were the chrome work, on bumpers, door handles, grille and the exhaust pipe. Nordic

Blue metallic was the prevailing colour scheme offset by a coach line leading back to a slightly bizarre Neon by Mini logo. Perhaps this was an early '90s realisation of the importance of the Mini brand. Mayfair wheel trims and a passenger door mirrors did not whip up too much excitement, especially as the Chevron velour upholstery hardly grabbed the attention.

British Open Classic • June 1992 • 1000 • £7195

Rover was after some Golfing allusion, plus a dodgy pun with this one, but the results were impressive. This was the first limited edition based on the 1.3 Mini and also the first time a British model had an opening sunroof. And what a sunroof, not some pokey plastic moon roof job, but a proper electrically operated, full-length fabric affair. The coat of arms made an impressive comeback on the rear panels and bonnet badge and heaven knows how they swung it, but Rover also stitched in a 'By appointment to Her Majesty the Queen' label into the front seats. Brilliant. Those lovely alloys were back and so was all the other chrome, although the door mirrors were colour keyed metallic British Racing Green. A wind deflector kept out draughts from above and inside there was true luxury. Countryman Tweed upholstery with leather seats and steering wheel.

Italian Job • October 1992 • 1750 • £5995

A special edition waiting to happen since 1969. Trouble is, The Italian Job turned out to be a big disappointment. Named after the film, which also inspired excursions in the name of charity to Italy, sought to capitalise on the seminal film's fun factor. It didn't. Despite a jaunty crossed British and Italian flag logo on the bonnet and rear panels they failed to excite. One reason was the standard 1275cc engine under the bonnet, a long way off Cooper tune. Their appearance was meant to resemble the cars featured in the film and though there was a red, white and blue options, British Racing Green, a colour never used on the screen cars. Bonnet stripes echoed the Cooper, rather than the bonnet strapped film star Minis and there were just two spot lamps, rather than three. The alloys were curiously painted white, as was the grille, which resembled a Mark I Minor. Inside was black tweed trim and the Mayfair's instruments.

Clearly Rover were building this model to a price, but if anyone genuinely wanted to look the Italian Job part they simply bought a Cooper.

Rio • June 1993 • 750 • £5495

Another mid '90s example of Rover getting lazy. A spruced-up Mini Sprite amounted to no more than special paint work: pearlescent Caribbean Blue, Black, or metallic Polynesian Turquoise, with Rio logos and black interior. Internal bonnet release and radio/cassette were at least useful.

Tahiti • October 1993 • 500 • £5795

If there is any significance to be gained by looking at the production figures, 500 units possibly reflects the lessening popularity of the standard Mini as buyers flocked to the Cooper. The nicest things about the Tahiti were the alloys and arguably the Tahiti Blue paintwork. Chrome bumpers were nice, but Rover penny pinched by not fitting opening rear windows. The interior was only notable for having new style seats whilst the trim was predominately finished in black. If anyone was interested, an automatic version cost almost £1000 extra.

35 • June 1994 • 200 • £6695

With the 35, Rover missed a prime opportunity, whereas as previous anniversary cars had made an effort to stand out from the mainstream Mini crowd, the 35 was understated to the point of anonymity. Sprite based, the colour options were white, pearlescent red and a metallic blue with a silver side stripe. Chrome was on the menu, dished out in the direction of bumpers, grille and door handles. Unique 35 logos on the rear flanks and bonnet badge were the only clues that this model was something special. Things perked up inside with so called Jamboree trim, a blue and pink concoction, which partly covered the seats and doors. And that was it.

Sidewalk • May 1995 • 1000 • £5895

The Sidewalk is the standard Sprite makeover. Once again there were three colour options from White Diamond through to Charcoal metallic and Kingfisher Blue. The latest in a long line of slightly bizarre logos included the obvious Side Walk, whilst a star design stamp proclaimed 'Authentic Mini'. How odd. Inside it was authentically Caledonian with a vivid blue tartan trim contrasted by red seatbelts.

EquinoX • April 1996 • £6195

Described as the 'Heavenly Mini EquinoX' this special edition was designed for no apparent reason, well none that Rover could explain anyway, around a zodiac theme. The decals comprised a large sun surrounded by the moon and stars, all very new age. As ever, three colours: Pearlescent Amaranth Purple, Charcoal metallic and Platinum Silver metallic. Chrome bumpers and grille were standard along with tinted glass and opening rear quarter lights. Inside the Sun, Moon and Stars theme was woven in Purple into the upholstery.

And that's not all the special editions, there is a whole raft of them after 1997 too, flick forward to see how the Mini became special again.

This is what the special edition syndrome had come to by 1996, the triumph of some sort of weird style over the substance of a jollied up Mini. This was the confusing image used in press advertising to communicate that the Mini was a fashion statement.

My Mini Cooper it's part in my Breakdown

October 1994. Mileage: 98,862 Amount spent: £1000 to buy a 1962 Austin Mini. Minis in my Life: 1964 Austin Mini Cooper. 1962 Austin Mini. MOT: Not for either Minis.

I was looking for a short cut to restoring the Mini Cooper and one presented itself in 1994. I still spent and inordinate amount of time looking at classified advertisements with Minis in them. What leapt out at me was the simple fact this was a Mark 1 Mini, which was already finished in Almond Green with a white roof. Suddenly I thought that another rapid restoration was on the cards. Not only that it was located just thirty miles away. I had to go and see it.

I remember it was a crisp and cold early Sunday morning when I excitedly left my house. Indeed, I was so excited about it that I forgot to take the keys out of my front door when I left. But I'll come to back to that later. I drove to a fairly remote house with outbuildings and met a fairly young man who had clearly started something, which he was now not inclined to finish. There was probably some parental pressure too to get shot of it all so that he could fund the next stage of his life. When I tugged the sheet back in the garage I found a Mini that had been repaired and resprayed to a reasonable standard. I knew that even in those far off days restoring a Mini bodyshell was now a furiously expensive and quite complicated thing to do. So I wanted this Mini especially as it came with boxes and boxes of spares plus a reconditioned A Plus engine from an Austin Mini Metro.

The seller seemed a little surprised that I agreed so readily, but to me this seemed like the perfect solution to a problem that I had already created. The ever patient Mrs Ruppert obviously didn't see it this way, not least because a trailer full of more Mini would be arriving within the week. Even so I was still so excited I couldn't wait to break the happy news. As I reversed into the drive I could see my front door keys in the lock. All I had to do was jump out and snatch them out. Mrs Ruppert got there first. Quite rightly she argued that there had been a breach of security. That meant I had to go out again and buy a brand new lock and fit it. I think that was probably a way of not having to discuss the arrival of yet another Mini.

As it turned out the Mini arrived on a trailer when I was away on a job. Mrs Ruppert pushed it into the garage with all the other Mini bits. It was now crammed completely full of Mini.

Just what I didn't need, yet another Mini and yet another Austin, or more boxes with bits of Mini in them.

18. **Punk turns to new romanticism and then plinky plonk electronica and finally computer generated drum machine dominated pappy pop, but the Mini still thinks the Beatles are at the top of the hit parade, meanwhile every other manufacturer is dancing to a brand new beat with a shopping hatchback for every possible taste, here's the mostly true story of what happened to the small car between 1977 and 1989.**
Minis made in 1977 214,134 • 1978 196,799 • 1979 165,502 • 1980 150,067 • 1981 69,986 • 1982 56,297 • 1983 49,956 • 1984 35,038 • 1985 34,974 • 1986 33,720 • 1987 37,210 • 1988 36,574 • 1989 40,998

The future may have been hatch shaped in Britain, but the boot was not going anywhere especially in many international markets. From February 1977 the booted Derby version of the Volkswagen Polo was introduced, which wasn't much to get worked up about. Then from 1981 the Polo got a revised body so that it looked at best like a van, but with windows.

Revised Polo looked like a mini estate car, or van.

In 1980 Ford's Fiesta buyers could now choose an entry level Popular with black door handles and vinyl trim. Beyond that the Popular Plus offered rear wash/wipe, centre console and cloth trim. GL had centre console, radio and clock. Then the Popular Plus replaces the base model in 1982 Popular Plus E with economy engine. There were S and Ghias too. Sorry about all that boring spec talk, but here's proof that Ford played to their strengths with a trim level for every budget. The facelifted model in 1983 just softened the edges a bit and featured a blunt front, which even added a few inches to the length. Not only did the car get bigger, so did the range of engines. Buyers could step up to a 1.3 and 1.4 litre lump under the bonnet plus there was even a diesel.

Over at Fiat in 1977 they moved on to the Series II 127s, which had a redesigned front end and a new 1049cc engine, produced in Brazil, that still sold alongside the older 903cc engine. Three levels of trim became available, the 'L', 'C' and 'CL'. A five door 127, the Panorama estate and a 1301cc diesel engine soon became an option. The final, series III arrived in 1981, but Fiat was more than pleased with the huge sales figures when production ceased in 1983. Plus they had the prefect replacement.

Fiat Uno was now the smart, modern and practical supermini that everyone wanted in the 1980s.

Now the Fiat Uno in three-door form might just have been pitched against a Metro, whereas the five door was up against the Maestro. Throughout the '80s and '90s a lot of hatchbacks would start to grow up and leave the Mini behind to fight it out with the tiny tot city cars. However, the creaky old 126 which by 1977 had a new 652cc, 24bhp engine was now looking unworthy of the Mini, because by far the closest Mini rival from Fiat was a small car with a cuddly name.

**The boxy Panda, yet another brilliant
small car from Fiat.**

Actually the Panda wasn't cuddly to look at all, resembling the crate it may have been delivered in. A riot of rectangular and flat panels, including a windscreen that was flat as the glass in your greenhouse. This was all part of a programme to make the Panda cheap to fix and easy to live with. As a piece of industrial design it was very clever and came with a 903cc engine, but also in several markets with the 126's barely adequate 769cc.

Moving across the Med to Spain a close relative of the Panda was badged as the SEAT Marbella. Although the company had close ties to Fiat, those had finished before Volkswagen took a majority stake. The Marbella wasn't nearly as nice as Fiat's version, with old unrefined engines and the original basic suspension. So not a particularly nice concoction with a bland front end and the lower half plastic mouldings making it look like a very cheap toy.

Hold on, almost forgot, the 126 was still alive when in 1987 it underwent a significant transformation when a water-cooled flat twin 704cc engine producing 26bhp was installed and the model was relaunched as the 126bis. Now capable of just reaching 70mph the engine was mounted horizontally instead of vertically. This new arrangement allowed significantly more space for rear luggage space and allowed the bodywork to become a three-door, accommodate a one-piece hatchback and a folding rear seat. Goodness me, was it really worth all that bother?

Clearly old Fiats refuse to die, they just get a crummy badge from some crummy communist car plant. The 127 was no exception when it was resurrected as the Yugo 45, 55 and 65. Made by the Zastava who were located in Serbia and partly owned by Fiat, the war in that region did not help matters as the company entered the '90s. For the moment though the unremarkable hatch styling with an unfeasibly high loading sill, cramped interior and dated engines did not make it very appealing. Especially as the build quality was marginal. The equally marginal price meant that some buyers could overlook such shortfalls, but eventually it would all end in tears.

Lancia Y10 was ahead of its time as a premium priced small car.

Back to Italy and the Lancia Y10 in 1985. Effectively a reworked Uno it bears comparison to the Mini because it only came with three doors. Premium priced and with Lancia's reputation for unreliability and rust to contend with, it was never a serious small car player. Available though until 1992. Lancia officially retreated from the UK two years later.

It is tempting to include the Talbot Sunbeam from 1977, so we might as well. Chrysler sold the Rootes Group of companies, Hillman, Sunbeam, Singer and Humber to Peugeot who then used the old Talbot name for cars marketed in the UK. Rootes had been working on what was their first supermini, the Sunbeam. Based on a shorter Hillman Avenger platform it had the now familiar flat-sided two box shape but with a sloped tailgate. It was

The Talbot Sunbeam 1.3 LS in appropriately French spec.

neat and practical and the smallest 928cc engine could be traced back to the Imp, whilst the bigger units were from the Avenger. This now seems like a class up from the Mini and perhaps the closest in spirit would be the Chryslered Samba in 1982. This was yet another version of the Peugeot 104 that the British buying public had already tired of in both Peugeot and Citroen flavours. So it didn't make much of an impression.

The Nova, here in Opel rather than Vauxhall trim.

My Mini Cooper it's part in my Breakdown

Vauxhall came to the small hatchback market even later than Ford. Some might suggest that the rear drive Chevette three door in 1975 was a good attempt at a homegrown small hatchback before all designs were farmed out to General Motors in Europe. Certainly it handled well, was successful in rallying and had a usefully practical boot. Sadly though it is the Nova (Opel Corsa everywhere else) from 1983 which is best remembered as one of the most significant entrants into the small car market. Two box styling like everyone else, but the bulging wheel arches was the only nice touch and might explain why first time driving youngsters liked it. Otherwise there was plenty to choose from with a big range of engines and also body styles, which also included saloons.

Daihatsu Cuore L60 representing what the company did best.

Daihatsu, in their role as the Toyota small car division, continued to come up with tiny cars such as the twin cylinder Cuore. There was also the Domino in 1983, which undersized the already compact Charade. It had a 617cc twin cylinder engine although in 1986 another cylinder was added and the engine size shot up to 846cc. The point is that in five door form it was six inches (15cm) longer than a Mini, yet the interior felt much more cramped.

My Mini Cooper it's part in my Breakdown

**The Suzuki SC100 also known as the Cervo Coupe
in some markets.**

Equally cramped inside was the Suzuki SC100, but then buyers could not expect too much from this tiny, but quite brilliant model. Badged as the Fronte in the home market, in 1979 the UK got a 1.0 litre engine mounted at the rear. Buzzy but fun, the stubby fastback styling was brilliant and incredibly there were even rear seats. The Alto from 1981 was a more practical proposition with either four or five doors. Big in Japan it always struggled in the UK with it's 3-cylinder engine. There were a couple of versions of the Swift and the SA310 from 1984 to 1986 was still very compact at 11 feet 9 inches (3.58m), but didn't find many takers outside of Japan.

Another minor player, Subaru, had one of the more interesting small cars in the shape of the Justy. Effectively an off road shopping trolley, except that no one would ever stray off the tarmac. The three-cylinder engine worked hard and the simple four-wheel drive system even harder.

Honda had the City in Japan, but British Leyland owned the rights to the name in the UK hence the Mini City. Which is why the Honda City became the Jazz. Available for not very long at all (1984-85), the very advanced toddler was subject to the overall import restrictions, which meant Honda would rather bring in more profitable Civics and Accords. Despite looking really rather boxy it would have made a brilliant Mini City considering how closely the two companies were in the

1980s. Rather than a Ballade badged as a Rover 200, surely this City would have made far more financial sense? Indeed, if the Metro had been a lot more like this the Mini might have been retired an awful lot earlier.

Honda City. It could have been a Rover City with a bit of persuasion.

Toyota replaced the largely overlooked 1000 (Publica) with the equally dull Starlet. Unlike almost every other supermini of the period, 1978, and despite appearances the Starlet was resolutely front engined and rear wheel drive. However, in 1984 Toyota did the decent thing and revamped the little car so that the front wheels now did all the work. Very compact and just two feet (60cm) longer than a Mini it at least had a five speed gearbox and just the one 999ccc engine option.

The Mitsubishi Colt is worth a mention because imported in 1978 it was the company's first front wheel drive model. Compact, tidy and spacious, after 1984 it would become especially so in 5-door form, but too large to be considered in the same class as the Mini. Equally, Nissan's Micra from 1983 was all grown up as a five-door hatch, but the three door was just about a Mini rival. It appealed to buyers that wanted reliability and indestructible mechanicals rather than style. Yet another '80s box on wheels that was deathly dull, but at least it started first time, every time.

**The quite dreary Nissan Micra. If you want
interesting then see below.**

With the Renault 5 in circulation and after the grim 104, Peugeot were obliged to do something more interesting. The 205 certainly looked good having been designed by the people best known for styling Ferraris. Pininfarina came up with a pert, pretty and well-proportioned small car that looked lovely as a three door, just as good when stretched to four and a bundle of fun when the roof was removed. At two inches over 12 feet long (3.7m) it was just the right side of compact, but it didn't just look good. Much was made of the car's suspension as it soaked up uneven road surfaces like a much bigger car.

**The Peugeot 205 in its purist three door and 1.1 litre
engined form.**

My Mini Cooper it's part in my Breakdown

There was plenty of grip around corners, good steering at speed, with fine brakes and an easy gear change. Everyone who got behind the wheel loved it, especially the performance ones. Replacing the original engines in a major 1988 revamp made a good car into a great one.

Just as Peugeot raised their game, in 1984 Renault went back to the 5 and revamped it. They did not fiddle much with the already neat, practical and stylish bodywork, but did go for a fully transverse engine like all the other superminis. Diesel power was becoming more important so that was added to the range in 1986 and the 5 settled down to life as an uncomplicated, faithful little hatch.

Mini Running Total 1977 4,237,448 • 1978 4,434,247 • 1979 4,599,749 1980 4,749,816 • 1981 4,819,802 • 1982 4,876,099 • 1983 4,926,055 1984 4,961,093 • 1985 4,996,067 • 1986 5,029,787 • 1988 5,103,571 1989 5,144,569

1996 – 1997 Mileage: 98,896. Amount Spent: £1400 on the Austin.
Minis in my Life: 1964 Austin Mini Cooper. 1962 Austin Mini.
MOT: Cooper no. Austin Mini Yes.

My Mini Cooper it's part in my Breakdown

I had to do something with the immense amount
of Mini now back in my possession, as there was now no
room to move. So I called up a local Mini spares specialist
who knew the value of what I had and a bloke came round
and offered me much less. We reached a compromise of
course, but even after he left with a van full of spares
there still seemed like an awful lot of Mini left.

I am not quite sure how I came across Mark Nolan
who ran Mini specialist Bank Garage in the
Cambridgeshire Fens. I think it was do with some
magazine story I worked on. Nolan is a colourful
Liverpudlian who had even spent time as a Formula 1
mechanic with the Fittipaldi team. That was good enough
for me. He was close enough to drop into for a cup of tea,
plus I would always see interesting Minis. Like what was
rumoured to be John Lennon's customised Cooper S.
Putting the Mini together would cost just £400 plus
'whatever'. The 'whatever' was around £1000.

We looked at all the bits and pieces and decided
that at least we could make a Mini with a Metro A Plus
engine. It reminded me of my first Mini, but would look
like my Cooper. However, I certainly couldn't use Cooper
badging, it had to be a plain Austin Mini and there was a
reason for this...

My Mini Cooper it's part in my Breakdown

The great thing about my Mini Cooper living at Mark Nolan's Bank Garage is that I could pop in and see a Radford modified Mark II Cooper, which had a famous owner. Apparently this one was rumoured to be John Lennon's. It was bought by Nolan near the Beatle's last British home in Surrey. Mind you, the Clubman Camper van in the background would have fun and probably weighed less than the loaded Cooper.

Inside the 'Lennon Cooper', which had all the '60s mod cons. Imagine no possessions, was one of his lines. However, not really sure if this was actually his Cooper, but nice to think that John and Yoko planning their anti-war, stay in bed for a week protests, from the front seats.

19. **Back from the dead, the Mini Cooper rises in the east first then the locals get it back and all because a lovely bloke called John Cooper refused to believe that the car with his name on should never just fade away...**

Despite reports to the contrary, the Mini Cooper did not die in 1971. John Cooper from his British Leyland franchise could still sell you a brand new Mini up until the mid '80s when he switched allegiance to Honda. Cooper had built a 1071cc model in 1975 featuring the traditional Cooper colour scheme, so the genuine Mini Cooper never really went away. Always thinking ahead John Cooper Garages developed the Metro Monaco in 1982, taking the new hatchback in 1.3 HLS trim and tuning it for 100mph performance. On the outside were Wolfrace alloy wheels and a bold Cooper logo and stripes from sill to waist height. It predated the introduction of the dire MG versions, but BL were reluctant to cover the car under their warranty so the project did not progress any further. But there were stirrings in the Far East.

My Mini Cooper it's part in my Breakdown

John Cooper had been selling performance conversion kits to Japan for some time and the President of Austin Rover of Japan was well aware of the interest in the cars. To boost demand he contacted Cooper and asked if it was possible to transplant an MG Metro into a Mini. Cooper obliged by bringing the unit together with a Mayfair. Exported to Japan, the locals loved it. A formal request was made to initiate production of 1000 units, but getting the model through type approval put senior management off the idea. Instead Cooper satisfied the demand for a go-faster, far eastern Mini by putting together a kit in a timber packing case, which fitted into the rear seat.

A Cooper for the '90s in full retro effect. The winged bonnet badge a mix of the original Morris and Austin Cooper items. Minilite type wheels, themselves copies of Cooper Formula items. This is the production model, with no extra driving lights, or the limited edition white bonnet stripes with John Cooper's signature on them.

In 1989 management changes at Rover coincided with the Minis 30th anniversary. They liked the conversion and asked for a couple of cars to be produced so that a warranty test could be carried out. After 20,000 miles, approval was granted and the company listened to John Cooper's suggestion for a celebratory model.

My Mini Cooper it's part in my Breakdown

Production of a Cooper-alike in the shape of the special edition Mini Racing and Flame, which had duo tone paintwork and Minilite type alloy wheels, was the result. Just in case anyone was in any doubt of their future intentions, a John Cooper Conversion Kit was added to the options list. This comprised twin SU HS2 carburettors, a Janspeed cylinder head, which had been polished and flowed, bigger inlet valves, hardened valve inserts and a 9.75:1 compression ratio. A twin box exhaust system and 3.1:1 final drive completed the performance picture. The output was boosted to 64bhp at 6000rpm and the 998cc engine became less of an also ran.

The full-scale resurrection of the Cooper occurred in 1990 when Rover again listened to wise old John Cooper and agreed to fit the 1275cc engine to the car. He built a twin carburettor prototype which went down very well with senior management, but the twin carbs presented a Type Approval problem. In the end the sub frame had to be moved 3/8ths of an inch (95mm) forward. All was then clear for Rover to take the Mini Thirty body shell and combine it with a 61 bhp, single carburettor, catalyst equipped 1275cc engine last seen in the old MG Metro. In performance terms it was nowhere near the old Cooper S, with a 12.2 sec 0-60mph time and a top speed of 92mph, but it was a move in the right direction. At first it was a limited edition of 1,650 cars, which featured white bonnet stripes. Minilite type alloy wheels, glass sunroof, driving lamps and door mirrors were all standard. Chrome also made a comeback with a slatted grille, bumpers and a winged Cooper bonnet badge. The two-tone colour schemes were back as the white roofs were contrasted by green, black, or red bodywork. The famous Cooper laurel logo decorated the rear side panel and a side stripe led to the tip of the front wing. On the inside there was half leather seat trim, red carpet and an equally red steering wheel. The first 1000 for the UK market came complete with John Cooper signature on the bonnet stripe.

By September of 1990 the Cooper became a proper production model. However, in the interests of economy the bonnet stripes, sunroof and spot lamps were dumped. Inside, the upholstery turned to cloth, the steering wheel went back to black, as did the carpets. If you wanted bonnet stripes, spot lamps and sunroof they could be ordered as extras.

Car magazine in their September 1990 issue undertook a monumental comparison, pitting the new Cooper against the ten best hot hatch rivals of the time. The line up was this: Mini Cooper v Alfa Romeo 33 16V v Citroen AX GT v Fiat Uno Turbo v Ford Fiesta RS Turbo v Mazda 323F GT v Metro GTi 16V v Peugeot 205 GTi 1.6 v Renault 5GT Turbo v Vauxhall Astra GTE 16V v Volkswagen Golf GTi, phew! Editor, Gavin Green placed the car first, "There's no doubt, on the Yorkshire assault course chosen for our shoot-out, it was the most inept. It groaned and whined when the others kept quiet; it bucked and bolted when the others gently cantered; and the seats are plain uncomfortable, seriously deficient in lateral support and rear seat movement. But I loved it...I suppose I loved it because I've always loved Minis. I also like small cars - any small car- and after more than 30 years, no-one has invented a smaller one."

LJK Setright also voted the Cooper in at number one, "The Mini shows that they are all too big, all slaves to showroom fashion. None shows the staunch independence that makes the Mini as refreshing as it always was, and makes it impossible for the others to bear comparison with it."

A 1.3i Cooper in full flight.

In March 1991 the Cooper got much nearer to the original car's sparkle with another conversion kit which finally turned it into an 'S'. The oil-cooled engine now produced 78 bhp and a handling package included low profile specially developed Dunlop SP Sport 165/60 R12 tyres and adjustable shock absorbers.

Performance Car tested the full 'S' equipped model in July 1991. The base car was a £6947, Rover Mini Cooper, the engine 'S' pack added £1878 and the Sports Handling Pack a further £671. "The bottom line is power up from 61 to 78bhp and torque up 67 to 78lb ft, these achieved at 6000 and 3250rpm respectively. What it means on the road is 0-60mph in a little over 10 seconds - quicker off the mark than the Vauxhall Nova SR or the VW Polo GT and a top speed close on 100 mph. Power and performance figures that match almost exactly those of the original car. Fuel economy remains outstanding; we averaged 36 mpg and we weren't hanging about." They really enjoyed driving it. "Few cars can match the Cooper S for sheer grip; those that can tend to be called Quattro or Cosworth...Those chunky Dunlops really bite an when they finally release their grip the S drifts through bends with astonishing poise, steering on the throttle. The tighter the turn the more the Cooper simply gets stuck in, sometimes lifting an inside wheel but never raising a doubt."

John Cooper himself rang up to ask how they were getting along with the car, "I didn't want the stripes on the bonnet, but otherwise it's got quite a bit of the old S about it. And it certainly handles. It gets the old adrenalin going, if you know what I mean..."

By October 1991 the Cooper was modified to comply with '90s emissions legislation as carburettors were replaced by fuel injection and a three-way catalytic converter. The new Cooper 1.3i was usefully quicker than the old model producing 63 bhp at 5,700rpm hitting 60mph in 11.5 seconds and on to a maximum of 92mph. The 1.3i came with those distinctive white bonnet stripes as standard once more. Inside there were 'Lightening pattern seat facings with leather bolsters and red piping. The red leather steering wheel was back along with equally bright carpets and even red instrument needles. In car entertainment was uprated with a R652 system, which as usual nudged the passenger's knees.

Inside a Mini Cooper 1.3i. Seats were trimmed in Lightening material with leather sides, plus red piping and a red Mylar strip for the doors and rear quarter casings. The driver held onto the red stitched leather steering wheel, put their feet on red carpets and looked at red needled instruments. Yes, there was a lot of red.

Enthusiasts did not have to wait long for the 1.3i to get the full 'S' treatment. A factory warranted Cooper conversion turned the car into the Si. 0-60mph in ten seconds and a ton (100) top speed made the Cooper something special again.

In March 1993 the emphasis was on beating the thief who had turned the Cooper into a 'hot' car for all the wrong reasons. Visible VIN (vehicle identification numbers) was now etched onto the front and rear screens. If that did not put them off then an alarm and engine immobiliser certainly would. Incredibly an internal bonnet release was finally standardised, as was a passenger door mirror.

**The limited edition accessory kit that is
the Monte Carlo**.

Special edition syndrome started to affect the Cooper 1991, although Rover cunningly disguised them as add on packs and kits. Firstly there was the Italian Job pack, which amounted to spot lamps, bonnet stripes and moulded boot liner. An RAC pack added tinted glass, sunroof and mud flaps. For the Full Monty Monte Carlo the finishing touches included sump guard, locking wheel nuts and a fire extinguisher. A Monte Carlo Anniversary pack in 1994 was largely cosmetic apart from a pair of spot lamps, and included white racing squares on the doors, decals and a coach line.

Car Magazine included this model in its September 1994 assessment of the 'Cheap Champs' picking five cars that dished up budget-priced fun by the bucketful. Gavin Green reckoned, "You don't have to go fast to have fun. Interesting cars aren't always good cars. It's possible to be kicked in the bum, get your eardrums bashed, be cramped, feel like you're riding inside a salt shaker - and still have a great time. I know this because I have just driven a Mini again....You wear a Mini, like a track suit, a pair of jeans or a suit (and the Mini is one of the few cars that can carry off all three roles). Never mind that the Mini isn't great transport, not by state of the art sensible (boring) 1990s standards. Instead, it's a little motorised chum."

Mini Cooper 35th Anniversary, seen here in the hands of 1968 European Touring Car Champion John Rhodes who is negotiating the chicane at the Goodwood racetrack. The car was finished in Almond Green and White paint work, just like the first Coopers.

In 1996 it was the Cooper's turn to celebrate 35 years in production hence...The Mini Cooper 35. Based on the standard Cooper 1.3i the paint scheme is pure '60s featuring Almond Green bodywork with a contrasting white roof, just as the original Cooper was presented back in 1961. There were also Gunmetal finish alloy wheels fitted with 165/60 R12 tyres, "Cooper' wheel centre badges and body coloured wheel arch extensions and door mirrors. There were also two fog lamps in addition to the standard main beam auxiliary lamps. On the inside the seats were inspired by the two tone originals with Porcelain Green leather upholstery, incorporating a Cooper logo embossed into the seats back; with colour coordinated leather steering wheel and gear knob. The Mini Cooper 35 retailed for £8195 and only 200 of these were built for the British market.

My Mini Cooper it's part in my Breakdown

The Mini Cooper can be viewed as little more than a slick marketing exercise. Certainly Rowan Atkinson writing about it in the November 1991 issue of Car magazine was not convinced. After laying into the limited editions, which multiplied during the '80s, Atkinson turned his attentions to the Cooper. "The depths of tackiness plumbed are still evident on the new Cooper. The nostalgia bred white stripes, white roof, tacky unpainted flared wheel arches, and driving lamps, just tinsel fripperies that attempt to distract you from the fact that they haven't spent any money at all. The only attractive Cooper element in my book is the stainless rather than black look radiator grille, which merely redresses an improvement of few years back. The original Mini shape is so good, so neat, that anyone who considers these nostalgia add-ons an improvement must be barmy. The car looks like a mobile Halfords promotion."

Cooper S still going strong in 1996. John Cooper stands next to Rover's cooking 1996 spec Cooper, his son Michael leans on to a John Cooper Garages 'Mini Cooper S' as Rover insisted on calling it.

Rover may have made a Cooper, but compared to what was now being offered by other manufacturers in the pocket rocket department, it was still tame. Luckily help was at hand.

Engineering Research and Application (ERA) was a great name from the past, which was acquired by the Jack Knight Group, and they put together a Mini that would perform a passable impression of a Cooper S. It turned out to be the fastest Mini ever built as the familiar 1275cc engine was boosted by a Garrett T3 turbocharger. The result was 94 bhp at 6120 rpm and a claimed 0 to 60mph time of 7.8 seconds and a top speed of 115mph. To cope with this extra power there were new front suspension arms and damper units with ventilated front discs with servo assistance. The spoked 6 x 13 alloys were shod with 165/60 13 low profile tyres. There were distinctive body modifications with a Dennis Adams styled kit which flared the arches, sills and added a deep front spoiler. Inside there were high backed sports seats, a new padded dashboard and a numbered plaque.

The 1989 ERA Turbo was endorsed by Rover, so you could order one through your local dealer and the first batch of 247 models was exported to Japan.

Then there was the Mini Cabriolet. The idea had been around for some time and Crayford produced the best-known versions in the 1960s. However, none was officially approved until June 1991. German Rover dealer LAMM Autohaus produced a Cabriolet based on the Mini Cooper and just 75 were imported into the UK as limited edition models. Although the running gear was all Cooper, the interior was Mini Mayfair, the dashboard timber and finished off with a body kit.

Rover followed this limited edition a year later with an even more official Cabriolet, which was launched in October 1992 at the Birmingham International Motor Show. Again based on the Cooper 1.3i it was developed by Rover Special Products and German coachbuilder, Karmann and built this time at Longbridge. The impressive strengthening work and comprised an extra sill made of thicker gauge steel, which covered the standard inner sill which meant that there were three sills in all. Tied to the extra sill was an extra strong cross member, which ran, as it does on the standard Mini, under the front seats. Also the foot wells on the Cabriolet were narrower than the standard car because reinforcement plates were welded into the area where the A pillars met the sills and floor structure. The A pillars also had a steel tube running inside them. And whilst the standard Mini has cubbyholes underneath the rear seat, a continuous sheet of steel reinforced the rear of the floorpan.

**ERA Turbo pictured outside the
British Embassy in Tokyo.**

Not only that, a U-shaped sheet steel structure surrounded the rear seats, and the B posts were also substantially reinforced. All that extra metal and the folding roof structure itself added 154lb (69.85 kilos) to the standard Cooper's 1521lb (689.9 kilos) kerb weight. The roof was colour coded, manually operated and folded back onto the parcel shelf. The rear windows wound down into the bodywork to disappear completely to make a truly open car. What a shame the Himalayan high hood, made all the passengers feel claustrophobic when perched at the rear. It looked fairly similar on the outside to the LAMM version because it too had a prominent bodykit. The alloy wheels were Revolution 12 x 5B five spokes, held on with lockable wheel nuts. There was extensive chroming on the door and boot handles, spot lamps, number plate lamp cover and 'Cabriolet' script kick plates.

The specification was, as befitted the most expensive production Mini ever, luxurious. The interior was dominated by a burr walnut dashboard, comprising three main dials and an analogue clock. The timber theme extended to the door caps, door pulls and gear knob. Cut-pile carpet covered the interior, unique high back, non-tilt seats were covered in Chevron trim. The driver gripped a leather steering wheel and was restrained by colour-keyed seat belts.

It's 1996 and the Cabriolet is just a few miles away from being deleted and from this angle, less chance of seeing the pram like profile.

There were just two colour schemes, Caribbean Blue with grey hood, or Nightfire Red with a red hood. Keeping it all safe and secure was an alarm, coded stereo, VIN etching on the class and a locking petrol cap.

Car magazine were not impressed when they reviewed the 1992 Birmingham Motor Show and the debut of the new model, "Absurd looking Mini Cabriolet looks like a pram without the handle, and doesn't look any less silly when someone climbs aboard, as an inspecting

Sir Graham Day proved on press day." When they got around to road testing it in their January 1994 issue the car hadn't got any prettier. "First I'll state the obvious: the Mini Cabriolet looks ridiculous and at £11,995 is ludicrously expensive. Good: now that's said, I can get on with enjoying myself." And so they did. "I've never driven a Mini that rides as well as this one...Even quite large furrows in the tarmac will not knock this car off line. You can achieve impressively high average speeds...In Britain, its outrageous price makes it an interesting chapter in the Mini's long running history, but no more."

That chapter in the Mini's life came to end in October 1996. Modifying the model to comply with the latest emissions, noise and safety regulations were too expensive. Meanwhile the Mini stayed in production, but for how much longer?

1997 – 1998 Mileage: 99,081 Amount Spent: MOT.
Minis in my Life: Austin Mini Cooper. Austin Mini.
MOT: Cooper no. Austin Mini yes.

My Mini Cooper it's part in my Breakdown

My nephew Graeme was just seventeen and needed a car to practice on and the Mini seemed the right car to use. My brother in law Stephen quite rightly had reservations. Weren't Mini's death traps? Designed in the 1950s before air bags and crumple zones, indeed the whole car was a crumple zone, it didn't seem to offer much in the way of protection. Probably quite a good thing if you don't want to produce yet another cocky, I'm invincible young driver. If you read the reports though, driving a Mini in the late Twentieth Century was on a par with piloting a coffin. According to safety researchers like Murray Mackay there was a lot to be worried about. Because the petrol filler cap stuck out, if the Mini rolled over then the cap would shear off. Also the door latch was nothing more than you would find on an internal door in your house. So that means if the bodywork stretched then the door would burst open and throw out the passengers. Front-hinged seats didn't help and of course there was not much of a crumple zone up front. That meant he engine would squeeze right up against the bulkhead and then keeping on going and land on the front seat passenger and driver's laps.

Clearly it was all very unsafe at any speed despite what Issigonis always said. He reckoned that because the handling was pin sharp it was driver's fault if they got into trouble. A few years later I had the opportunity to interview Russ Swift the legendary stunt driver. Best known for parking a Montego in a perpendicular fashion for a Rover TV advertisement and entertaining the public at car shows with his Mini antics. I asked if he thought they were safe. I don't remember much about the story he told me involving a Mini leaving the road at speed, but I can't forget the sight of him rolling up his trouser leg to reveal a spectacular scar.

I suppose my brother in law was right. That didn't stop him using the Mini when he was between cars for low level commuting. However, he'd forgotten that old cars don't have heated screens, and that water leaks were a way of life.

My nephew didn't mind though and he reckoned that the Cherry Bomb exhaust made it sound like a Lamborghini. After nine months in which he passed the test and not that many miles were added, the Mini came home.

Oh and if you are wondering why the odometer started moving again? Well that's because amongst several other parts, the instrument binnacle was being used in the Austin Mini. It was time to start thinking about rebuilding that Cooper. Again.

I had started to lose bits of trim and the plastic cover on the air vents had gone missing. The vinyl had been stripped from the dashboard when repainting and needed replacing. Still had the original seat cover which itself was now breaking up.

20. **The BMiniW Years, just what happened when the Germans got their hands on the iconic little car and despite it's limitations and dimensions made it better for the first time in a generation, oh and also started to soften us all up for their own version by turning the retro dial up to 11.5 and dropping an options bomb into the price list, then just when you thought it was safe to buy a Mini again, a big fat Phoenix waddled in and flogged the last few.**

1993 model Mayfair, with 1275cc fuel injected power and optional alloys.

When the Metro got the K series engine in 1990, pundits wondered why the Mini did not get the transplant to give the car a new lease of life and meet stringent emission regulations. The official reason is that it won't fit and even if they re-engineered the engine bay, the car would fail the strict European type approval regulations. So in June 1992, the Mini entered an important new phase of production as it changed into the Mark V.

Powering it was a 50 bhp 3- way catalysed version of the 1275cc engine last seen in the Metro. Replacing the City as the entry level Mini was the Sprite.

Specification wise it was a late model City re-run complete with full width wheel trims, chrome bumpers, chrome Mini badge, Sprite decals on the rear side panel and harlequin trim inside. The new Mayfair also mirrored the old 998cc model with chrome effect grille, colour keyed door mirrors and chrome finish on the Mini and Mayfair badges. Inside there was chevron decorated velour trim. Outside, the wheel trims were identical to the Sprite's although Minilite style alloys as seen on the Cooper could be ordered as an option.

Inside the new Mayfair with for the first time, a full width burr walnut dashboard, incorporating a glovebox, radio/cassette and clock plus front seats from the Metro.

The Mayfair received a major interior facelift in March 1993 when a full width burr walnut dashboard was fixed into place. For years customisers had been inserting their own planks of wood into the fascia and finally Rover had decided to do the same. Maybe they had forgotten that the Riley Elf had featured such a fascia and that came with two glove boxes. Three dials were mounted on a slightly proud section, whilst the radio sat mid dash with an analogue clock above it and in front of the passenger was the novelty of an opening glove box. Both the Sprite and Mayfair also benefited from larger front Metro seats, restyled door bins, a boot mat, new badging and remarkably after all this time, an internal bonnet release. Other security measures included a visible Vehicle Identification Number etched onto the glass and alarm/immobilisers fitted as standard to Mayfairs.

As the Mayfair went further up market, the company that sold it went on the market. On the 31st January 1994, British Aerospace was reported to be selling Rover to BMW for £800 million. The history of the motor industry in Britain took another twist, but the Mini was in safe hands, not least because the BMW Chairman was a distant relative (Cousin once removed) of Issigonis who fully appreciated the importance of this marvellous little car. Well, there was more to it than that, but for the time being Sprites got a little brighter in June '95 when a chrome lock set (door handles and boot release) was fitted. Inside new fabric trim was topped off with new fabric trim, black carpet and a radio cassette with a removable front panel.

The Mini was rarely matched against its rivals in the '80s and '90s, mainly because there were no rivals. In fact, pint sized contemporaries of the original 1959 Mini were pretty thin on the ground after thirty years. Hardly surprising then that in May 1992 Car magazine borrowed the oldest surviving Mini from Rover, 621 AOK and pitched it against the car which came closest in spirit to the old 500, and even shared its name, the Fiat Cinquecento. LJK Setright refereed the bout.

Of course you can't really compare cars separated by 33 years and Setright does not try. The title of the feature is: 'Will there ever be a better Mini than the Mini?' to which the answer has to be a resounding, no. "There is a new fashion for cars - to be as short as possible. The fact that none of them not even the titchiest of the Japanese tax dodgers, is as short as the Mini makes me wonder where the progress has been made. The Mini was just 10ft long in 1959; even the Fiat 126 is longer than that, and the Cinquecento is longer still." Setright soon discovered the flaws in the 'new' Cinquecento, not least that it had ambitions to be a conventional motorcar. Worse still there was no spark of originality, or genius which distinguished the earlier 500s and 600. However, the conclusion was that, "It is merely an extraordinarily convenient car which quickly becomes a surprisingly endearing one."

BMW might have been in charge, but not much had changed since 1959. The Minis looked identical, the production methods were the same and even some of the workers on the line dated from '59.

If anyone had any doubts that the Mini had fallen into the wrong hands when BMW took on Rover, they needn't have worried. Bernd Pischetsrieder BMW's Chairman was a confirmed Mini fanatic, who didn't just love the Mini but believed it had a future. Interviewed for Car Magazine in their February 1996 issue by Gavin Green, Pischetsrieder had very definite views on the image and the future of the Mini. "The Mini has a brand image which is totally apart from Rover. I think it's crazy to call the car the Rover Mini, or even hint that's what it's called. The car has been called an Austin Mini, a Morris Mini, a Wolseley Mini, a Riley Mini and God knows what else. With all due respect, that's bullshit. A Mini is a Mini. And because it's a brand name, it could be a family of cars.

Alec's [Issigonis] idea was to minimise resources. The new car must also be limited to the essentials. It'll be recognisably a Mini, even though it will be all new. The Mini is the only lovable small car. The others are just like bars of soap."

The next generation of Mini was underway when the BMW Chairman set the small car agenda, but it was enjoying several false starts. Project R59 involving both BMW and Rover engineers was to have resulted in a British styled, but German engineered Mini relying on existing small car set-ups. The project was renamed E50 when Munich assumed control as the car went over budget and beyond its sign off deadline so that the launch date went from 1998 and on to 2000.

This is what the Mini had become by the late '90s, a fashionable magnet for options. In this case a chequered roof decal, bonnet stripes, exterior bright packs, white alloys, driving lamps and chrome wheel arch spats.

Meanwhile, Rover made sure that the existing Mini was dramatically reengineered for the first time

288

since 1959. In effect the Mini had been pickled since 1969 with the introduction of wind up windows, concealed door hinges and Clubman fronts being the last radical changes. 1st October 1996 was the launch date and the Paris Motor Show was the revised Mini's debut. The changes signified BMW's recognition that the Mini was a brand in its own right (New Mini badges and not a Rover logo in sight) and that buyers enjoyed individualising their cars with a large range of options. The Mini had arrived as a premium price niche product. According to their press release: "Throughout the 1990s, Mini has been moving steadily upmarket. In the key export markets of Europe and Japan, Mini has long been perceived as a desirable status symbol, bought for its heritage and unique, ageless style. The 1997 programme moves the UK versions of the car in this same direction, as there are no longer any 'entry-level' models such as the previous Sprite, or low price Special Editions.

"Typical Mini buyers are now less likely to be families seeking a second, or third car, but increasingly tend to be single, well-educated professional and managerial people desiring a fashion statement.

"The 1997 Mini sees an important step-change in the development and projection of the Mini brand by reverting to a classically simple and straightforward range that emphasises the strength of the brand, taking it firmly upmarket." So there you have it. But never mind the marketing ambitions, or cosmetic frills which we ill come to later, the most significant changes were in the most important area of all, under the bonnet.

Rover followed this limited edition a year later with an even more official Cabriolet, which was launched in October 1992 at the Birmingham International Motor Show. Again based on the Cooper 1.3i it was developed by Rover Special Products and German coachbuilder, Karmann and built this time at Longbridge. The impressive strengthening work and comprised an extra sill made of thicker gauge steel, which covered the standard inner sill which meant that there were three sills in all. Tied to the extra sill was an extra strong cross member, which ran, as it does on the standard Mini, under the front seats. Also the foot wells on the Cabriolet were narrower than the standard car because reinforcement plates were welded into the area where the A pillars met the sills and floor structure. The A pillars also had a steel tube running inside them. And whilst the standard Mini has cubbyholes underneath the rear seat, a continuous sheet of steel reinforced the rear of the floorpan.

The view under a '97 Mini bonnet with multi point fuel injection, radiator sited at the front of the engine, repositioned oil filter and a bigger alternator.

The 1275cc Cooper engine was standardised for the '97 models, with multi-point fuel injection. This was controlled by the MEMS 2J engine management system

My Mini Cooper it's part in my Breakdown

(as developed for the 2.5 litre KV6 and MGF 1.8i VVC engines) to give a fully programmed sequential injection. Each injector was pulsed at the optimum time to independently fuel the to cylinders that it served. This provided precise control of the fuel input and distribution to achieve very low emissions without any loss in performance. There was also a direct electronic ignition system, which used quad dry-coil twin-spark technology, which triggered each spark twice, once on the compression stroke and once on the exhaust. This meant that the high-tension voltage does not have to be switched between cylinders. The cylinder block itself was modified to delete the distributor housing and it also involved a redesign of the oil galleries and relocation of the oil filter. This allowed the radiator to be moved from its traditional side mounting to a more conventional position in front of the engine as part of the pass-by noise reduction programme (see further). Also new under the bonnet was the replacement of the 45 amp alternator with a 65 amp one and the use of a poly vee belt alternator/water pump drive for greater durability and reliability.

All these changes resulted in the cleanest A series unit ever, matching the power and torque figures of the previous Cooper unit, but at lower engine speeds. For lower internal noise levels, a 2.76:1 final drive ratio raised the overall gearing by 16% compared to the previous Cooper and the higher kerb weight, by 3.5%, meant that the actual performance suffered, but not by a huge margin. The old Cooper had a maximum speed of 92mph, the new 90mph, and getting to 60mph took 11.5 secs in the old days and 12.2, for the '97 model. Fourth gear was now claimed to be the equivalent to most fifth gears as it cut engine speed at 70 mph from 3,888rpm to 3,333rpm. As a result of all these changes, the automatic transmission, which had always been a costly item to produce, was dropped.

Apart from the mechanical changes, probably the most welcome changes were those relating to safety and security. Often criticised for being easy to steal as well as being small and vulnerable, although many owners will testify to the car's strength and manoeuvrability, Rover addressed these shortfalls. So secondary safety equipment involved some complex engineering. A driver's airbag was fitted as standard and seatbelt pre tensioners (actuated by pyrotechnic devices in the inertia reel units) and side door

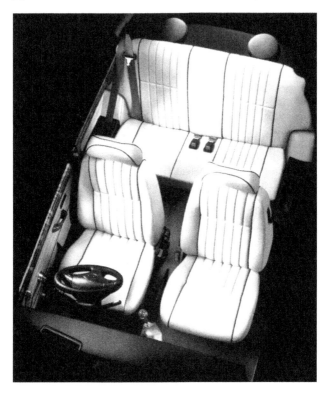

Inside a '97 Mini with stone beige leather, wood accessory pack and wood gear knob. Note the chunkier air bagged steering wheel, plus column stalks, in the familiar Routemaster bus driving position.

intrusion beams were part of the core specification on both models. The airbag required a total redesign of the steering column enabling the fitment of column control stalks which finally brought the lighting controls within finger tip control of the driver.

1997 Minis came in just two flavours. The Mini and Cooper. Mini pictured with an optional canvas sunroof and Cooper with optional sports pack.

On the security side there was a full perimetric alarm system, plus an engine immobiliser, operated by a remote control. Even if the owner forgets, or delays the setting of the system, the engine immobilser automatically activated after a few seconds. A fascia warning light flashed once the system was activated as a visible deterrent. The new steering column also incorporated a new lock.

The Mini became quieter thanks to European Community directive 92/97/EEC which dictated that all post October 1996 registered cars must not exceed a noise level of 74dB(A), down from 77dB(A). That might not sound much, but according to Rover it represented a halving of the prevailing noise levels. To achieve this the '97 Mini's higher gearing, front mounted radiator with electric cooling fan and a rear exhaust silencer box were all part of the package. Inside there were numerous sound deadening measures including damping pads in the roof, plus extra absorption effect of the new foam-backed fabric headlining which helped to tune out the 'boom' effect at higher engine speeds. What a relief, but it did not end there. Extra sealing around the top of the bulkhead and the A-post areas kept engine noise out and new sound insulation around the fuel tank and boot area eliminated any possibility of whine from the high pressure fuel pump. The rear seat bulkhead was now solid as the blanked off aperture was deleted from the pressing. Improved acoustic insulation from road noise resulted from a new moulded one-piece floor carpet.

Rover or rather BMW did not miss a trick when it came to specification for '97 Minis. The kitchen sink really was available. In total there were 37 different 'personalising' items. Rover viewed the situation like this: "For example, retro enthusiasts might choose the prefect finishing touch of a 1960s-style grille to go with a 'Classic' paint and trim combination. 'Thoroughly modern' Mini buyers may choose high tech treatment, with 'chrome' wheel arches complementing of the special alloy wheel sets. The natural extroverts may opt for a striking decal treatment, such as the chequered roof panel. The potential is bounded only by imagination and budget, and, of course, the personalisation process can continue right through the customer's ownership of the car." To make sense of all that, here is the factory packages.

Sports Pack comprised 13in 6J 'Minilite Style' alloy wheels with 175/50 R13 tyres. Faired in a body coloured wheel arch spats to cover the wide tyres. Koni shock absorbers. Four front auxiliary lamps. Large bore chrome tailpipe finisher. Extra fascia gauges for oil temperature and battery condition. Unfortunately the Pack only looked good and Rover admitted that the extra aerodynamic drag of the wide tyres reduced the top speed to 84mph. In fact the Cd (drag co-efficient) went down from the standard car's 0.49 to 0.54 and o to 60mph time slipped from 12.2 to 12.8secs.

Chrome Pack 1: Retro style chrome grille, front bumper over riders and corner nudge bars. **Chrome Pack 2**: Chrome wiper arms, door mirrors and tail pipe finisher. **Interior Pack**: (colour keyed red, blue, or green), leather header rail, parcel shelf finisher, steering wheel, hand brake grip and gear knob. **Alloy Pack**: alloy door pulls, door releases and window winders. **Decals**: Union Jack roof, Chequered roof, "Zipper' side stripe, Chequered bonnet stripes. **Wood Pack**: Cappings, door pulls, door releases, window winders. **Interior**: Engine turned fascia panel, "Cooper' black leather trim, 'Luxury' beige leather trim. Special option "Classic' leather trim in retro 1960's Mini interior trim colours of Porcelain Green, Horizon Blue, Cumulus Grey, Tartan Red. **Exterior**: Special Option Classic Paint, Almond green, Surf Blue, Whitehall Beige, Yukon Grey. **Engine Dressing**: Polished rocker cover, sump guard. **Wheels**: 12' Sports style in Silver, charcoal, or White. 12" Premium. 12" Revolution 5 spoke. 13" revolution 5 spoke. 13" Sports. **Sunroofs**: Electric glass, electric full-length canvas. Standard paint colours: Solid - Flame red, White Diamond, Electric Blue. Metallic - Charcoal, Platinum Silver, Kingfisher Blue, British Racing Green. Pearlescent - Nightfire Red, Tahiti Blue, Amaranth (purple), Volcano (orange).

Sport pack equipped Cooper, on the move, but slower because of all those extra bits.

Car Magazine were not over impressed by the Mini revisions when they reviewed it under the title 'Going quietly to the grave.' After recounting all the important mechanical updates, Paul Horrell summed up the major objection: "All this engineering cost, spread over a comparatively tiny number of cars, means a price hike. Rover reckons Mini buyers aren't interested in cost anyway, so it has elected to go for a boutique strategy: big prices, big range of optional trimmings and accessories. So you can't now buy a Mini for under nine grand. Gulp." After criticising the lengthy final drive and the sports pack, which made the Cooper slower, the sum up was expected. "...In the year of the Ka, don't try and justify it as a sensible buy. It just isn't."

Autocar were more positive. Writer Colin Goodwin zeroed in on the appeal of the car "You don't buy a Mini these days because it is a small car, you buy it because it is a Mini." Precisely. All the options were not seen as handicap, there was much appreciation for the soundproofing and the fact that fun aspect of driving a Mini had not been lost. "Rover has provided us with the safest, most livable-with Mini to date. It's just up to you how you finish the job."

In fact all those option packs were a taste of things to come when BMW would launch their own MINI. In a way they were testing to see if buyers really would spec up a Mini to nonsensical levels. Not only that the Mini would be regularly re-promoted with each special edition.

In 1998 the Paul Smith was as the name suggested, styled by fashion designer Paul Smith in his own colurs, Paul Smith Blue with Citrus Green detailing and black leather upholstery. Also that year a limited edition (100) Mini Cooper Sports became available in either Brooklands Green or Black, all with a green leather interior. What set them off was a twin coach-line to a throwback BMC rosette on the rear panel. Not only that there was sports pack style arches and 6x13 inch alloy wheels.

My Mini Cooper it's part in my Breakdown

Mini Sport 500 LE on the move.

1999 was an even busier year in the special edition business. The Cooper S Touring had a tuned 86bhp engine. Then the Cooper S Sport 5 not only had the Sports pack but a Jack Knight 5 speed gearbox. Then the Cooper S Works arrived with a 90bhp engine, the most powerful fitted to a production Mini. It had 'S Works' badges and decals.

Mini 40 was created to celebrate 40th glorious years of Mini production. It had extended wheel arches and 13-inch (33cm) sports alloy wheels and could be bought in Island Blue, Mulberry Red or Old English White.

The John Cooper LE was another birthday car and also celebrated the 40th anniversary of the first Cooper Formula 1 World Championship win. Painted in Brooklands Green with Old English White roof, bonnet stripes and matching mirrors. Inside there was red leather and a CD player.

Which brings us to the year 2000. By March, Rover was still making a loss, but BMW had got what they came for. This included the inside track on how 4 x 4s vehicles should work, so they sold Land Rover to Ford. Not only that, BMW now understood just how to market a small car. BMW retained the Mini name and the planned new model, granting Rover temporary rights to the brand and allowing it to manufacture and sell the run-out model of the old Mini. The sell-off was completed in May with the MG and Rover brands going to the British consortium

My Mini Cooper it's part in my Breakdown

Phoenix. The full sorry story of this episode can be found in the British Car Industry, Our Part in its Downfall. For the time being the Brits are in full control and still carrying out BMW's dastardly marketing plan.

The Classic Mini Se7en was introduced in April 2000 in Solar Red, Old English White or Black, the last non-Cooper Mini and a recreation of the original Seven. It had cream fluted fabric with red leather front cushion, red PVC seat backs and head restraints. The dashboard was body coloured with a black leather gear knob and hand brake grip were the extra touches, plus it rode on pepperpot alloy wheels. The Cooper Classic added a leather steering wheel, seat sides and bolsters this time with PVC piping. It rode on Minilite alloy wheels. The Classic Cooper Sport was available with Platinum Silver roofs and came in a choice of four colours: Solar Red, Tahiti Blue, British Racing Green and Anthracite. It had unique seats which featured black and nickel leather with matching head restraints and black PVC piping, the plastic also being applied to the seat backs, borders and casings. The door furniture was lightweight alloy, the fascia had a metallic finish with a top rail that was leather covered along with the handbrake grip. The gear knob was a polished alloy item and the sport steering wheel a nickel and black job with duo tone leather.

The Cooper Sport 500 LE, officially the last of the line had all of the above from the Classic Sport but with official glovebox mounted 'Cooper Sport 500' plaque. This reads 'This Mini is one of the last 500 built to the original Sir Alec Issigonis design.' Somehow the austere Issigonis might have felt that actually a Cooper Sport 500 with all the fripperies and was not entirely in keeping with his original vision of building a simple car for the masses. Maybe instead of this flared arched, over optioned Mini monstrosity (his imagined thoughts, not mine), it should have been a simple Classic running on 10 inch (25.4cm) steel wheels, with sliding windows in Tartan Red, Farina Grey or Speedwell Blue with Austin badges. Or Clipper Blue, Cherry Red, or Old English White with Morris badges. Because for the first two years of production you could have any colour you liked provided it was those ones. Sir Alec would have approved of that. I think.

My Mini Cooper it's part in my Breakdown

What actually happened was that on the 4th October 2000 the last Mini built at Longbridge was a Red Cooper Sport. It was presented to the British Motor Industry Heritage Trust in December. That is the official story anyway, but I know the real one because I was there and I could see from a distance that '60s shouting songstress Lulu was perched on the bonnet. And the truth is that this harmless little Mini is unlikely to have been the very last. After all this was a big press relations event and photo opportunity to promote the last Minis and their new owners. According to the workers production had stopped a few weeks before and a car was picked not quite randomly to represent the last of the line. Meanwhile Getta Bloomin' Move on! (Self Preservation Society) from the Italian Job was ringing around the factory floor.

**The end of an era. Production finishes. Mini Cooper
Sport pictured unlikely to have
been the very last one made.**

I know the tune intimately not just because I've seen the film a few times, but Her Majesty's motoring press were also given a pack that contained The Italian Job original Soundtrack sampler. It contained two tracks, the aforementioned Self Preservation Society and the infinitely better, On Days like these, sung by the peerless Matt Munro. Sadly that was what I took away from that

My Mini Cooper it's Part in my Breakdown

day and not the genius of the design. Or the fact that it had helped change the way all small cars were built, or that a total of 5,387,862 Minis had been manufactured. The only message seemed to be that the Mini had once been the star of a film, which was never critically acclaimed, and only means anything to British TV viewers who have been force-fed it in the days before the multi channel revolution. To me that was sad.

What was even sadder is that there wouldn't be another Mini. Not that Rover was not above suggesting where the little car could go in the next millennium. It is worth reading a few words that Sir Alec Issigonis wrote in 1973. This was included in a report that produced for BL Chairman Sir Donald Stokes outlining the requirements for a new model.

"A new Mini replacement must set new concepts of car design as the original Mini fourteen years ago. To replace the Mini with a new one that is neither lighter nor offering more internal accommodation seems pointless..."

With these words in mind it is worth looking at a couple of the later and publicly revealed proposals. So three years after BMW's buyout of the Rover Group the ACV30 was unveiled on January 18th 1997. The official line was that the AVC30 Anniversary Concept, to give it the full title, was built to commemorate the 30th anniversary of Mini wins in the Monte Carlo Rallies of 1964, '65 and '67. That helps explain the red and white livery. In truth the whole point was to help the Rover and BMW design and marketing departments decide how retro styling would go down. Built in just four months, the aluminium body panels were formed in Germany.

According to Rover at the time the basic and mechanical packaging of the car had been decided. So the running gear of the MGF sports car was mated to the front and rear sub frames including its 1.8 litre, 115bhp double overhead camshaft, 16-valve K series engine. This was mounted in the middle of the car and controversially would drive the rear wheels. Inside and outside though the design was far from decided. Well, according to the publicity, Chris Bangle, no stranger to controversy himself, and at the time BMW design chief, described the front end to Car magazine as a 'mouth spitting out four breadsticks.' It was roughly a foot longer than the original Mini. Apparently the interior was production ready and eventually it would be taken away by BMW and incorporated into their equally retro take on what their MINI should look like.

The ACV 30 built to celebrate the 30ᵗʰ anniversary of the Monte Carlo Rally hat trick of wins. In the background is Rauno Aaltonen's Monte winning Mini Cooper LBL 6D.

A few months later in March '97 at the Geneva International Motor Show, The Rover Group unveiled the Spiritual. Rover believed that this concept followed the same radical thought processes used by Sir Alec Issigonis with the three door Spiritual platform leading to a potential family of small cars. Indeed, the Spiritual Too was a larger, one box, five door family car. It even mimicked the dimensions of the original being just 3.1 metres long (as near as dammit 10 foot). It was designed to meet prevailing crash and emissions requirements.

Mini Spiritual and Spiritual Too, which could and perhaps should have been the next Mini.

Just the ACV30 broke with tradition the Spiritual's powerplant was a flat, three cylinder unit mounted under the rear seats and driving the rear wheels. The theoretical stats was a 45bhp output, 62mph arriving in 13 seconds and the fuel consumption calculated at an astounding 104mpg. The fuel tank was positioned under the front seats with the spare wheel, battery and radiator where the engine would usually be. Suspension was provided by the Hydragas system as used in the Metro and it weighed in at just 700kg (1,575lbs). The Spiritual Too weighed in at 900kg (2,025lb) and measured from front to back at 3.5m (11 feet 4in). The other difference was a slightly larger four cylinder, but still flat engine.

As we now know the ACV30 sort of became the MINI and the Spiritual certainly didn't.

My Mini Cooper it's part in my Breakdown

June 1998 Mileage: 99,725 Amount spent: MOT
Minis in my Life: Austin Mini Cooper, Austin Mini MOT:
Fail

With the Austin Mini back home is was now time
to see what I could use from the fully working Mini to the
fairly knackered Cooper. So I rolled up my sleeves, got out
my spanners and started to rebuild it. I then drove it up to
my local MOT and waited for the verdict. Sadly the fail
sheet did not make good reading.

Offside headlamp not working. Nearside
headlamp too high. No indicator light inside vehicle.
Nearside rack gaitor split. Nearside lower ball joint worn.
Offside rear radius arm excessive movement. Main brake
pipe fouling steering rack. Nearside handbrake cable
unattached. Rear brakes out of balance. Offside rear tyre
below 1.6mm. Blowing at front end of exhaust pipe.

It actually would not have been all that daunting
to make the Cooper roadworthy, but I'd had enough. Or

perhaps it was just that the family was growing, I had work to do and a house to repair. Yes, life got in the way again for another eight years.

The Cooper starts to clutter up the garage again and it's my fault...

21. **Superminis come of age and leave the old Mini standing, so what were the models that the Mini wasn't actually up against, and where did all those micro people carriers come from? ...So here are all the pretend and alternate Minis both supersized and the superskinny hatches that bothered the price lists between 1990 and 2000.**

Minis made in 1990 46,045 • 1991 35,007 • 1992 26,197 • 1993 20,468 • 1994 20,417 •1995 20,378 • 1996 15,638 • 1997 16,928 • 1998 14,311 • 1999 11,738 • 2000 7,070

Yet another decade and the Mini just would not go away. Hardly surprising as the car was entering a renaissance with the Cooper while all sorts of tricks was used to keep it strictly legal. However, the tiny tot war was heating up, so who else was poised to take the Mini's crown?

The Peugeot 205 was still going strong and would last until 1996, when the larger 206 arrived. The 206 was good but not so charming. Decent standard specification, diesel was the biggest hit, not least because it returned 49mpg. Proper small car duties though belonged to the Peugeot 106 from 1991.

Peugeot 106, but underneath it's a Citroen AX.

Citroen made their own versions of the 106 in the shape of the much squarer AX, which ran from 1987 to 1997. Light, almost flimsy, always frugal but never less than fun. Then there was the Saxo, which was Citroen's other spin on the Peugeot 106, which was a safe and sound buy. Despite being a tiddler it was available with four doors and proved a big hit with young buyers as free insurance in the UK certainly helped.

Citroen AX. Underneath it's a Peugeot 106.

Over at Renault the 5 soldiered on until 1996. The Campus 1.4 had a 5-speed gearbox, but specifications were now basic, as it became Renault's entry-level model. Above the 5 was its replacement the Renault Clio from 1991 and successfully sold to the UK as the car that Nicole drove. Indeed, Nicole wasn't wrong, the Clio had lots of appeal, was comfy, nice to drive and cheap to run. Upgraded in 1998 being still cheap and chic enough to impress

The Fiat Uno continued until 1994 when the Punto took over. Well packaged and stylish but it had the flimsy build quality of old and didn't seem like the impressive step forward that the Uno had been. Reworked and restyled in 1999 it still had patchy reliability. Also distinguished by its firm ride, which meant it bounced into and out of potholes.

My Mini Cooper it's part in my Breakdown

Fish faced Fiesta, also available with a Mazda badge and a longer warranty.

Old school Ford Fiesta continued through to 1997 despite the arrival of the new model in 1995. It was adjudged to be fun to drive though not more spacious or more practical compared to the old model. Very odd styling, best described as ugly/dull, or dead fish. Restyled in 1999, but still the same old Fiesta underneath, so that meant limited rear room and no decent diesel. People still bought it though because it was cheap and easy to own rather than being cutting edge.

Long running Daihatsu Charade struggled to be taken seriously. The models from 1996 were better to drive. Mechanicals tough, trim not so much. Ultra reliable? Certainly. Cheap? Yes. However insurance was a high group 8. A charade? Absolutely. Then there was the Sirion from 1998 was a small hatch with a big spec and low road tax. Surprised look styling, silly name, but a sensible little supermini even though it felt cheap and looked very narrow.

South Korea came into the small car market with the Kia Pride in 1991. At least it didn't break down because the Pride was a rehashed '80s Mazda 121. Certainly cheap but not a lot to be proud about really. Basic, boring, and some might think it was only marginally better than walking.

The proper 121 from Mazda in 1991 was an oversized egg of a car, which was well built, with good equipment. Even odder canvas sunroof model was effectively an up to date 2CV. At least it looked different because the revised model from 1996 was just a rebadged Ford Fiesta but with a three year warranty when the Fiesta made do with one.

Kia Pride, with whitewall tyres. Yes whitewall tyres.

Mazda still did odd though with the Demio in 1998. Interesting if confusing styling which looked a bit like a small 4 x 4 that has mated with a people carrier and then not grown up. That makes it a crossover, before anyone knew what they actually were. So there were few takers.

Mitsubishi's Colt from 1996 had now become a larger than average small hatchback and was largely bought as a practical two seater coupe' by OAPs who wanted reliability and quality.

Nissan Micra, badged as a March in Japan. Seen here without dual controls, L plates and Bert's Driving School on the roof rack.

My Mini Cooper it's part in my Breakdown

The original Nissan Micra remained a driving school favourite. From 1993 built in Britain, but the Micra no longer looked like a box, but rather like it belonged in a toy box. Cute to some the Micra was spacious practical and affordable. Very easy to live with and it never broke down.

Suzuki Wagon R+. Effectively a mini minibus.

No one would have thought there was a niche' for a 4 x 4 shopping cart and the continued existence of the Subaru Justy confirmed this. Few buyers had a dirt road drive to Tescos, so were better off going for the otherwise identical Suzuki Swift without the 4 x 4 plumbing. Then again, in 2000 the Suzuki Ignis came along, a fun little runabout which looked like a micro 4 x 4 but wasn't and that didn't matter. Enthusiastic 1.3 petrol engine managed 44 mpg and was fairly quick. Decent high driving position and equipment levels excellent with light controls and quick electric power steering. Meanwhile, the Suzuki Wagon R+ from 1997 continued to be the most successful of the micro MPVs. Bigger and the better than the other boxes and also more practical. Buzzy 1.0 engine, but 1.2 less frantic.

Toyota Yaris, the shape of minis to come.

One of the more conventional tots in circulation was the Toyota Starlet. Revised in 1996 making it better than the old one, but that was not saying much. Finally replaced by the Toyota Yaris in 1999, which was one of the very best of the new breed of shoppers. Sliding rear seats very clever, although the interior seemed a little cheap. Never mind, this was the future of the small hatch, cleverly packaged, well built, and cheap to run.

In 1994 SEAT left their low quality image behind with the VW based Ibiza paella flavoured Polo which is actually a lot nicer than it sounds. Underrated, keenly priced and frugal (48mpg from the 1.9D). From 1999 the Ibiza was based on a more recent Volkswagen Polo and it was better looking than the old car.

Also a big part of the growing VW family was Skoda and their Fabia in 2000, which was good, value, spacious and also based on a Volkswagen Polo, but significantly bigger. Single-handedly Volkswagen had managed to transform the Skoda brand image from basket case to the solid, dependable and value for money choice of the Great British Car buyers who spent their own hard earned money. However, if you wanted the real Polo thing then the little bread van was still about until 1994. A new Polo arrived in 1994, which was solidly built, didn't look remotely like a small commercial vehicle and was nice to drive. Revised in 2000 with new insides and slightly changed

Volkswagen Polo, one of the Mini's oldest rivals and by the '90s offered a multiple threat as the basis for Skodas and SEATs.

outsides, despite being pricey it was the choice of those who were happy to pay for prestige in what was steadily becoming bigger than the old Golf.

Vauxhall still had the Nova until 1993 that had been nothing more than box suddenly become chic and cuddly. Cheeky styling made it lovable and decent interior room made it practical.

**The Nova becomes the Corsa.
It always was an Opel.**

Sharper handling from 1997, but the whole point was that it was cheap to buy and run. Vauxhall also entered the micro people carrier market by taking the

My Mini Cooper it's part in my Breakdown

Polish built Suzuki Wagon R in 2000, putting less equipment in it but not forgetting their badge and model name, Agila. Its 1.2 engine was from the Corsa, but it was never as lively. Of course, the Mini was technically up against all the other Rover badged products. There was of course the Roverised Metro, which at least had almost modern K series power in 1.1 and 1.4 sizes. Both better than the crude diesel engine it rattled around with. Five speed gearbox was not just desirable, but standard from '93. It had a terrible image, but parts and running costs were cheap, some would say that this was BL's longest running joke. Then along game the 100 in 1995 that was the last go by Rover at tarting up the tired Metro. Cancelled by embarrassed BMW owners in 1997 when they found that just kerbing the wheels could cause instant death.

**Rover 100. Even though it looks
remarkably like a Metro.**

Then there was the Rover 200 from 1995 was supposed to be a small family car, but actually it was even smaller than that and rather more of a supermini shopper. Fairly well built and classy but never remotely fashionable. It was though, great to drive. Never the cheapest option and bought mainly by mature drivers who still wanted to drive something which was made in Britain. Then it got a makeover in 1999 and became the 25 that meant a price rise because of its fancy new grille and so slightly resembled the big grown up 75. However, still very cramped inside, especially for those stuck in the back.

So after looking all those grown up superminis, what were the genuinely mini, city cars up to?

Well, the Fiat Panda was, apart from the Mini, the most ancient town centre assault vehicle of all. It still had lots of old school charm and Lira like running costs, delivering up to 48mpg, and group 1 insurance. The Seat Marbella was still around, effectively a Panda but without the charm. A sort of holiday hire car from hell, which left the UK market in 1993, followed by the Panda two years later.

To every small car lover's delight, the Cinquecento made a comeback in 1993. Fiat's baby three-door hatchback at just 10' 7" (3.22m) long and just 4' 9" (1.44m) wide was the perfectly sized City car. Interior room is limited, but that's not surprising. It was a lot more right angled than it had been previously but the Polish built Cinquecento was still a small car with real character that is fun to drive, cheap to own and promised 47mpg. Has become the quintessential first car immortalised by the 'Inbetweener' generation. The Seincento from 1998 onwards was a restyled, safer and better built/equipped Cinquecento. Roomy and practical, but not as instantly lovable and certainly not as sharp to drive as the old Cinquecento either.

Until the Ford Ka came along in 1996, City cars only had to be small. It didn't have to be roomy, exciting to drive, or look very stylish. Luckily the three door Ka was all these things. Best of all it wasn't just at home in the City, it felt perfectly happy on the open road too. A truly practical little package which was also a low cost, no worry Ford. Arguably the closest in spirit to the original Mini although it could also be regarded as self-consciously attention seeking. The 'Kay A' as it was sometimes pronounced, was A1 when it came to refinement, but for some it is just a less practical Fiesta with wonky looks. The engine was an old 1.3 unit that could be traced back to old Anglias and was painfully slow, but most importantly it was always fun to drive.

Fiat Cinquecento.

City cars often look like little delivery vans and shrunken people carriers, but Giorgetto Giugiaro, the man who brought us the original Golf at least dared to be different. We are talking about the Daewoo Matiz in 1998. It had a very tight turning circle which combined with light power steering means that manoeuvring was never a problem, even though a car magazine managed to make it fall over by going backwards quickly. Never mind, the engines were very eager and therefore nippy where it mattered and there was almost a sporty roar to the three-cylinder engine.

Daihatsu made more of an effort in 1997. The Cuore came fitted with a little Mini reminiscent 850cc engine, which was very noisy. Then when the unit was increased to 998cc from 1998 the Cuore became slightly better. Easy to drive and live with, but without the personality of many small cars of the time and a lack of dealers hampered sales. Then there was the Daihatsu Move which had micro MPV styling that effectively meant all the passengers could wear top hats, if they wanted to, or were undertakers. Very much in the Japanese K, or Kei type mould to fit in with Japanese government rules and regs for parking. A weird little van, but certainly not alone.

Ford Ka. Quirky, fun to drive, almost the Mini reinvented.

There was also the Suzuki Wagon R from 1997, which we have already mentioned when it was badged as the Vauxhall Agila. This version had real character and a very enthusiastic 1.3 engine, which means that when driver's strayed out of town it, could cope with higher speeds. Well built with a decent level of standard equipment, it is the revised model from 2000, which looks less toy-like. So is that it then? Well, it may look daft, but for some people, the sheer size and expense of buying, owning and running a full size MPV is also daft. The truth is that the interior was large for such a small car, with plenty of headroom and legroom for four adults. Tall passengers didn't have a problem at all and there lots of cubbyholes and the small but practical boot could be boosted by the split/fold rear seat. As for the Suzuki Alto from 1997 there was never a lot to recommend this dated Indian built tot. Slow, noisy, cramped, only reliability and low costs are the redeeming features. Otherwise the Alto was a bum note of a car and buyers would always have been better off with an old Fiesta.

The Hyundai Atoz from 1998 was another perpendicular car with a peculiar name. Plenty of equipment and despite limited rear space it was an easy car to live with. The Hyundai Amica from 2000 was a marginally more modern Atoz and much the same comments apply really. It bounced around on hard suspension and there really wasn't a huge amount of room inside.

As for Perodua Nippa from 1997 which at the time was the
cheapest new car on sale, it didn't have a lot going for it with zero spec levels and zero appeal. However, ultra low running costs, only partly redeem this Malaysian remake of an old Daihatsu.

The cute Renault Twingo. Left hand drive only.

The Renault Twingo was a distinctive hatch that the UK market missed out on. Anyone interested had to cross the English Channel and buy a left hand drive example. The Initiale spec one had driver, passenger and side airbags, ABS brakes, CD player, climate control air conditioning and alloy wheels. Some may consider left hand drive a disadvantage, but it was a tiny car and if you used it in town then drivers simply stepped safely onto the pavement.

Seat's Arosa from 1997 was closely related to the Volkswagen Lupo which arrived a couple of years later. However, the Arosa was better value and the sensible choice. Engines range from the purely economical petrol and diesel to those tuned for performance. It was fun to drive whether it is around town or out on the open road, but only with the larger engines. Refinement could be difficult to achieve in a city car like this but outside noise was kept to a minimum. The boxy cabin should mean plenty of room and at the front there are no complaints, but rear legroom was at a premium. That boot certainly struggled to take a weekly shop although the rear seats do split and fold to help out.

Which brings us to the Lupo in 1999. To sum it up this is a high quality small car that realistically only seats two. Fun to drive, quite civilised and felt like a much bigger car. Practicality was limited and it was never cheap to buy, but hey it was a VW. There was a surprisingly wide range of petrol and diesel engines from the slow to the seriously sporty.

One car alone rewrote the tiny car rulebook in the 1990s and takes us right back to the beginning of this book. Mercedes Benz, the inventors not just of the car, but also the small simple groundbreaking car, bought the company that designed the Smart and then made it much better.

Available from 1999 in left hand drive only, it could be argued that buyers were paying rather a lot for two seats, but that's also the case with a Ferrari. There is no simple tick box when it comes to buying a car it's emotional and the cute Smart tapped right into that, creating a fan club and hardcore community right from the off. Owners swapped stories, pet names and even their body panels with like-minded smarties. The Smart though isn't just a social club with a groovy mascot, it really did deliver as a small car.

From the Pure model upwards the Smart delivered as a City Centre assault vehicle with that 600cc turboed Mercedes engines returning around 60mpg. It is safe too with all those clever electronic devices like electronic traction control and electronic stability control to stop it falling over. Full size driver and passenger airbags, ABS brakes, 'Tridion' safety cell-reinforced steel frame and integrated side impact struts are also reassuring. Available in three trim levels the Passion had air conditioning and alloy wheels, there was the back to basics Pure and almost sporty Pulse.

The Smart Pure, two seats and steel wheels, all you really need.

December 1999 is when the Smart officially landed in the UK, but for much of the previous twelve months it was available as a grey import. The specification was upgraded with double wishbone front suspension and longer spring travel with wider section front tyres, and electronic brakeforce distribution. Also the tailgate could be opened from inside, the seats had more padding, there was a bigger driver's door mirror and the rear wiper now washed and could operate intermittently. Golly.

More important was the fact that this genuinely small and innovative car actually didn't change the way we drove in the short term. It wasn't even copied, or even that successful. Although the Mini took a while to be taken seriously and sell substantially, the Smart was a slow to catch on and remained something of an expensive oddity. For the time being at least, the Mini still had two more seats and a decent boot.

Minis Running Total 1990 5,190,614 •
1991 5,225,621 • 1992 5,251,818 1993 5,272,286 •
1994 5,292,703 • 1995 5,313,081 • 1996 5,328,719
1997 5,345,657 • 1998 5,359,968 • 1999 5,371,706 •
2000 5,378,776

June 2006 Mileage: 99,747 Amount spent: £1000
Minis in my Life: Austin Mini Cooper. MOT: Expires
June 2007

Eight years on and Bank Garage doesn't exist anymore but my local Threeways, certainly did. The Cooper was essentially complete, but there were plenty of parts that needed to be replaced, released, greased or revived to get back on the road.

The engine was always OK, even though it wasn't the proper one. I regularly turned it over and it always started quickly and easily until the battery started to fade.

There was an issue about all the rust in the fuel tank. We couldn't find a replacement for some reason and hoofing it out of the car was all very complicated so it was easier to mount a filter in the fuel line to keep all the flaky bits from getting into the fuel system.

It took a lot of fettling and time to get the Cooper running properly, including sorting out the brakes and getting the engine to meet the emissions. However, once finished and MOT'd there was an advisory that refused to go away, exhaust gases leak from the front of the exhaust pipe. There was also a nagging doubt that wouldn't go away, here was a Cooper that may have be running, but it was only half finished. I felt I was letting myself and the Cooper down. I didn't want to leave things undone. I had already failed to fully restore a BSA Bantam, which was painted, but the two-stroke engine was largely in bits with various parts missing. So I now had to clean up my garage and my pitiful attempts at making my Mini better.

It looks OK from a distance, but this is an A Plus engine from a Metro. The exhaust pipe continues to spring leaks and it's got just the one carburettor making this Mini wrong on many levels.

22. **The national and international response to the Cooper, or just how Johnny Foreigner and what was left of the Brit motor industry made their own go faster shopping trolleys, welcome to world of alternate Coopers, many of which were much better than the old Coops which got increasingly arthritic and pointless as time went on, so welcome to the confusing world of go faster tiddlers which were turbo'd, injected and decaled to performance infinity and beyond.**

You could be forgiven for thinking that the Cooperised Mini was a first. The simple fact is that before John Cooper, there was Carlo Abarth. Founding his company in 1949 he became known as 'The Wizard' who established his reputation in motorsport but he also diversified into building sports cars, silencers and tweaking standard production models, especially Fiats. It was the introduction of the 600 in 1955 which gave them the impetus to create the 850TC and later the 1000TC. Fiat would supply incomplete cars that were missing front brakes, crankshaft, carburettor and exhaust and Carlo finished them off.

Fiat Abarth 850TC ready for action. Wow.

However, by 1958 Fiat were able to introduce a 500 model with 'Sport' badges having been inspired by some epic performances on the track, notably a first, second, third and fourth in class at the Hockenheim 12 hour race. This model was fitted with an uprated version of the standard engine enlarged to 499.5cc, with a revised camshaft, valves, cylinder head and fuelling. As a result it now produced a very creditable 21.5bhp. With a distinctive red stripe down each side the Sport was difficult to miss. Another feature was a solid roof to improve rigidity, whereas the standard production models had canvas rollbacks. Rigidity was less of an issue than sales and marketing when the Sport became available with a hole from 1959.

For those who didn't want a rounded 500 there was always the option of the more spacious 850, which was revised in 1968 with the 850 Special which was a saloon with the coupe's engine and front disc brakes. Obviously buyers could go for the larger and more elegant Coupe, but was that really a Cooper rival? Probably not.

Tame compared to an Abarth, the 500 Sport as featured on the front of a Fiat brochure.

My Mini Cooper it's part in my Breakdown

Abarth continued in the same vein throughout the 1960's with their own interpretation of 500 and 600s. The 595 built until 1971 produced 27bhp, which would deliver 85mph and beat an 850cc Mini, but certainly not any Cooper, However the 595SS and 695SS was more of a Cooper botherer with uprated suspension, wider wheels and optional front disc brakes. Not as sophisticated as the Cooper or S, or as quick even with the 690cc engine. Most though ended up modified further for track use.

Abarth also dabbled with the 850 and the OT part of the OT850 stood for Omologato Tourismo which meant it was type approved for competition and again buyers could order disc brakes and higher states of tune, to a massive 53bhp. There was also an impressive tally of entertaining Abarth specials until competition commitments bankrupted them and sent the company sliding into the welcoming embrace of Fiat in 1971. From then on the little scorpion badge has identified a Fiat that ought to go faster. Actually that wasn't actually a guarantee because often the arachnid was just decoration.

As well as Abarth there was also the Austrian Steyr-Puch who also built Fiat based models, but with their own power unit. So the 650 TR II was in effect a 500 but with their air-cooled engine, which would get to 85mph.

Back to Fiat and the 128 that was crying out for more power that finally arrived in the shape of the 1290cc 67 bhp engine to make the Rally in 1972. Rather than being celebrated as the first hot hatch it is remembered as forming the basis for the X1/9.

The 127 Sport joined the range in 1978 with the 1049cc engine tuned to give 70bhp plus improved brakes, a larger anti-roll bar and as the name suggested, a suitably sporty interior and exterior trim. In 1981 the new 1301cc unit producing 75bhp made it a bit quicker.

By the 1980s it was the Uno Turbo from 1985 that carried the performance flame for small Fiats. With fog lights in the bumper, Turbo graphics down the flanks, alloy wheels, and a spoiler on the tailgate there was no mistaking this for a humble SL. The 1299cc produced 105bhp, the engine size boosted to 1301cc in February 1988. A new model in 1990 ushered in an even bigger

1372cc engine with an intercooler, multi point fuel injection and 118bhp which was badged as the Turbo ie. All very boy racer, but very capable and a class act compared to an XR2.

Fiat 127 Sport. That's a hot hatch isn't it?

When the Uno turned into the Punto in 1994 there was more Turbo fun as Fiat christened it the GT and turned up the wick to produce a more substantial 126bhp that translated into 124mph and 60mph coming up in 7.9 seconds. The comprehensive specification apart from the compulsory alloy wheels and body kit, included electric windows, roof, headlamp wash and remote locking. Output was upped to 130bhp in 1997. But never mind all that, because overall it was a disappointing and unreliable package that did not look or feel very special.

Lancia were still around with their rebadged Fiats pushed upmarket and it also had the image (thanks to the Integrale) to justify the go faster versions. So the tiny Y10 measuring just 11 feet one inch (3.37m) was first given a turbo in 1985, which also had a twin choke carburettor and produced 85bhp from the 1049cc engine. It wasn't that exciting to look at or drive. Effectively replaced by the normally aspirated GTie with a 1301cc engine, this time pushing out 78bhp. Slightly more interesting to look at with driving lights and alloys wheels on the outside, whilst inside Alcantara upholstery, rev counter, central locking, electric windows and a remote hatch release made life more informative and comfy.

Those looking for a direct Mini Cooper rival when it comes to dimensions and possibly charm couldn't miss the Cinquecento Sporting. It was however bigger than the Cooper, but it was faster overall, yet slower at getting to 60mph. The buzzy 1.1 litre engine did its best to produce 54bhp and had a top speed of 93mph and would get to 60 mph in just over 14 seconds. Despite being very agile with sharp steering the offset pedal layout and rubbery gear change didn't make it easy to drive or enjoy. Better built than a Mini it nonetheless seemed far for fragile, flaky and prone to breakdowns. Then came the broadly similar Seicento in 1998. It wasn't half as cute as the boxy old Cheekycento and seemed quite bland. You could though order an Abarth sports pack that just meant a lot more Scorpions scattered around the car and positioned in the middle of the 14-inch (25.4cm) alloys.

**Fiat Seicento Sporting, Schumacher edition.
Schumi not pictured.**

BMW were always in the performance game but the 1950s were a tricky period. However the 700 built from 1959 to 1965 was the model that bridged the gap between 'bubbles' and real BMWs. A flat twin 697cc motorcycle engine was rear mounted and the pretty body designed by Giovanni Michelotti. Initially a 2 + 2 coupe', there was also a saloon and cabriolet. It was the twin carburettor Sport models with a heady 40bhp that delivered a more than acceptable 80mph. Surprisingly tidy handling, despite rear engines, but the pre-engaged starter meant it was almost refined. Lots built 188,121, but few came to Britain and even fewer coupes or cabriolets.

The smallest car that Ford made in the '60s was the Escort so we might as well include the Mark 1 when it comes to comparing Coopers and Cooper S. A 1298cc engine powered the Super, but the GT in 1968 had a new cylinder head, high lift camshaft, revised manifold and dual-choke Weber carburettor producing 72bhp. Clearly Ford was serious about making performance versions of this exciting small car, like the Twin Cam. This had the running gear from the Lotus Cortina, but in an Escort shell that was 300lbs lighter. Eventually built at Halewood the uprated mechanicals were installed into specially strengthened bodyshells with generously flared wheel arches. Like the Cooper S it went on to dominate motorsport.

As these special Escorts grabbed attention and increasingly sales Ford set up an Advanced Vehicles Operation in Aveley to hand build them. The first was the RS1600 in 1970 with a new 16 valve Twin cam Cosworth unit. Then inspired by victory in the World Cup Rally they launched the Mexico with a larger 1558cc engine for everyday reliability, whilst the RS2000 had the 2-litre Pinto engine and bold side graphics and was a less specialist performance model built in Germany. While the Cooper had stagnated and morphed into the 1275GT, Ford had continued to develop the Escort to the point where the performance Mini became irrelevant.

With the arrival of the more compact Fiesta, Ford as was quick to offer performance packs. First there was the Series X in 1977. There were all sorts of options from RS catalogue both cosmetic and realistic. So 7 x 13" wheels, extended wheel arches, front air dam and rear spoiler made the Fiesta look more aggressive. The next stage was to go for larger diameter brake discs that would certainly help when the 1100 engine kit was specified which raised power by over 20%.

**The XR2, designed with the young
driver/buyer in mind.**

The slightly dreary 1300S delivered 69bhp, but then from 1980 a Supersport 1980 Limited edition based on it added alloy wheels, shaded body stripes, black plastic wheel arch covers, front driving lights and comfy Ghia seats. The first properly serious go faster Fiesta was the XR2 that arrived in 1982. It effectively created the 'pocket rocket' version of the hot hatch. It offered style and performance with low Ford running costs and reliability. Built from 1981-83 with a 1598cc, 84bhp and a four-speed gearbox, it had the looks if not the outright performance. So it came with front and rear spoilers, round headlamps, side stripes, decals and pepper pot alloy wheels.

A facelifted XR2 in 1984 had a new 1597cc engine and now produced a more useful 95bhp connected to a five-speed gearbox. Then in 1989 it got the boost it needed and was renamed XR2i in line with its fuel injected engine. As well as 110bhp the XR also benefited from firmer suspension and wider wheels. Here was the working man's hatch, hardly sophisticated, but certainly easy to live with and cheap to run. More hardcore though was the introduction of the Fiesta RS Turbo in 1990. The 1.6 engine felt the benefit of a Garrett TO2 Turbocharger that boosted the output to 133bhp. It came with extra driving lamps, tailgate top spoiler, electric windows, central locking, glass sunroof, Recaro seats and most important of all - vents on the bonnet. It could top 130mph and get to 60mph in 7.7 seconds.

XR2i, an aggressive and unsophisticated car. Great.

Briefly, the fast Ford performance crown rested with the Fiesta RS 1800. Introduced in 1992 it looked like an XR2i but had a bigger 1796cc engine producing 128bhp. It was reasonably quick, registering 124mph as a maximum speed and gets to 60mph in just a fraction over 8 seconds. When that model left the showrooms for good in 1995 that was effectively the end for the XR, RS and any pretence by Ford at offering a quick small hatch ended. When the XR2i was cancelled and replaced by the more anaemic 1.6Si with 89bhp. However, from 2000 the Fiesta 1.6 Zetec S and Ghia offered a 101bhp worth of small Ford which had a decently long list of standard fixtures, but wasn't quick or remotely interesting to look at it. After decades of leading the performance pack with clever marketing and branding that appealed to a certain kind of value buyer, Ford had lost their nerve. Beaten down by high insurance premiums and the Essex boy racer image that no longer helped a global company, the hot hatch was sadly abandoned.

Honda didn't really have a small fast car until the Civic GT briefly troubled the price lists for a couple years from 1985. The three-door car had big bumpers, side skirts and GT decals on the rear three quarter panels. It may have packed 100bhp but it never caught on. Slightly more serious was the Civic 1.6i VT in 1990 which made great use of the 148bhp VTEC engine. In the dull Civic no one noticed, but when installed into the tiny CRX coupe it grabbed a lot more attention. The CRX 1.6i vt replaced the old 16 valve, 130bhp model in 1990.

Citroen, who had been quiet on the small fast car front, took advantage of the lightweight AX to fit an 85bhp 1360cc engine and call it the GT. The AX had slightly extended wheel arches and packed out sill, but not much else to set it apart. In 1991 the 100bhp GTi had as the name suggested, fuel injection. Reasonably nippy getting to 60mph in just over 8 seconds and a scary 118mph. What came next though became something of a legend amongst teenage drivers, helped initially by free insurance packages for the standard non-performance versions on the UK market.

Citroen Saxo VTS. Every adolescent driver's dream.

My Mini Cooper it's part in my Breakdown

The Citroen Saxo from 1997 onwards was available in warm, VTR, and hot, VTS, versions. Well actually the warm VTR was actually fairly tepid as the 90bhp 1.6 engine was already available in SX and VSX trim. The point was that the VTS had body coloured bumpers and wheel arch extensions, with alloy wheels, fog lamps and sports seats. Mind you, 116mph top speed and getting to 60mph in 9.3 seconds was not too shabby. Trading up to a VTS meant 120bhp that translated into a 127mph top speed and gets to 60mph in just over 8 seconds. ABS brakes though was standard, along with a passenger airbag, leather trimmed steering wheel and a map reading light no less. A responsive, nimble and fun to drive package and not just for teenagers either.

In the 1980s Daihatsu concentrated in the Charade as their performance car and the three cylinder 993cc engines were turbocharged to push the output to 68bhp. This '84 to '89 model had bucket seats and spoilers, but the suspension was beefed up to cope a year later. However, it was the oddly nomenclatured GTti in 1987 with a normally aspirated engine that produced a much more useful 99bhp. Here was a proper high speed shopping trolley that made Minis look very anaemic as it registered a 113mph top speed and got to 60mph in under 8 seconds.

Indeed, the GTti went away in 1993 and then very briefly came back as the more logical GTi with a new shape body in 1997. For just a year the now four cylinder 1296cc engine produced 97bhp and came with ABS brakes as standard. Like all Daihatsus the standard specification was decent and included 14-inch (35.5cm) alloy wheels, electric mirrors, drivers airbag and a Pioneer audio system. No one was really interested though as the company was more successful at selling cheap reliable shoppers. That didn't stop them downsizing to the Cuore in 1997 and offering the completely bonkers Avanzanto TR-XX R4. This model came with four wheel drive, 16 valves, sports suspension, alloy wheels, sports seats and spoilers. The tiny 659cc four-cylinder engine produced 64bhp and managed 89mph and would get to 60mph in just under 12 seconds. So not sparkling

performance but different and the 4WD meant that it
wouldn't fall off the road too easily.

Mazda's 121 was the tiny one, but the 3-door 323
was used as their high performance weapon of choice. The
1500GT from 1983 wasn't that special and only had
85bhp, plus it was also available as a saloon and five door
hatch. The 1600i with 103bhp was a bit more focused and
three door only. However, the 1600 Turbo 4 x 4 and
limited edition Rally version from '86 to '87 had 148bhp
and is a forgotten precursor of the Subaru Impreza and
Mitsubishi Evo.

**Sunbeam Stiletto, a fastback bundle
of rear engined fun.**

NSU got Bertone to design them a pretty coupe
called the Sport Prinz. It wasn't that quick, managing
75mph from its 583cc, later increased to 598cc. Pretty,
but pretty ineffective, despite finally getting front disc
brakes in 1965. More important was the new Prinz model.
Ever since 1911, NSU riders contested the motorcycle
events, with frequent success. To commemorate this, the
company launched the 1200TT in 1965 with front disc
brakes and wider track. Developed from the standard TT
model for competition use, the NSU TTS in 1967 had a
1000 cc engine with a power output of up to 85 bhp. By
1972 the small NSUs were no more and five years later
NSU ceased to be as a result of the Wankel issue.

My Mini Cooper it's part in my Breakdown

If the closest domestic rival to the Mini was the Imp, there really wasn't too much in the way of a high performance equivalent. The excitingly named Hillman Imp Californian was a fastback with a steeply sloping rear roofline and no opening window tailgate, but at least it looked great. No, the quick Imps were Sunbeams, which were uprated to cope with the extra output. The saloon was badged as the Imp Sport from 1966 and had a meaty 55bhp twin carburettor engine, with high lift camshaft, larger radiator, oil cooler and better brakes. And then there was the Stiletto that had the same powerplant, but period details made it stand out such as a leather steering wheel and black vinyl roof. The final hot offering from the Rootes group was the rare Singer Chamois Sport saloon.

**Sunbeam Talbot Lotus, three marques,
one hot rear drive hatch.**

When the Imp went, the replacement was the Chrysler Sunbeam in 1977. The warm one was the Ti with twin carburettors and a 1.6 litre engine last seen in the Avenger Tiger. Badged as a Talbot from 1980, the seriously quick Sunbeam was the one with name Lotus in front of it. Built to qualify for rallying some 2300 were made with a 2.2 litre 150bhp Lotus 16 valve engine connected to a five-speed ZF gearbox. Didn't actually sell that well despite the pedigree and the last 150 cars were registered a year after production finished in 1981. Those cars were repainted and reappointed by Avon coachworks and incredibly sold at a discount through a dealer in Nuneaton.

There were plenty of performance oddities around before and after the Cooper's reign. The Messerschmitt TG500 Tiger, an aircraft canopy on four wheels was a singularly terrifying way to reach 75mph in 1958 and faded away in 1961 just as the Mini Cooper was launched. The DAF 55 Marathon coupe in 1968 provided 63bhp and some rallying success. Then the DAF 66 in 1972 used the Marathon name across the range from '73 but it never bothered the Cooper, but had some of the stripy detailing of the 1275GT. Honda's S600 in 1963 was a coupe' with a very advanced twin camshaft, four carburettor light alloy cylinder head engine. These early Honda models did poorly in their home market but were technically interesting and showed that Honda could move on confidently from motorbikes to small interesting sports cars. The Z Coupe from 1970 looked like a little hot hatch but was just a rebodied N600. But then there was a lot of rebodying going on in the '60s.

Ogle SX1000, the hubcaps are the biggest clue to its origins.

Taking all the important innards of a Mini and then plumbing it into a plastic coupe body was a popular pastime in the 1960s. From 1962 you could supply the

Mini or Cooper parts to Ogle who would put them into their pretty glass fibre SX1000.

For the DIY brigade there was the rather more successful Mini Marcos GT, which was the only British car to finish the 1966 Le Mans. Launched just a year earlier by the company which bore Jem Marsh and Frank Costin's names. The Mini Marcos was not a pretty sight, but it was tremendously successful on the track and as a commercial product. It had a complicated parentage, based on a Paul Emery designed prototype, with a Mini Van floor pan and built by Marcos parent company Falcon for amateur racer Dizzy Addicot and called the DART. It was hurriedly prepared for production hence the oddly styled monocoque body. Mini sub frames were bolted in through metal plates with wooden floor reinforcement. Also from the same gene pool sprang the MINIJEM which was almost identical had competition success with sales that topped 350.

The Marcos had a chequered history, got a tailgate in 1971 and after the bankruptcy of Marcos passed through a variety of owners. Marsh relaunched the Marcos Mk V in 1991 as a result of a huge order from Japan. The MINIJEM had an equally unfortunate career going out of production in '76 when the UK kit car industry collapsed. However, it was later revived in the early '80s as the Kingfisher.

Marcos made the most popular Mini based kit car.

My Mini Cooper it's part in my Breakdown

Universal Power Drives built forestry tractors. In 1968 they constructed what is probably the best mid engined Mini incarnation ever which they called the Unipower. Originally built by Andrew Hedges with an aluminium body for racing driver Roy Pierpoint, UPD bought the rights and entered production. At £1200, prior to the required Mini, or Cooper engine being fitted, it was not cheap. This was a sophisticated tubular steel chassis, GRP bodied, mid engined sports car. Suspension was all independent with coil springs. With 998cc power the Unipower could get to the magic ton, but with 1275cc on board, 120 mph was a possibility.

The Mini Sprint had a roof that looks like it has been used as a skateboard by an elephant. The thing is that very few of these are the genuine Minisprint article. The story goes back to Cars and Car Conversions magazine, the monthly bible of the inveterate club racer and go faster freak, when contributor Clive Trickey demonstrated just how low a Mini roof could go. The design passed through several hands, at one point being called the Walker GTS before coachbuilders Stewart and Arden called it the Mini Sprint in 1967.

What happened was that a Cooper S Minis were stripped and the roof pillars were increased in rake and reduced by one and half inches (and a similar amount was removed from the middle of the car. Then all the external seams were removed for a smoother look and 40 square inches (258 sq cm) less of aerodynamic resistance. The wings were reshaped and rectangular headlights fitted. The driver sat a little more comfortably because the seat frames were lowered and reclined.

One of the prettiest and best engineered Mini specials was the Broadspeed GT. Tuning genius and respected Mini racer Ralph Broad came up with a fast backed Mini and put in on sale in 1966-67. With lowered Hydrolastic suspension, well-engineered and structurally sound roof conversion, it really looked the scaled down Aston Martin part. Five versions were offered, a basic 850cc at £808, a GT based on the Cooper at £915 and a 1275 Cooper S badged as a GT de luxe for £1,068. These models had reclining seats, a folding rear seat for extra luggage, pile carpets a comprehensive fascia and plastic bumpers with rubber and chrome inserts. Not only that, a Super de Luxe was offered with a more highly tuned Broadspeed Stage III engine (100bhp) and a full race GTS version to special order. Only 28 were built, many ending up in Spain.

The beautiful Broadspeed GT.

Of all the coachbuilders and specialists involved with Minis in the '60s, Radford was arguably the most successful and innovative. Inspired by the work of Hoopers who had conjured up an eye catching wicker worked special for Peter Sellers, made their own version. Harold Radford who was used to installing cocktail cabinets into Rolls Royce limousines did much the same with their first effort in 1963, producing the Cooper Mini de Ville Grande Luxe. It was described as 'The chauffeur driven Mini' and featured redesigned white leather seats, an instrument binnacle in front of the driver, two-tone silver over charcoal Rolls Royce paint, electric windows, Webasto sunroof, stereo radio and lamb's wool carpets. It cost £1100 and with all that extra weight of the gadgets was disappointingly slow. Radford never made that mistake again and used Downton tuned engines to make up the shortfall and leave a standard Cooper for dead.

Industrial Designer David Ogle had underground trains and helicopters to his credit when he turned his attention to building and marketing a small sports car. First revealed in 1962 with a 997cc Cooper engine, the bodywork was made from GRP, which enclosed the Minis floor pan, which was also reinforced. Badged as the SX1000 it flopped in America, the market was intended for, but sold steadily in the UK as the Lightweight GT and Mini 850 GT. After Ogle's untimely death and sixty-six examples were built the manufacturing rights were sold. The resulting Fletcher GT with an ugly new nose was equally unprofitable and just four were sold.

Crayford Sprint. Open air Mini Motoring at its best.

Crayford were legendary coachbuilders, who opened up (cut the roof off) almost every significant car built in the '60s. Amongst the many attempts to build a fresh air Mini theirs was the best. The Sprint was announced in September 1963 when any Mini could be converted for £129. They installed floor section box members, door pillar and scuttle reinforcement with transverse stiffening and waist level stiffeners. The side screens could be retained for the sliding windows, but there were also removable versions.

My Mini Cooper it's part in my Breakdown

A Radford hatchback, which was built for Peter Sellers.

And finally, oddball Isle of Man based Peel operation also brought out a Mini kit car in 1965 called the Viking. Putting the useful Mini bits into an oddly proportioned, but far less spacious pint sized coupe seemed pointless. Apparently they sold fifty but it is hard to see how.

Back with the proper manufacturers like Peugeot who fancied their chances taking on, well not the Cooper anymore but the faster Fiestas, there was an overlooked slightly warmish hatch based on the promising chassis of the 104. The ZS from 1979 to 1984 was the three-door version with a 1360cc engine boosted from 72 to 80bhp. The stubby three door struggled for attention in an era when the much more brash Ford XR2 grabbed all of the attention. Which brings us to the 205 GTi, which took over from where the original Golf GTI left off.

The 205 was small, light with a powerful engine, which handled sweetly. This was the hatch, which also dominated the '80s from launch in 1984. It didn't have much power, but initially didn't need it. The 1580cc engine had Bosch fuel injection produced 105 bhp using a close ratio 5 speed gearbox. However it came a proper hot hatch when the engine was uprated to 115bhp in 1987. That's also the point when buyers were also offered a 1.9 version. The 1905cc engine pumped out a seriously useful 130bhp. So it needed rear disc brakes, chunkier alloys and low profile tyres. By 1992 the 1.6 had been discontinued and the 1.9 neutered slightly by a catalytic converter, which reduced output to 122bhp.

**The Peugeot 205 GTi, the true
definition of the hot hatch.**

There was even a racing version called the T16. Just 200 were built between 1983 and '84 to qualify for motorsport with extras for competition. Two seat, four wheel drive, with a mid mounted 1.8 turbo engine. Road versions produced 200bhp and Group B rally versions up to 450bhp.

Then Peugeot's spin on the Citroen AX was the rather wonderful 106 Rallye in 1994 which proved that less was so much more, the 1294cc engine producing 100bhp and not a great deal else. Body mouldings and wheel arch extensions covered the white sports steel wheels. Inside there were red carpets and seat belts with sports seats. Here was the essence of a hot hatch which wasn't clumsy or complicated but with refreshingly bold styling. By 1996 it was so good it had been discontinued.

However, the 1.6 GTi brought back vivid memories of well, the original 205 GTi. This time the 1587cc engine produced 120bhp with standard ABS brakes and colour-keyed paintwork were the main elements. The standard kit list was quite long but didn't contribute to the maximum speed of 127mph and getting to 60mph in 8.7 seconds. Yes, you didn't need loads of kit to make an interesting car and to prove the point Peugeot brought back the Rallye concept in 1997 as a limited edition. This time they fitted a 103bhp version of the engine, which still managed to reach 121mph and get to 60mph in 9.4 seconds. 200 were available finished in either Indigo Blue or Bianca White.

Logically, the follow up to the 205 GTi was the 206 GTi and although it was not nearly as stylish or pretty as the old car, it was still a very good hot hatch. The 1999 3 door had the 1997cc engine and it produced 137bhp. There were nice little touches like the chrome tail pipe, driving lights, aluminium gear knob and pedals to set it part from all the other 206s. However, the fact that it did 131mph was enough for it to stand apart. It just didn't have the same tickle its tummy lovability even though it was quick and handled tidily. Maybe by the late '90s there were far too many accomplished hatches?

Renault Gordini. The 5 with performance knobs on.

The Renault 5 always leant itself to going much quicker and the Gordini was that version, although in the home market it was branded Alpine. Available from 1976 producing 93bhp from the 1.4 litre engine it also benefited from a five-speed gearbox. The Gordini managed a creditable 110mph and came with alloy wheels, bucket seats and front spolier, with fog lamps plus body stripes and decals. Along with every other manufacturer in the 1980s, Renault added a turbo. So the Gordini Turbo was born in 1982. It needed a chassis makeover to handle the power, (110bhp) plus wider alloy wheels. Renamed Le Car 2 Turbo in 1984 the model was replaced the same year by the all-new 5. For the time being the hottest model was the 90bhp 1721cc GTX. Well actually it wasn't.

Then there was the Renault 5 Turbo 2 that was completely mad, but then it was meant to be. Homologated for competition use, the 1297cc, 160bhp turbocharged engine was shifted to the boot. It had bulges and air intakes just like a supercar. The proper racing ones even had aluminium body panels and a turbo helped produce a significant 240bhp. Back to reality the civilian version of the 5GT Turbo went back into the brochures in 1986. Still with a 1397cc engine the bhp started at 115 and was increased a year later to 120bhp. Great fun to drive, incredibly responsive but often broken down, or refusing to restart after a blast.

Renault Turbo. Late '80s excess at its very best.

Of all the performance Renaults the Clio Williams is rightly regarded as the ultimate '90s hot hatch. Built to celebrate Renault's association with the Williams F1 team, it felt sensationally quick as a 7.5 second 0 to 60 mph time should do. Not only that it was more than up to hard braking and sudden changes in direction without any drama. Powered by a 1998cc fuel injected engine producing 150bhp it was a lot of fun and best of all; the Williams really looked the part, wearing attention seeking gold alloy wheels. But there was more than one Williams.

My Mini Cooper it's part in my Breakdown

First off there was a limited edition of 400 imported into the UK in 1993. Finished in metallic blue with Williams decals and four gold Speedline eight spoke wheels. Inside there were sports front seats with lumbar adjustment, electric windows, remote central locking and an alarm. In January '94 the Williams 2 was more of the same. Finally, the July 1995 Clio Williams 3 arrived in two batches of 150 the second in September 1995. To justify a higher asking price it came with ABS brakes, electric tilt and slide sunroof.

Oh, and then there are the other performance Clios from 1993 that didn't have the drama and sense of occasion of the Williams, but could be considered the Cooper and Cooper S of their day when it comes to performance. The 1.8RSi had the 1794cc in 110bhp state of tune and looked fancy enough with its spoilers and skirts, sports seats and electric tilt/slide roof. Meanwhile the 1.8 16v had a multi point fuel-injected version that put out 137bhp and was only a bit slower than a Williams recording a 130mph top speed and racing to 60mph in 8 seconds.

With the new generation Clio the RSi made do with a reduced engine size of 1598cc, but still managed to get 110bhp out of it, but it was now the top spec 1.6 ahead of the Etoile and Initiale. However, two new performance Clios indicated just how far the hot hatch and come and how outclassed the reborn yet pensionable Cooper now was. In January 2000 the Clio 2.0 16v Renaultsport 172 screeched onto the scene with, as the name suggested, 172bhp. It had a specification similar to the RSi plus a more convincing body kit, 15-inch (38cm) OZ alloy wheels, aluminium pedals and standard metallic paint. Here was a truly exciting hatch, which oddly still wasn't as quick as a Williams in top speed terms, but registering a 6.9 second to 60mph time, it certainly was keener to accelerate.

Renault Clio Williams, pretty much the Mini Cooper of the 1990s.

In the same month that the Mini ended its production, October 2000, the Clio 3.0 V6 Renaultsport, which recalled the great days of the Renault 5 Turbo 2 by putting a huge engine in the boot, was unleashed. The 2946cc V6 produced 230bhp, and like the old 5 was an interesting amalgam of bulges, gaping mesh covered intakes and huge alloy wheels, in this case, 17 inch (43cm) OZ Superturismos. It also had a six-speed gearbox and may have had less power than the old 5, but at 147mph it was much quicker, more response and even more of a scaled down supercar.

Rover produced a few Cooper alternatives over the years. The first act was sticking the famous octagon badge onto the Metro in 1982 to make it, yes you guessed it, the MG Metro. Firmed up suspension, finned alloy wheels and some extra power, 72bhp up 10bhp from the standard car, pushed it to 100mph. Oh yes and it had red seat belts. In fact later versions went rather over the top in the MG logo department both inside and out. Then in 1983 Rover then decided to emulate the Cooper S with the MG Metro Turbo. It could just about cope with the extra oomph, but it was restricted to 93bhp so that the four-speed gearbox would survive the extra power. It wasn't that quick though with a maximum speed of 110mph and getting to 60mph in 10.3 seconds. It should have been universally loathed as an insult to the MG badge, instead it was a late triumph of badge engineering and the best selling MG, that wasn't a Midget or MGB.

MG Mini Metro, certainly not the Cooper of the 1980s. This is the fancied up, all white, Tickford version.

SEAT, seemed like the manufacturer least likely to make a hot hatch despite Porsche giving them a hand in the 1980s. Actually the 1985 Ibiza wasn't that bad because not only did Porsche design the overhead-cam engines, Giorgetto Giugiaro penned the subtle and clean bodywork. With the largest 1714cc engine it only just managed 107mph and it didn't handle that tidily either. Once Volkswagen took control, things got much better until the Germans donated the Polo and it was rebodied as an all-new Ibiza.

The resulting three-door Ibiza was a quality product with firm suspension, agile handling and VW engines under the bonnet. Whereas the contemporary Golf GTI was sluggish and far from sharp, a range of responsive ibizas proved to be a much more accomplished and better value alternative. In the beginning, that's 1993, there was a 1984cc 8-valve model, which produced 115bhp. However for those who wanted a bit more in 1994 a 1.8 GTi blasted out 130bhp. It even had EDS traction control. Revisions in 1997 saw the introduction of a 16 valve 2.0 litre with 150bhp and also Cupra Sport versions. These were often finished in yellow and added an onboard computer, wider wheels and arches. SEAT also initiated a rally programme and for a while, this was the hot hatch for those who wanted value, performance and a dash of competition kudos.

In the 1980s Datsun became Nissan and the Cherry was the one they made go pop. The three door Turbo from 1983 wasn't that powerful the 1488cc engine producing 114bhp in a fairly scruffy and laggy manner. It did have a front spoiler with Turbo written on it in orange. Indeed Turbo was also written on the side and tailgate so that no one could miss it. Just to confuse matters it was renamed the ZX a year later. Then in 1985 it was tarted up with black side panels and wheel arches, bucket seats and bizarre blue spectrum patterns inside. Even more bizarre though was the Nissan Cherry GTi Europe, quite possibly the worst car ever made. It had the distinction of being the first Japanese car to be built in Europe, well half built anyway. The trimmed out bodies were sent to Italy and the Alfasud plant in Naples where they installed the 1.5 flat four 75bhp engines. In theory that sounded quite good, Japanese build quality with Italian flair, the reality was breakdowns and disappointment. A seriously shoddy car and a mistake that Nissan would never repeat, setting up a proper factory Tyne and Wear to make boring, but unburstable Bluebirds.

Subaru still did four-wheel drive and instead of making the Justy dangerously quick they applied a turbo to the 1800 model and produced a 136bhp 4 x 4 three-door hatch. Few though really cared about such things until the Impreza arrived and started winning world rally championships.

Mitsubishi chose the Colt as the basis for their Turbo experiments in 1984. Combining a turbo and petrol injection boosted the output of the 1597cc engine to 123bhp. It was actually very quick with a top speed of 114mph and quite brutal acceleration getting to 60mph in 8.7 seconds. Mitsubishi then moved onto a more sophisticated follow up with the GTi in 1988. This had a new twin camshaft 16-valve 1.6-litre engine that produced 125bhp with a top speed of 122mph. It was well built, expensive and consequently rare.

In 1985 Suzuki added an extra cylinder to their Swift range and just as importantly cut the wheelbase on the GTi by 4 inches (10cm). This had a 16-valve engine producing 101bhp that meant a useful 112mpg and 0 to 60mph in a decent 8.6 seconds. Another forgettable dud that didn't hit the spot in the '80s because it was too pricey and not nearly showy enough.

Toyota never managed to sprinkle any actual performance stardust on the Starlet, but the Corolla 1.6 GTi-16 in 1987 was a relatively compact 13-foot (3.96m). It had disc brakes all round and the engine produced 123bhp. No one seemed to know it existed but getting to 60mph in 8 seconds dead was standard hot hatch timings for the day. Yet another far eastern hot hatch failure.

Like many of the large manufacturers who could afford it, Vauxhall played the rally homologation card with the Chevette HS. Late to the performance party and unfashionably rear wheel drive, but that only added to the sporty fun. In 1976 plumbing in a 2279cc engine with special 16 valve twin camshaft cylinder heads produced a useful 135bhp, all controlled through a Getrag gearbox leading to a 120mph maximum. Wider alloys and front and a rear spoiler looked good. However, few made, around 400 according to Vauxhall. In 1979 even fewer (50) of the Chevette HSRs were built and Vauxhall upped the output to 150bhp and it spent most of its life rallying. Shame that Vauxhall did not exploit the HSR branding with mass-produced road cars instead of leaving it all to the XR Fords.

However, Vauxhall's main performance tool was always the Astra GTE in the '80s but the Nova also got that moniker so we will go with that as the more pint sized equivalent of the Coopers that were not around when they first came out. In 1983 the first go faster Nova was the SR. It had 1297cc 69bhp, which was neither here nor there. What buyers really liked was the front and rear spoilers, grey mouldings down the flanks, sporty steel wheels and tinted glass. Inside there were grippy sports seats and a comprehensive array of instruments. In case you are bothered, apart from a centre console, there was a rev counter, voltmeter, oil pressure gauge and a four spoke steering wheel. It was replaced in 1989 by the 1.4SR that now had 72bhp. A revamp a year later also resulted in uprated springs, dampers and rear anti-roll bar.

Opel Corsa GSi, same as the Vauxhall Nova GTE and also GSi.

The 1.6i GTE from 1988 was of course similar to the SR but had Bosch fuel injection, and fashionably body coloured grille, bumpers, rear spoiler and door mirror housings. A reflective GTE between the tail lamps was a nice touch as were the wider sports steel wheels, revised suspension and close ratio gearbox. It produced 101bhp and would get to 60mph in just over 9 seconds. It wasn't that lively, but it looked the part and that was the important thing. Indeed there was a name change in 1990 when it was redesignated the GSi with mods as for the SR.

When the Corsa went curvy in 1993 the GSi provided the excitement. It had 1598cc engine producing 105bhp, which meant 60mph in 9 seconds. ABS brakes are standard with alloys, sports suspension, leather steering wheel and gear knob. It got an Ecotec 4 16 valve engine a year, which produced 104bhp and was then discontinued in '95. It came back as the Sport in 1997. Just to confuse matters the SRi came back with the revised Corsa in 2000 with both a 1.4 and 1.8 engine. It was the same month that the Cooper left the new car listings for good. There probably isn't anything significant in that, except that the Corsa was by now quite a dull little shopper and the SRi no longer set the pulse racing and when it went missing, no one missed it.

When it comes to reviving the spirit of the Cooper the Volkswagen Golf is always credited with bringing proper compact car performance back to the masses. That may well be right, even though that overlooks Ford's complete understanding of what makes buyers tick when it comes to go faster badges. However, the Golf is too big to be compared with the Mini, especially when there is the Polo to consider. Trouble is, it didn't get the 'hot' treatment for several years. With the arrival of the bread van Polo came the slightly funky three door coupe', although really it was just another less long hatch and anyway resembled the old Polo Mark 1. Launched in January '83 it might have had some red paint surrounding the grille like a GTI, plus front and rear spoilers, a centre console and plastic trims on wheel arches and sills, but underneath the bonnet was a 1093cc 50bhp, 4-speed slug. VW tried to sex it up a bit with a 1272cc, 55 bhp engine in September '83, but even calling it Coupe S, sticking four lights on the grille, a rev counter, sports seats and steering wheel inside, could not hide the fact that this was another slow if slightly prettier slug.

Volkswagen Polo GT. Not that exciting or that quick.

It was a good job that the GT came along in November '90. Multi-point fuel injection was connected to the 1272cc engine and it pumped out a mighty 72bhp. 60mph came up in 14.5 seconds and top speed was 95mph. Fitted with a catalyser and rectangular headlamps, wraparound indicators, red inserts in the bumpers and a three spoke steering wheel, things were starting to look serious for the old Polo. In fact the really serious Polo was the intercooled and supercharged G40, which produced 113bhp. The performance was a highly respectable 122mph top speed and 60mph arrived in 8.1 seconds. The suspension was firmed up and lowered by an inch, the alloys were 5.5 x 13" BBS items, there was GTI like wheel arch extensions and side rubbing strips too. Inside cloth with a sporty check design on it, plus a four speaker HO5 Panasonic pull out radio/cassette made owners feel special.

Then after what seemed like over a decade, well 14 years anyway, the Polo was suddenly brought up to date, but sadly there seemed to be no space for a G40 or GT. No, that had to wait until the revised Polo in 2000 when it got the full GTI treatment with a 1.6 litre engine. As exciting as that was this may not have been the best application for that power unit.

Volkswagen Lupo GTI. Like the Cooper for the new millennium, but without the charisma, competition history, or contrasting roof colour.

349

My Mini Cooper it's part in my Breakdown

In the last year of Mini Cooper production Volkswagen revived the concept of the tiny performance car by launching the Lupo 16v Sport. The 1390cc engine produced 100bhp that in the small stubby shape of the Lupo meant a decent 117mph and 60 mph arriving in just under 10 seconds. Distinguished by its body kit, alloys and ABS it was a great little package, also available in SEAT Lupo trim too. However Volkswagen went one better with the Cooper crushing 1.6 16v GTI. The 1598cc engine produced 125bhp pulling along a relatively light body meant that it could get to 125mph maximum and 60mph in 8.3 seconds. It was fancied up and sat on 15-inch (38cm) alloy wheels, centre exhaust, aluminium pedals, Xenon headlamps, sports seats and remote locking. Yes, the original GTI was back and the Lupo is probably the closest in spirit, cuteness, clarity and performance to the original Cooper. Shame it never got to win a rally, star in a film or be considered remotely cool.

June 2007 Mileage: 99,956 Amount Spent: £MOT cost plus a down payment on an engine and gearbox rebuild. Minis in my Life: Austin Mini Cooper MOT: Yes

My Mini Cooper it's part in my Breakdown

Another year and the Cooper manages to scrape another MOT, but not without an increasingly long list of advisories. These now read, offside rear brake recording little or no effort. Parking brake efficiency below requirements. Oh and that damned exhaust leak from the downpipe.

In the corner of the garage on a trolley was the original Cooper engine and gearbox. It was a leaky old thing and I may have forgotten to mention this earlier, but the twin carburettors had been replaced by a single SU. The owners probably took them off firstly because they can be a pain to balance and secondly it seems like an easy way to save a few miles per gallon. The reality is that a sweetly tuned 998cc engine and twin carbs will be more economical than a single SU trying to cope with an iffy engine.

When the Cooper first arrived in my life the twin SU carbs were in a cardboard box in the boot, which is where they stayed pretty much for the next thirty years. I thought it was time they took their rightful place on top of a rebuilt block.

So it all started with the engine, not that it had been started for quite some time. I've wrestled with them before and in my teenage years managed to hoof them out of engine bays without a conventional lift. That may now explain my recurring hernia issues. Never mind I had got the Cooper engine onto a trolley where it leaked oil for at least a decade. A Metro A Plus engine may have had the same displacement as the engine, but it was no replacement.

According to Threeways Garage a respected engine builder had moved into my village. So I popped round for a chat. Steve Parker was a chain smoking, bearded and avuncular chap with a lifetime's experience spent poking around the inner recesses of any engine you cared to mention. Indeed, he had an anecdote for every type of engine you've never heard of which would mean that dropping off a part would turn into a nicotine tinged story involving colourful 1970s privateer racers and a drunken boat yard owner with outboard motor troubles.

Suffice to say he was never boring and a highly skilled engineer who quickly discovered that all sorts of unsuitable modifications and common parts had been used to keep the 998cc lump running over the years. Obviously absolutely everything needed overhauling. The number of parts required runs to a couple of densely packed A4 sheets. I won't bore you with the list, effectively the whole thing was blueprinted. From a rebored block to new pistons, big end shells, valves, guides and camshaft there were new ancillaries too. So oil and water pumps, alternator, dynamo and clutch were included. The gearbox was rebuilt and the radiator refurbished. I also went for a Lumenition ignition kit to get rid of the points. Nine times out of ten that was the reason most Minis didn't start. Easy enough for me to sort out when I was younger, but I didn't want to muck around in the dark at my age. Also the modern electrickery would all be hidden, so no one could point and say I was cheating.

More to the point, all this work wasn't going to be cheap...

23. How to Build a Mini, this is the part where the author was allowed to visit the factory and observe first hand the really quite antiquated way that Rover was still building the Mini in the mid 1990s which must have given owners, BMW, palpitations every time they went near Longbridge, indeed there were blokes with hammers knocking shells into shape and incredibly not much had changed in over 30 years which included some of the workforce...

I wrote this chapter after a Longbridge factory tour in the summer of 1996...

Rationally the Mini has been outclassed, outdated and overpriced for some time, but it remains unique. The incredible thing is not just that the Mini has managed to survive this long, but also the fact that it is built in the same place, in the same way, in some cases by people who have spent their entire working lives on the Mini production line.

"Where are the robots?" Yes it must be another party of Japanese visitors coming to terms with the concept of unautomated car production. With a few crucial exceptions, making a Mini is virtually unchanged after nearly forty years of production. Although Issigonis designed the Mini so that it was easy to build, hence the prominent exterior seams, it is not an especially easy, or quick car to assemble. What the Mini requires is good old-fashioned workmanship.

Pam Wearing, Corporate Communications Manager and employee since the British Motor Corporation days doesn't need reminding that she has been around the factory almost as long as the little car. "If you live in Longbridge and all your family worked at Austin, it is inevitable that you are going to join them, but I've never regretted coming here." Not surprisingly as we enter the Old West Works where the body shells are put together, Pam meets and greets everyone on the line like old friends, because they are.

Reg Phillips Manufacturing Manager steers me around this time warp, "We've still got some of the original equipment from 1959, like the jigs for the windshield and fenders (wings) although the main carousel went last Christmas." What strikes you is the large number of real people involved at this stage of the process. Whereas the rest of the Rover plant is sparsely manned and robotised, the Mini is virtually hand built. The body pressings that make up the shell are hand welded which means that pinpoint accuracy is impossible. So each body has to be fettled, tweaked and teased to perfection. This takes experience and Bill Banner with an astonishing 40 years on the track works in the 'boneyard' putting the bodies right.

"I've seen almost no changes over the years, which is a good thing, because building a Mini is highly skilled and I really enjoy being on final rectification. There isn't a fault I can't cure and the quality of the car just gets better."

There aren't many women around, but Lyn Croft became the first gas welder ten years ago and is now in charge of the Final Quality Audit. Using her eyes and gloved hands no body leaves the plant without her authorisation. "I love it here, the blokes are all such brilliant characters who like a laugh, but are respectful with it."

Bearded Brian Dipple fits that description having worked on the Mini line since January 1960. Like the others he hasn't seen too many changes over the years, "Things are a lot more stable today, back in the '70s it was down tools every five minutes for one reason, or another." Hasn't he ever got a little bored at all? "Never, some people say it was because I come from Bromsgrove and we're a bit simple, but I enjoy the work and wouldn't want to work on any other car. In the early days we called the Mini the 'Bubble', to keep the model secret. That's because we were told by BMC that we were building a bubble car, so the name stuck: working on the bubble, bubble trouble." As Brian chuckles I reflect on the fact that he has probably had something to do with just about every Mini I've owned and he's a lot friendlier than a robot.

"I've shown dozens of Japanese visitors around here over the years and they always ask where the robots are and they sort of freak out when you tell them there aren't any." Pam Wearing leads me out of the Old West

My Mini Cooper it's part in my Breakdown

Works and past the surreal sight of dozens of bare metal shells waiting for paint. The next stop is Paint Shop 3 that is rather more high tech. Now the Mini takes its turn sandwiched between much more modern products like MGFs's and Rover 100s which trundle along together on a monorail. The bodies are degreased, rustproofed, primered and painted. The Mini Coopers with their contrasting coloured roofs go through the painting process twice, once to be sprayed say Almond Green and secondly after the body is 'bagged up' in brown paper enabling the roof to be painted white.

It is then a short walk to the final assembly track where Rover 100s and Minis mingle before all the vital organs are plumbed in. Suddenly it is much like any other car plant as trim and mechanicals are added to the constantly moving shells.

There are no workers at Rover, only 'associates' and the benefits of teamwork, a legacy from the company's link with Honda, are constantly stressed by Geoff Powell, who is the Principal Engineer Mini Technical Support. But Geoff is not a dour salary man, like everyone else he genuinely loves Minis. He's got a classic Cooper at home, another he is restoring and drives to work in an old MGB. "It's got such a great character and really stands out from the crowd. We also never stop developing it on the line, everyone is encouraged to come up with ways of building it better. Compared to a 1959 Mini the only parts which are identical are the roof and windscreen surround."

Minis are carefully lowered onto the engine and subframes then fitted in place by four associates another '59 throwback, because the opposite happens with most modern cars as these parts are bolted up into the shell. After that there are electrical diagnostic checks and the Mini is run on a rolling road before being parked in a holding area and trailered to your local dealer. It has taken around 50 hours to build a Mini, roughly double what a modern supermini spends inside a factory. Production is running at over 400 a week and more than half of that number goes directly to Japan. They can be credited with keeping the car alive, although far eastern Minis have a slightly different specification. A peek under the bonnet reveals an air conditioning unit shoehorned into an impossibly small space. Inside there's a bracket for a distress flare and what looks like a squash ball is pushed onto the edge of the bumper to avoid scraping sensitive Japanese shins.

Outside of the Ferrari, Morgan and Aston Martin factories it would be hard to find workers, sorry associates, with such a passion for the cars they build. Brian Dipple who's been on the line since 1960 said he would retire when the Mini did, "And that won't happen".

I don't want to spoil the ending for you, or Brian, but it did. So here's how they used to build Minis in the old days.

Building a Mini in 15 Easy Stages

1. Body Panels: Rover Group Body and Pressings in Swindon produced the majority of the panels, although the doors dashboard and front valance is made by Camford Pressings of Llanelli.

2. Grille and Fenders: Three jigs were used to spot-weld the front end of the Mini together.

3. Floor: The floor pressings are joined to the front end and then put onto the build line.

4. **Monosides**: All the major panels now box in that familiar Mini shape as the sides, rear end and roof are welded into place. In this case by a giant.

5. Doors, boot and bonnet: All the opening panels are screwed into place and the body trundles down an illuminated line to highlight any imperfections and any rough areas are sanded off.

6. Final Line: Off line work is carried out for specific models and markets, or instance cutting out the sunroof for a British Open model, or detail changes for Japanese and other export specifications.

7. VQ Final Quality Audit: Every 'body in white' is checked for faults and won't leave the works until rectified and rechecked.

8. Dispatch: Every body, still welded to its carrier is moved to a holding area where they are stored until summoned by computer to the paint shop.

9. Paint shop: Primer, underseal and final paint finish. A thoroughly modern approach to painting a very old body.

10. Two Tone: A Cooper goes through the painting process twice on account of the contrasting roof colour.

11. Final Assembly Bodywork: Glass, badging, stripes, lights, bumper and sundry other items are affixed.

12. Final Assembly Interior: Dashboard, loom, air conditioning, headlining and hundreds of other parts, which conform to the Vehicle History Card that identifies the model and tells the associates which parts need to be fitted.

13. Running Gear: As the shells are suspended twelve feet high the A series engines built at the East works factory and the sub frames, made by GR Smithson & Co of

Wolverhampton move along a lower track. As the shell moves above it four Rover associates, position the body over the running gear and exhaust system, then on the moving line, fix them in place.

14. Checks: Once the wheels have been bolted on the Minis are treated to a full diagnostic test, comprising a rolling road, emissions, wipers, horn, lights, accuracy of the instruments and performance of the brakes.

15. Completion: Finished Minis are parked outside the factory in the blazing summer sunshine awaiting the transporter that will take them to your local dealer (this was 1996 remember).

2008 – 2009 Mileage 00003 Amount spent: £3150 on engine rebuild...
Minis in my Life: 1964 Austin Mini Cooper
MOT: Yes...but...

So let's start yet again with the MOT fail sheet. Horn does not function. Front brake application uneven. Oh and that irritating minor exhaust leak had turned into a pretty major one from the front. This was now all more than irritating especially as the engine was the wasn't the right one.

I didn't want an extra filter in the fuel line. The body actually looked OK, but I knew that just beneath the surface there was more rust than I could shake a bottle of Kurust at. If I wanted a Mini that I would be happy to own and drive and even put a cheesy, meaningless **Rüpp***Speed*® sticker on, I had to do something about it.

364

My Mini Cooper it's part in my Breakdown

Here was the start of chain of events that would culminate in the Mini Cooper being packed off to Ipswich in a Transit. In one respect the old motor was coming back together, mentally though I was starting to fall apart, just a bit. The bills had been quite gentle up to now even if cumulatively they would amount to a tidy sum. However, I'd already paid over £3000 to get what is on the face of it a relatively simple four-cylinder engine fixed.

So it had taken me thirty years to realise that sorting out a small car properly would cost a very large amount of money. The oily mechanical bits are always the simplest and cheapest parts of the restoration, whereas the bodywork is the pricey bit. If anything was going to suck the money right out of my wallet it was new panels, welding, paint and all the associated expensively cosmetic operations.

I felt rather queasy.

Yes that is a Mini Cooper disappearing inside a Mercedes Sprinter Van.

24. How not to build a Mini, because so far a very tired and rusty Mini Cooper has been sporadically and shoddily rebuilt over far too many years, bodged by the owner, then poked at by garages who are often reluctant to give it an **MOT**, but most shocking of all the Cooper hardly gets used at all, meanwhile other Minis have turned up and donated parts, so here is the abridged story in words, pictures and occasional invoices to explain where it finally went right, or possibly wrong.

It's 2009 and here was my opportunity to build a **Rüpp***Speed*® Mini Cooper. In my head I could see a bloke, certainly not me, but possibly called Spencer Haze who had taken on a pretty decent used Cooper then specced it up according to his late '60s, early '70 sensibilities. Spencer Haze is a fictional creation who lives inside my head, as well as a rather grand designer 1970s bachelor pad in North London. As a mover, shaker and generally groovy guy having fun in 1973 he could have easily afforded an S. However, I think the Cooper came his way as the settlement of a gambling debt, or it was part exchange against a Jag he was flogging. Then he decided to keep it as a spare. Easy to nip around town and park up without attracting too much attention. Obviously Spencer would want a blueprinted engine so it was quick away from the lights. As a result I think he would have approved of what happened next.

First the good news. The engine came back from around the corner in one piece. One great big, spanking new, cling filmed piece. Painted, primed and fitted with all new sundries. It really was pristine and fantastically detailed. The trouble was, with such a perfect and perfectly expensive engine, putting it inside a body that was fairly rotten and less than pristine would be stupid. So reluctantly, instead of cutting corners, or cutting my throat, I decided to do what the imaginary, very loaded Spencer Haze would do. Spend, spend, spend.

My Mini Cooper it's part in my Breakdown

Ted Sparrow was back in business and had reconstituted the East Anglian Mini Centre and presumably put bigger locks on the workshop doors. He was keen to have another crack at the Mini Cooper and there was no one else I could trust to do the work. By December 2009 the Mini had been bundled off and the scale of the job was only just becoming apparent.

On the surface the Mini Cooper looked fine, but even that was a bit of a fib. The paint had micro blistered so it that it had a bumpy acne like quality, mainly on the roof. The chap who was designated to spray the Cooper said that the only way to stop that happening again was to go back to bare metal basics. What that meant was a full sand blasting.

Once blasted the shell then revealed all sorts of horrors. Patches, old rivets and holes where the metal used to be. Now the list of new body parts was going to grow exponentially.

The stripped down Cooper shell will soon feel the cruel sting of sand on its body.

Sandblasted body looks OK but....

That's not good, a great big patch of metal below the windscreen.

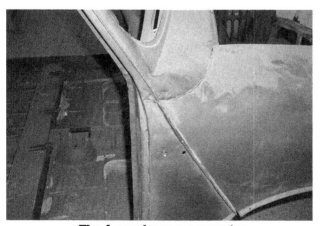

The A panels were a mess too.

Ted asked me to pop down and look at the damage and authorise more money to be thrown in the general direction of the Cooper. It was now 2010 and things started to stop more often as various parts became more of a challenge to find. As of September 2010 the workshop was waiting for an inner wing. Once the top half had been sorted then it was due to go onto the 'spit' so that it could be rotated and the holey underside sorted.

When October arrived the bills were really starting to mount up. An interim quote of £2 to £2.5K plus VAT for labour alone covered the collection, strip down and sandblast of the body. It also paid for the sub frames being blasted, cleaned and powdercoated. Not surprisingly the actual bill for this in April 2010 was £2500 rather than £2000.

The list of parts required and to be paid grew ever longer. So the Cooper needed two new inner wings, inner A panels, A panels, the door sills and two repair pieces for the door arches. Incredibly there was money coming in. That Metro engine and gearbox which had been hoofed out was sold by Ted for £200. Unfortunately I still had to write a cheque for £1652.48, which took me up to January 2011. Then three months later and I was writing another cheque for £2083.33.

A pattern seemed to be emerging. Every time I spoke to or emailed Ted it cost a couple of grand. So I thought it was best to stop. I did though pop to the workshop in February 2012 and must have stayed there a bit too long because the next month I was faced with a total bill of £5,148.14.

I suppose I did get plenty of relatively cheap body parts that cost a fortune to weld into place. At the rear was a boot floor, an extended boot hinge rail, rear valance, valance fillers for both sides of the valance. Oh and the old boot was pretty rotten, but the boot lid from my very first 1963 Mini Super De Luxe seemed to have survived intact, so I donated that. It was still Surf Blue, but along with the rest of the car would look better in Almond Green. The rear wheel arches needed replacing along with the sub frame mount panel and bracket.

Up front it was largely carnage even after the inner wings had been done. So obviously it needed wings, wheel arch stiffeners and a whole windscreen scuttle panel to attach them too and also both closing panels on each windscreen corner. The entire front panel that provided the fixing point for the grille was replaced too. I thought the doors were slightly bubbly and may just need new skins, but also on the bill were repairs kits for the bottoms. With the whole shell back in one piece it was then resprayed in Almond Green with an Old English White roof and the paint job alone amounted to £1650. But there was more.

The Mini Cooper being welded back together.

Mini Cooper now with fresh war paint.

Remember my invisible friend Spencer Haze? Well, I thought he would have gone for a roll cage. I could see him doing a bit of gentleman racing at the weekend. Most likely it would have been no contact hill climbs, but

My Mini Cooper it's part in my Breakdown

also a Spencer was such I forward thinker I would guess
that he was trying to set up track days for the thrill
seeking cool cats of the 1970s. So it would have helped to
have a safe, track friendly car. So Spencer and me bought
a front and rear cage, which needed to be slightly, no
considerably refabricated to fit.

This was the point at which I resolved not to talk
to Ted anymore or visit the Mini Cooper. I looked at what I
had agreed to build which was essentially a brand new
1964 Mini and was that what I wanted? Not really. I've
never owned a brand new car, sold a few certainly, but
had no inclination ever to buy one. Ideally the paintwork
would be sprayed in a unique finish called patina.
However, a distressed finish wasn't something that any
sensible person would do. Although it is possible to buy a
brand new 'road worn' (bashed about, scratched, faded,
dented, played a million gigs) electric guitar, there is no
such thing with cars or antique furniture. Those are called
fakes and this Mini Cooper was definitely the real thing.
The dilemma is you either let it rot and become an MOT
failure or replace the important bits to make it safe so that
you can drive to the shops. Sympathetic restorations are
fine with separate chassis pre war bangers where the
bodywork just hangs onto the cast iron underpinnings.
However, a monocoque bodied car needs to be completely
rebuilt to make it safe and driveable. Did that reasoning
make me feel better?

Course not. Late one evening when I believe
alcohol may have been involved I sent an email to Ted. In
it I said I wanted my old Cooper back. The one that wasn't
so shiny or original, but useable and rusty. I wouldn't
worry that someone would try and nick it or tap it in a car
park. It was a stream of drunken consciousness, which
might have ended in tears. I didn't expect the late night
rate to be taken at all seriously. Instead I heard nothing
and didn't even get a bill for a couple of grand. I thought
great, maybe it will all go away then. Instead, what
happened is that the Mini went away and was pushed to
the back of the workshop.

Ted read between the lines, reckoned I wanted to
sell it and decided to prioritise something else Mini
shaped. That was silly of me.

My Mini Cooper it's part in my Breakdown

By the time I had pulled myself back together and decided that life was too short not have fun in a brand new Mini hand built to my own and Spencer's specification. So I pinged off an email to Ted to ask after the old Cooper and got a bill for £2,068.49 by return. It was days from being mothballed and being liable for a weekly storage rate.

So what had I paid for this time? Well new fuel lines had to be fitted and brand new ones on the rebuilt sub frames with engineering work on both the radius arms. Otherwise it was list of fairly cheapish bits to help make the Cooper roll and stop again. Wheel bearing kits, suspension bushes, rear wheel cylinder, brake caliper seals and the like. More expensive was the wiring loom and dynamo as the old one was like rotten spaghetti and just as appealing. Ted also recommended that as suspension technology had moved on I'd be well advised to pay £143.67 for a Gaz shock absorber set and another £86.18 for an Adjusta Ride kit. I also got a glimpse into just how costly retrimming the interior might be. Not that it was that bad, but the headlining was looking grim, so a cream crackle headlining would be £130.93.

We weren't quite there yet and there was plenty still to do and the latest exchange of information in October 2012 suggested that it was estimated that another £2000 to £2500 of labour, plus VAT would be required to put it all together. That was just an estimate. In a less lucid moment I had suggested to Ted that once he had all the bits then I would then take it home and bolt the whole thing together. Where of course it would all have remained for the next few years, or until my estate was put in order and the whole lot auctioned off.

Instead I took the easy and more financially costly route. Even if emotionally it was still tying me in knots at the sheer ridiculous expense of it all and the fact it had taken over thirty years to get this far. Fortunately Mrs. Ruppert told me to pull myself together and get the Mini Cooper together and hang the expense.

Well there was a lot more expense coming. When 2013 arrived I decided to pop down and see the Cooper and apart from the fact that it could be pushed out on a set of wheels because the sub frames were fitted. Otherwise it didn't look much different from the last time I had seen the painted shell a year previously.

**Now fitted with sub frames, wheels
and a roll cage**.

There was then much still to do, or sorry pay for. Mechanically it still needed clutch and brake master cylinders, clutch slave cylinder with all the associated pipes and gaskets. Driveshafts and couplings were needed too. Inside some bits of trim and the knackered grey wheel arch liners needed replacing whilst the rear seats just needed a good clean. The passenger seat was not too bad, but the driver's one always had been doing the splits for years and an upholstery fellow who was recovering the headlining would take a look. Certainly the carpet had seen better days and anyway it was the wrong colour. On the inside the original door and window seals were very sorry looking items. Outside the door had needed lower chrome fixings for some time as well as the sliding window chrome channels and felt runners that had almost crumbled away.

Then there were things I thought I'd kept but had clearly lost, so amongst many other small items. The interior light units I'd had, and there were several, had all disintegrated or been trodden on by me. So a good second hand one was needed and heaven knows what that would cost. Ted though should have boxes of them, so I'm not

My Mini Cooper it's part in my Breakdown

worried. Not sure about the washer bottle pipes and jets, or sundry bits of chrome that I seem to have mislaid. I did have an exhaust that wasn't very good and cost about a tenner (£10) brand new. I gave that to Ted, but agreed to upgrade to a single 'box stainless steel job that should last forever and sound like the end of the world. And part of making it last forever will be the massive injections of Waxoyl. Then there is a debate about the heated rear window.

Mark 1 Minis didn't have them, even though they desperately needed one, but in the age when a heater was option that was never going to happen. However, the Cooper did come with a stick on Smith Industries one that never worked and was peeled off sometime in the late 1980s to be replaced by nothing. Ted told me that you could now buy a rear window with the elements bonded in. It was 'only' £170. That's a bargain when you consider that it's impossible to buy the stick on ones anymore, even if they used to be £4.99. I just couldn't face spending all that money, even though it would be more than worth it when the condensation arrived. So foolishly I said no, thinking perhaps I could make a heated rear window out of some wire and sticky backed plastic. I also turned down the chance of having some hairy material glued to the roof and door panels which stopped them clanging, rather than reducing the wonderful cacophony that is the inside of a Mini Cooper with the engine switched on.

All this would cost £1600 plus VAT just for the parts. In addition the Cooper S reverse rims that it came with would stay. Spencer Haze would definitely approve of those, but in order to match the rest of the car they would have to be shot blasted and painted Old English White. The approximate cost of that would be £250, hopefully not per wheel.

Just two more finishing touches that I could think of was a new chrome rooftop aerial and a clip on rear view mirror. The complete refit was scheduled to take up to 10 days and it would inevitably cost some £2000+. There was a lot more spending to come.

So that's how much it costs to build a brand new Mini Cooper. Then again a brand new MINI Cooper at the time of writing is £14,900.

My Mini Cooper it's part in my Breakdown

So what do I do now?

Originally I had entertained thoughts of driving the finished Mini Cooper across Europe to Issigonis birthplace in Turkey. When I scaled back my ambitions it just amounted to running the engine in by visiting significant (Longbridge, the Weybridge dealer, John Cooper's garage, finding some previous owners, if they were still alive. None of that would actually happen. In the end and this is the end, I was just glad that it was all in the same place,

So what have I learnt? Well I won't be doing this again. Mainly because in another thirty four years time I'll either be dead, in a home, or detained at His Majesty's pleasure because I have infringed some future law about automotive abuse.

I am certainly not cut out to restore a car with a chequebook. It is far too stressful for a cheapskate like me. I'd much rather use spanners and get dirty. I shouldn't care whether I cross thread, dent, damage, or defile a bit of old metal. That's why I am looking at all the left over bits and wondering whether instead of building another factory fresh car, I went for something earthy. Yes, I could throw something together and really call it a **Rüpp**_Speed_® Mini.

Pass the spanner and in the words of Sir Les, 'here I go again...'

2022 update:....

Still have the Cooper. Thousands of miles covered. Head gasket went a couple of years which was irritating, considering that it was supposed to be all new. A starter motor and the odd bulb. That's all part of the joy of owning and running an old car. Less bother, inevitably cheaper than something which may be comfy, but is dull.

The moral is: buy an old car and use it.

James Ruppert Is under the delusion that he can time travel. Having said that, he lives mostly in 1979 with no direct access to the modern world except through the medium of Telex and a telephone landline. Always interested in motoring history (grade 1 CSE), he bought all sorts of MOT borderline Bangers that were prehistorically awful. Once sold cars then switched to writing about used ones. Spent many years driving around the country looking at car lots and talking to blokes who sold them. Wrote for newspapers including The Independent, The Sunday Times and Evening Standard. Best known as a writer for Car magazine, Autocar, Performance Car, Supercar Classics and many others. Dreamt up the word Bangernomics in 1990 and wrote a story about buying and running an £80 Eastern Block Banger. Book of the word came out in 1993 and has found that banging on about marginal motoring only makes a marginal living. Please consider the following titles for inclusion on your bookshelves to help pay for food, fuel and automotive tat.

Order Books from www.bangernomics.com

There might also be T-Shirts and maybe other branded goods available with quite possibly some wonderful colour images from this book.

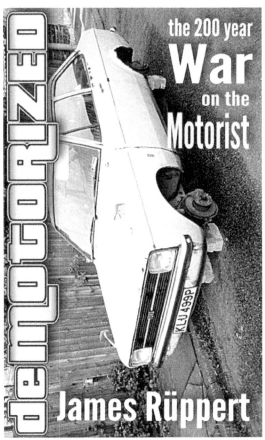

Demotorized. This is the not quite definitive history of how parking became an industry, governments overtaxed motorists, carmakers lied about how safe and environmentally friendly they were and tested their emissions on monkeys and humans. Also why robot cars are so dangerous and electric cars are not the answer. Also, who is behind the ongoing plan to Demotorize the world. Printed in 2020 it predicted the future with terrifying accuracy. Buy it before it gets banned.

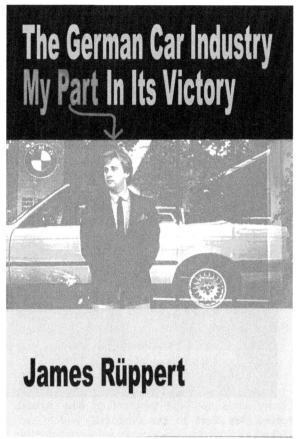

The Award Winning and so good the BBC based a documentary (Das Auto) on it **The German Car Industry, My Part in its Victory**. Winner of the Mercedes-Benz Montagu of Beaulieu Trophy for the best motoring book of year. Contains Yuppies, BMW 3, 5, 6 & 7-Series (yes that's all there was back then) and references to contemporary 1980s music.

The

The British Car Industry
Our Part In Its Downfall

'Brilliant'
Classic Car Weekly
•
'Beautifully written
with considerable
wit'
Daily Telegraph
•
'Charming'
Classic & Sportscar
•
'Informative, well-
written and
extremely funny'
Daily Express

James Ruppert

Critically acclaimed and best selling **The British Car Industry Our Part in Its Downfall**, which has been described as "Beautifully written with considerable wit" by the Daily Telegraph and The Daily Express said, "It's informative, well-written and extremely funny" which was really nice of them. The story of the motor industry from 1945 to 2005, explaining just why you can't buy a British built family hatchback from a British owned company. Plus all the cars, James's Dad bought.

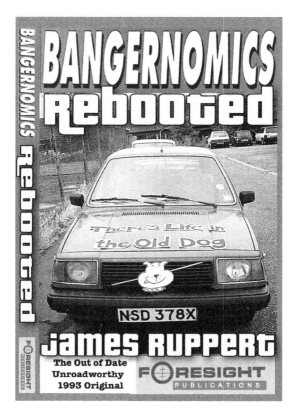

In the beginning, 1993, there was Bangernomics and now there is **Bangernomics Rebooted** which contrasts the absurd expense of buying a new car with the supreme good sense of buying well used. At a stroke depreciation no longer became an issue, running costs were slashed and there were no finance charges to be endured. Here is the original book, republished and effectively rebooted. So it is absolutely useless to any car buyer unless they have access to a time machine.

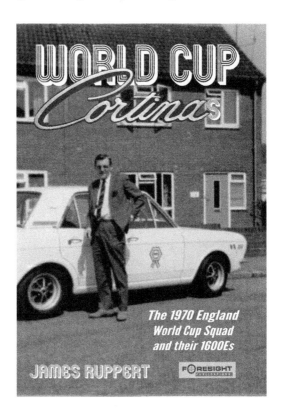

World Cup Cortinas In 1970 something very remarkable happened. Not only had England qualified for the World Cup in Mexico because they were defending champions, but most important of all Ford had loaned every squad member the greatest saloon car in the world. A book about what happened to those Ford Cortinas and how footballers bought better cars when they earned more money and no longer owned the same motors that your mum and dad drove.

Channeling the absurdist spirit of Spike Milligan" said Classic Car, others just called it "Witty", that's **My Mini Cooper Its Part in My Breakdown** which has the full history of the world's favourite small car, plus the history of what came before but not after. Also details the on-off restoration of a Mini Cooper that cost £200 in 1979. The expense of restoring the bodywork and mechanicals ought to put off most sane people. Except that original minis are always worth far more than you could imagine.

Ruppert's Bangerpedia deals with the confusing line up of noughties models. The Bangerpedia does this with a fairly ridiculous rating system involving Slog the Bangernomic Dog. The briefest of guides to each of the 700+ models includes some fairly marginal buying advice, a sarcastic appraisal and an almost definitive indication as to whether it will fit into a garage, or not.

The world of motoring is in a desperate crisis. Demonised, despised and attacked from every wrong thinking government, local authority, pressure group and even car manufacturers themselves. Bangernomics is here to bring motoring back to the masses, saving time, money and automotive headaches. Squashing together the original Bangernomics, Bangernomics Bible and Bangernomics Diet into one easily digestible guide to buying and running an older cost efficient motor.

Only **Bangernomics can save the World.**

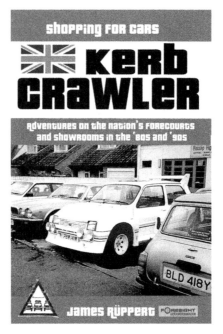

Shopping for cars can be a full time job, well it was for me anyway. In the pre Interweb age it meant actually going to look at cars for sale. It meant talking to the blokes selling the cars face to face. You learned loads lot doing it that way. With the benefit of hindsight and a time machine, some cars look cheap now, but they could well have been pretty expensive then. Find out how I got sued by one of the 'stars' of the Italian Job, was told off by the Deputy Prime Minister, find out what the worst car Sir Ian Botham ever owned was, and that time I lent my car to Bjork. Plus there are excursions around the UK that includes buying a car in Scotland and posting it to to Japan. Also looking for Bangers in Northern Ireland whilst trying to avoid the troubles. Then there is Princess Diana's Escort Ghia and the true origin of the word Bangernomics. There are Cop cars, Army surplus and even the true meaning of motoring life...

My Mini Cooper it's part in my Breakdown

He was a man running out of time and that time was 1973. Spencer Haze is a comic superhero who first hit the 21st century in the year 2000. First on the 4Car website, then later in national newspapers and car magazines. Some say he was even on the television and might well have been real. Here is just about every frame he ever squeezed into, plus a TV script and random pictures that have never been seen before. Here is everything possibly no one ever wanted to know about a fictional bloke called Spencer who loved cars, people and the absolute truth. There are a couple of full stories, loads of articles he appeared in.

The only pro-motorist car mag in the Universe*

It costs nothing, but contains everything you need to be a more anarchistic, bolshie and less co-operative car driver.

*www.freecarmag.com